JUNIOR
LISTENING EXPERT

A Theme-Based L. ...or Young EFL Learners

Level **4**

JUNIOR
LISTENING EXPERT

Level 4

Series Editor	Dong-sook Kim
Project Editors	Yu-jin Lee, Hyun-joo Lee, Ji-hee Lee
Contributing Writers	Patrick Ferraro, Rebecca Cant, Susan Kim
Illustrators	Kyung-ho Jung, Eun-jung Shin
Design	Hoon-jung Ahn, Ji-young Ki, Hye-jung Yoon, Min-shin Ju
Editorial Designer	Jong-hee Kim
Sale	Ki-young Han, Kyung-koo Lee, In-gyu Park, Cheol-gyo Jeong, Nam-jun Kim, Woo-hyun Lee, Jin-su Ha
Marketers	Hye-sun Park, Kyung-jin Nam, Ji-won Lee, Yeo-jin Kim
ISBN	979-11-253-4047-8
Photo Credits	www.fotolia.com
	www.dreamstime.com
	www.istockphoto.com

Copyright © 2023 NE Neungyule, Inc.
First Printing 5th January 2023
2nd Printing 15 February 2023

INTRODUCTION

Junior Listening Expert is a four-level listening series for EFL learners, particularly older elementary school students and junior high school students. Systematically designed to improve listening skills, its audio material is offered in a variety of formats, covering a wide-range of topics.

Features

Theme-Based Units

Every level contains twelve units, each covering a lively topic such as food, lifestyle, sports, IT, or social issues. A variety of listening formats expose students not only to everyday dialogues, but also to more advanced informative material.

Systematic Design

Each unit is composed of five closely related sections that allow students to develop their listening skills step-by-step. As students pass through each of the five sections, they have the opportunity to evaluate their progress and build confidence in their listening abilities.

A Variety of Question Types

A variety of question types are provided, including identifying the main idea, finding specific details, and making inferences. These serve to familiarize students with the standard types of listening test formats.

A Focus on Critical Thinking

Students are not only exposed to social issues through the listening material, but are also encouraged to think about these issues and form their own opinions.

Format

Getting Ready

This section utilizes a quiz to introduce the key vocabulary words and expressions that will appear in the unit. It is designed to facilitate easier understanding for students preparing to tackle challenging topics in English.

Listening Start

In this section, students have the chance to check their listening comprehension and master key expressions by answering questions and taking dictation. This prepares them for the Listening Practice and Listening Challenge sections.

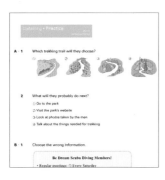

Listening Practice

Students are given the opportunity to practice a variety of listening question types in this section. It enables them to develop the different listening skills required for each question type.

Listening Challenge

This section presents students with two long listening passages and a pair of checkup questions for each passage. This section challenges students to understand a higher level of English and upgrade their listening skills.

Critical Thinking

This section encourages students to think about a social issue related to the unit's topic. After listening to different opinions about an issue, students develop their own opinion, which they then express in a speaking activity.

Vocabulary List

This section provides easy access to key vocabulary. It contains the new vocabulary words from each unit.

Dictation

This section focuses on helping students improve the accuracy of their listening skills by requiring them to take dictation.

Table of **Contents**

Outdoor Activities

Getting ★ Ready

A

Choose the correct word for each definition.

ⓐ trail   ⓑ limit   ⓒ indoor   ⓓ rescue
ⓔ shallow   ⓕ struggle   ⓖ destroy   ⓗ float

1 not deep: _____
2 to damage something badly: _____
3 a path through the countryside: _____
4 located or used inside a building: _____
5 the act of saving someone from a dangerous situation: _____
6 the greatest amount or level of something that is allowed: _____

B

Choose the best sentence for each blank.

ⓐ Stay where you are and wait for rescue.   ⓑ That picture was taken after a paintball game.   ⓒ You don't know how dangerous the mountains are in winter.   ⓓ It was more amazing than I expected.   ⓔ Players are divided into two teams and fight each other with paintball guns.   ⓕ Children will participate in activities like hiking and outdoor cooking.

1 W: What should I do if I get lost in the woods?
　M: _____

2 W: What activities are included in the summer camp program?
　M: _____

3 W: How do you play paintball?
　M: _____

1   What is the man mainly talking about?

① Good places for family camping trips

② Tips for planning a family camping trip

③ Tips for better relationship with family members

④ Good points of going camping with family members

2   According to the woman, what are two good points of horseback riding?

① It helps you stay healthy.

② It exercises the whole body.

③ It's a relaxing thing to do.

④ It makes you more confident.

3   Who did NOT follow the guideline for rafting?

①
I put my helmet on tightly.

Mike

②
I wore shoes with no shoelaces.

Katie

③
I remained seated while inside the boat.

Jessica

④
I relaxed my body when I fell in the water.

Eric

A - 1 Which trekking trail will they choose?

①  ②  ③  ④

2 What will they probably do next?

① Go to the park

② Visit the park's website

③ Look at photos taken by the man

④ Talk about the things needed for trekking

B - 1 Choose the wrong information.

> ### Be Dream Scuba Diving Members!
>
> · Regular meetings: ① Every Saturday
>
> · Activities: ② Training in indoor pools and in the sea /
>
>   ③ One tour abroad each year
>
> · Membership: ④ $50 a month (tour fees are not included)

2 What event will Dream Scuba Diving Club hold this Saturday?

① An overseas scuba diving tour

② A welcome party for newcomers

③ Scuba diving practice at a nearby beach

④ A basic scuba diving class for beginners

C - 1 What does a team have to do to win a paintball game?

    ① Find the other team's flag first

    ② Shoot all the other team's members

    ③ Come back with the other team's flag

    ④ Take the paintball guns from the other team

2 Why does the woman like paintball?

    ① It is full of thrills.

    ② It is a good workout.

    ③ It is fun to shoot a gun.

    ④ It is interesting to make strategies.

D - 1 What would the man say about his hot-air balloon ride?

    ① It was more boring than I expected.

    ② It wasn't bad, but it was too expensive.

    ③ It was a lot of fun and the time went by so fast.

    ④ It was nice to see beautiful scenery, but scary.

2 Check [✓] T for true or F for false.

	T	F
(1) The hot-air balloon ride costs $150 for two people.	☐	☐
(2) The balloon took off before sunrise.	☐	☐
(3) The basket could carry 20 people.	☐	☐

A - 1   What are they mainly talking about?

     ① Tips for climbing mountains in winter

     ② The dangers of climbing mountains in winter

     ③ The good points of climbing mountains in winter

     ④ Advice for when you are lost in mountains

2   How does the man feel now?

     ① angry   ② worried

     ③ excited   ④ disappointed

B - 1   Choose the wrong information.

> ### Memo
>
> Summer Camp
> ① Place: Bear Lake
> ② Date: from July 7th (for 4 days)
> ③ Activities: Hiking, Outdoor cooking,
>   Swimming, Canoeing
> ④ Price: $400 per child

2   Why did the woman register only the older daughter for the camp?

     ① Her younger daughter is afraid of water.

     ② The price is expensive.

     ③ The camp has an age limit.

     ④ Her younger daughter is sick.

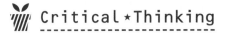 Critical★Thinking

National Parks

1 What's the woman's opinion?

① Park officers should take more care of the park.

② National parks should raise their entrance fees.

③ Hikers should change their ideas about protecting nature.

④ Hikers shouldn't be allowed to enter national parks.

2 What will they probably do next?

① Set up their tent

② Pick up the trash

③ Move to a cleaner place

④ Join an environmental campaign

What do you think?

1

Check [✓] if you have the same opinion. You can add your own opinion in the blank.

☐ Hikers must try not to harm nature.

☐ The government should severely punish hikers who destroy nature.

☐ National parks shouldn't be open to hikers because they damage the environment.

2

Talk about the following questions with your partner.

• Have you ever seen trash left behind by hikers in national parks? How did you feel about it?

• What would be good ways to protect nature in national parks?

02 Entertainment

Getting ★ Ready

A

Match each word with the correct definition.

1 something that you must have   •   • ⓐ plot

2 a TV program that is shown again   •   • ⓑ rerun

3 the storyline of a drama, movie or play   •   • ⓒ gossip

4 talk about other people's personal lives   •   • ⓓ necessity

5 to send out programs that can be watched on TV •   • ⓔ nominate

6 to suggest something to be considered for a prize •   • ⓕ broadcast

B

Choose the best sentence for each blank.

ⓐ It's supposed to be broadcast at 8 p.m.   ⓑ I like watching programs related to animals.   ⓒ You shouldn't have missed yesterday's episode.   ⓓ Do you mind turning to Channel 11?   ⓔ How does the competition on this reality show work?   ⓕ The evening news is on Channel 11 now.

1 M: Do you know when *Doctors* is on?

   W: _____

2 M: _____

   W: People will be voted out one by one on each episode.

3 M: Did you watch *Henry V* yesterday? I didn't.

   W: _____

1 Why could they NOT watch the music program?

① It was replaced by a news broadcast.

② They turned to the wrong channel.

③ They misunderstood what date it was on.

④ They misunderstood what time it was on.

2 Which kind of program does each person like?

(1) Adam: _____   (2) Betty: _____   (3) Chris: _____

| ⓐ news | ⓑ documentaries | ⓒ talk shows |
| ⓓ cooking shows | ⓔ soap operas | ⓕ comedy shows |

3 What is the woman mainly talking about?

① The negative effects of watching TV

② Useful TV programs for children

③ Things that may happen without TV

④ The relationship between TV and weight

A - 1 What did the boy do yesterday evening?

①  ②  ③  ④

2 How will the boy watch *Love Triangle*?

① Watch a rerun

② Download it from the Internet

③ Rent the video from a shop

④ Borrow the tape from the girl

B - 1 What did the man suggest to the woman?

① Practice singing hard

② Record a debut album

③ Participate in a reality show

④ Watch the new reality show

2 Which is NOT true about *Star*?

① It is similar to *American Idol*.

② There are 12 competitors.

③ The winner gets a $20,000 prize.

④ The judges are famous singers.

C - 1 What are they mainly talking about?

① Entertainers that they don't like

② The bad points of variety shows

③ The important roles of viewers

④ Programs that copied foreign ones

2 What will they probably do next?

① Go to the movies

② Watch a comedy show

③ Call the broadcasting companies

④ Open a community site

D - 1 Choose the wrong information about tonight's Fun TV schedule.

① 19:00　*Focus*

② 20:30　*Jimmy's Show*

③ 22:00　*With Anne*

④ 23:30　*Specialists, Season 1*

2 What type of program is *With Anne*?

① a quiz show

② a soap opera

③ a music show

④ entertainment news

A - 1 What are they mainly talking about?

① Violence in TV cartoons

② Ways to make good TV cartoons

③ Uneducational TV programs for kids

④ The bad effects of watching cartoons

2 Who has the same opinion as the woman?

① Parents should care about what programs their children watch.

Jack

② TV stations should show fewer cartoons.

Nora

③ TV stations need to consider showing educational cartoons.

Paul

B - 1 What will they probably do next?

① Introduce the show's host

② Announce the winner of an award

③ Have an interview with some actors

④ Say how they feel about receiving an award

2 Choose what makes each drama special.

(1) *Witches*: _____   (2) *The Boys*: _____   (3) *Dream*: _____

ⓐ exciting story   ⓑ excellent camerawork   ⓒ fantastic special effects

ⓓ great acting   ⓔ interesting characters   ⓕ wonderful sound effects

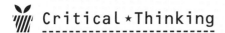

Entertainers' Privacy

1 **What are they mainly talking about?**

① Should paparazzi be stopped by law?

② How can we protect entertainers' privacy?

③ Who is responsible for entertainment gossip?

④ Should entertainers' private lives be in the media?

2 **Which is the man's opinion?**

① Entertainers should give up their personal lives.

② The media should protect the private lives of stars.

③ Some entertainers use the media to get attention.

④ Entertainers themselves are to blame for gossip.

What do you think?

1

Check [✓] if you have the same opinion. You can add your own opinion in the blank.

☐ It's natural to give up privacy once becoming a star.

☐ I want to know every detail of my favorite star's private life.

☐ If I were an entertainer, I wouldn't want my life to be open to everyone.

_____

2

Talk about the following questions with your partner.

· How would you feel if your life were open to the public?

· How much information about entertainers should be provided by the media?

Daily Life

Getting ★ Ready

A

Match each word with the correct definition.

1 to put something into a liquid for a while • • ⓐ dye
2 to increase the time or size of something • • ⓑ soak
3 to change the color of something with a special liquid • • ⓒ region
4 to pay money to receive copies of a magazine regularly • • ⓓ extend
5 a particular area or part of the world • • ⓔ subscribe
6 the opinion that people have about someone or something • • ⓕ reputation

B

Choose the best sentence for each blank.

ⓐ My food was cold when it arrived.   ⓑ I can't decide between cutting it short and getting a perm.   ⓒ One issue is $5, so it's a 10% discount.   ⓓ I didn't know the condition of my hair was that bad.   ⓔ We had a rush of orders.   ⓕ We don't charge an annual fee.

1 W: How would you like to have your hair done today?
   M: _____

2 W: How much is the annual fee of this card?
   M: _____

3 W: What made my delivery arrive so late?
   M: _____

1   Why did the man call?

① To make an order

② To add some food to his order

③ To complain about his food

④ To ask when his food will be delivered

2   Choose the wrong information.

Speed Movers

20 years of experience!

① Moving services (including overseas moving)

② What we do: packing, moving, cleaning, unpacking, arranging

③ Working hours: from Monday to Saturday, 9 a.m. to 7 p.m.

④ Contact number: 143–9012

3   Choose the two services that the woman is going to get.

① cut

② perm

③ hair dye

④ hair treatment

21

A - 1   Choose the woman's wallet.

①   ②   ③    ④

2   How did the woman's feeling change?

① worried → relieved

② upset → nervous

③ surprised → excited

④ worried → disappointed

B - 1   Why did the woman visit the photo studio?

① To have her pictures developed

② To pick up her photos

③ To make a photo album

④ To have her picture taken

2   Choose the photo album that the woman wants.

①    ②    ③    ④

C - 1 What is the man mainly talking about?

   ① How electromagnetic waves work

   ② How we can avoid electromagnetic waves

   ③ How dangerous electromagnetic waves are

   ④ How electromagnetic waves affect our lives

2 Write T for true or F for false about electromagnetic waves.

   (1) Small TVs produce fewer waves than big TVs.   _____

   (2) When using a cell phone, they come mostly out of the screen.   _____

   (3) They stop flowing if you turn off electronic devices.   _____

D - 1 Choose the wrong information.

> **No. 3232**
>
> Name: ① James Pitt
>
> Address: ② 160 Clinton Street
>
> Period: ③ 1 year (from October)
>
> Payment: ④ by credit card

2 How much is the man going to pay?

   ① $27   ② $30

   ③ $48   ④ $60

A - 1 Why did the man call?

① To change his card

② To change his billing address

③ To get an e-billing service

④ To ask about the benefits of his card

2 Which is NOT a benefit of the Green Card?

① hotel discounts

② restaurant discounts

③ gasoline discounts

④ no annual fee

B - 1 Who is following the woman's advice correctly?

①
When I wash white socks, I put salt and toothpaste in the water.

Ian

②
Before washing my sneakers, I put them into water with lemon juice.

Kate

③
I rub shampoo on my shirt collar before washing it.

Lily

2 Which is NOT likely to be mentioned next week?

① Cleaning the sink

② Cleaning the carpet

③ Washing the floor of a bathroom

④ Removing fish smells from a house

Visiting Banks

1 **What are they mainly talking about?**

① Why should overtime work be paid?

② What time should banks be closed?

③ Should banks be open during weekends?

④ What is hard about working at a bank?

2 **Who has the same opinion as Janet?**

①

Banks should extend their working hours on weekdays.

Jack

②

Some of bank branches should be open on the weekend.

Matt

③

For people's convenience, all banks should open on weekends.

Laura

What do you think?

1

Check [✓] if you have the same opinion. You can add your own opinion in the blank.

☐ It's not fair to ask bankers to work on weekends.

☐ Banks should extend their hours if they will not open during weekends.

☐ Paying bankers extra money will encourage them to work on weekends.

_____

2

Talk about the following questions with your partner.

• What do you think about banks' hours?

• How long do you think banks should stay open?

Food

Getting ★ Ready

A

Match each word with the correct definition.

1 not cooked   •   • ⓐ dip
2 very difficult to cut and chew   •   • ⓑ tough
3 to put something into a liquid for a moment   •   • ⓒ nutrient
4 to judge the value, quality, or importance of something •   • ⓓ raw
5 a substance in food that helps plants and animals grow •   • ⓔ evaluate
6 a small amount of food eaten before the main part of a meal •   • ⓕ appetizer

B

Choose the best sentence for each blank.

ⓐ I waited for an hour to be seated even though I had a reservation.   ⓑ That's why olive oil is widely used in diet programs.   ⓒ It's helpful in reducing cholesterol levels.   ⓓ I've already lost my appetite.   ⓔ I feel honored to be served in this restaurant.   ⓕ I'd like to have the potato salad as an appetizer.

1 M: What are health benefits of olive oil?
   W: _____

2 M: Can I take your order?
   W: Yes. _____

3 M: How was the restaurant you visited yesterday?
   W: Terrible. _____

1 Choose the food each person describes.

(1) _____   (2) _____

①   Bibimbap

② Sushi

③ Bulgogi

④ Shabu-shabu

2 Choose the wrong information.

Table No. 103

① **Appetizer:** 1 chicken salad with French dressing

② **Main Dish:** 2 rib-eye steaks ③ (2 well-done)

④ **Drink:** 1 glass of red wine

3 Choose the foods that should NOT be eaten together.

(1) Cucumber: _____   (2) Tomato: _____   (3) Black tea: _____

| ⓐ sugar | ⓑ lemon | ⓒ honey |
| ⓓ pepper | ⓔ carrot | ⓕ orange juice |

A - 1 Why does the man decide to buy olive oil?

① He thinks it tastes better.

② He wants to reduce his cholesterol levels.

③ He needs a cheaper oil.

④ He wants to lose weight.

2 Which is the best way to store olive oil?

① Placing it in a dark cabinet

② Putting it in the refrigerator

③ Putting it near a sunny window

④ Keeping it in a wet place

B - 1 What is the relationship between the speakers?

① waiter – cook

② cook – customer

③ waiter – customer

④ manager – waitress

2 What are the two things that the woman did NOT like?

① The waiting time was too long.

② The food was too expensive.

③ The restaurant was too noisy.

④ The food wasn't tasty.

C - 1   Which is NOT true about Spanish food?

① Garlic and red pepper are widely used.

② It often includes seafood.

③ There are many rice dishes.

④ It is very similar to Indian food.

2   What is true about the EL Cruce restaurant?

① It doesn't have a reservation system.

② It became popular in recent years.

③ It closes at midnight.

④ It provides dance performance on Fridays.

D - 1   What is the man mainly talking about?

① How to eat cabbage in a healthy way

② What happens when you heat up cabbage

③ Which vegetables doctors suggest we eat

④ What nutrients cabbage contains

2   Who is NOT following the man's advice?

①

I sometimes put lemon juice in my cabbage juice.

Cindy

②

After I make cabbage juice, I drink it quickly.

Ben

③

After I boil cabbage, I throw out the water and eat just the cabbage.

Joshua

A - 1   How did Americans feel about sushi at first?

① curious

② negative

③ favorable

④ indifferent

2   What are the two successful strategies of Mr. Taka?

① He made a new type of sushi dish.

② He used only fresh ingredients.

③ He held free food tasting events.

④ He decorated his restaurant in a Japanese style.

B - 1   What is true about the Michelin Guide?

① It judges restaurants based on food only.

② It was first published by the owner of a tire company.

③ It has changed its name to the Red Guide.

④ It is a guide to French restaurants around the world.

2   How did the woman's feeling change?

① annoyed → satisfied

② angry → depressed

③ surprised → excited

④ embarrassed → disappointed

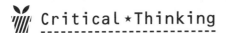
Critical ★ Thinking

GM Food

1 What are they mainly talking about?

① What GM food is

② How beneficial GM food is

③ How GM food is made

④ Whether to eat GM food or not

2 Who has the same opinion as the woman?

①

I won't eat GM food until it's proven safe.

Anne

②

I prefer GM food because it has so many advantages.

Ted

③

GM food could prevent people around the world from going hungry.

Mark

What do you think?

1

Check [✓] if you have the same opinion. You can add your own opinion in the blank.

☐ GM food could cause negative side effects in the long run.

☐ GM technology should be encouraged so that we can produce more food.

☐ I don't want to eat GM food until it's proven to be 100% safe.

_____

2

Talk about the following questions with your partner.

• When you buy food, do you care about whether it's GM food or not?

• Do you think GM food should be produced? Why or why not?

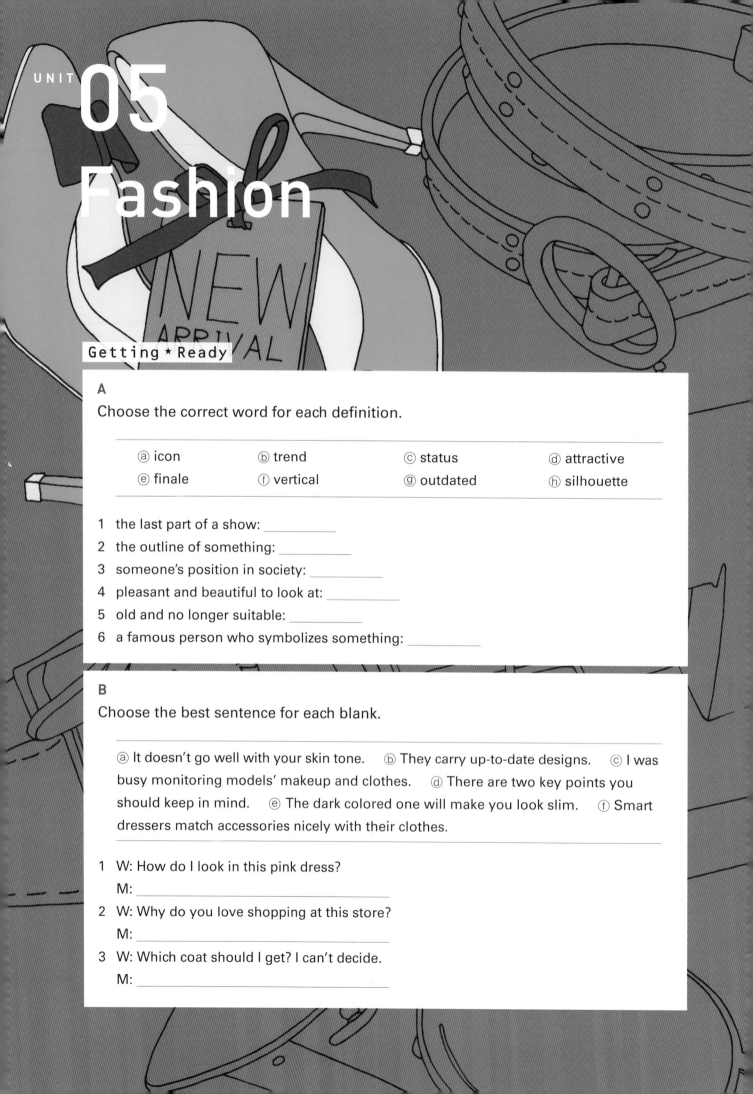

Getting ★ Ready

A

Choose the correct word for each definition.

ⓐ icon	ⓑ trend	ⓒ status	ⓓ attractive
ⓔ finale	ⓕ vertical	ⓖ outdated	ⓗ silhouette

1 the last part of a show: _____
2 the outline of something: _____
3 someone's position in society: _____
4 pleasant and beautiful to look at: _____
5 old and no longer suitable: _____
6 a famous person who symbolizes something: _____

B

Choose the best sentence for each blank.

ⓐ It doesn't go well with your skin tone.   ⓑ They carry up-to-date designs.   ⓒ I was busy monitoring models' makeup and clothes.   ⓓ There are two key points you should keep in mind.   ⓔ The dark colored one will make you look slim.   ⓕ Smart dressers match accessories nicely with their clothes.

1 W: How do I look in this pink dress?
   M: _____
2 W: Why do you love shopping at this store?
   M: _____
3 W: Which coat should I get? I can't decide.
   M: _____

1   According to *Fashion World*, which is the fall season trend?

①    ②    ③    ④

2   Choose the right advice for each person.

(1) Jane Stewart: _____   (2) Susan Morris: _____   (3) Kate Smith: _____

ⓐ Consider your skin color.   ⓑ Match accessories with your dress.

ⓒ Wear a shorter dress.   ⓓ Choose a bright color.

ⓔ Take off some accessories.   ⓕ Wear a dress with a slim line.

3   What is the man mainly talking about?

① What fashion editors do

② Why it is good to be a fashion editor

③ What is needed to be a fashion editor

④ How fashion editors develop their careers

A - 1   What is the relationship between the speakers?

① designer – interviewer

② designer – fashion model

③ photographer – fashion editor

④ makeup artist – fashion model

2   Why did the woman agree to do the show?

① To earn money

② To show her talent

③ To build her career

④ To help raise money

B - 1   What is the woman mainly talking about?

① The right colors for your skin tone

② The best accessory of this season

③ The right style for tall, thin people

④ Ways to make you look slim and tall

2   Who is following the woman's advice best?

①    ②    ③    ④

C - 1 What is this report about?

   ① Tips for wearing skirts

   ② The popularity of skirts for men

   ③ Japanese men's thoughts about fashion

   ④ The popularity of designer brands in Japan

2 Who has the same opinion as the man?

① Men should dress like men.

Toby

② Wear designer brands, and you'll be a fashion leader.

Jen

③ It's good to try wearing something new.

Mike

D - 1 According to the woman, what is the man's problem?

   ① He always wears cheap clothes.

   ② He looks too thin in his clothes.

   ③ He is not interested in fashion at all.

   ④ He doesn't have clothes that fit him.

2 Choose the tip that is NOT from the woman.

   ① Copy a TV star's style.

   ② Consider your body shape.

   ③ Read fashion magazines.

   ④ Match accessories with clothes.

A - 1   Check [✓] T for true or F for false about fast fashion.   T   F

(1) Its prices are cheap.   ☐   ☐

(2) It reflects the latest styles right away.   ☐   ☐

(3) It focuses on both designs and materials.   ☐   ☐

2   How does the man feel toward fast fashion?

① proud

② negative

③ favorable

④ indifferent

B - 1   Which is NOT true about Yves Saint Laurent?

① He was born in the 1930s.

② He was a designer for 50 years.

③ He showed "the safari look" in his first collection.

④ He was the first designer to use black models.

2   Why is Yves Saint Laurent considered to have changed the world?

① He made blue jeans popular.

② He designed pants suits for women.

③ He turned clothes into works of art.

④ He protested for women's rights.

 Critical ★ Thinking

Extreme Styles

1   **What are they mainly talking about?**

① The best current fashion trends

② Styles that they want to wear

③ Styles worn by movie stars

④ Styles that they don't like

2   **Who has the same opinion about miniskirts as the man?**

①
> They look good on anyone.

Tara

②
> Some miniskirts are too short.

Bob

③
> They only look good on slim women.

Judy

What do you think?

1

Check [✓] the styles you don't like. You can add your own opinion in the blank.

☐ Women wearing miniskirts   ☐ Men wearing earrings
☐ Women wearing high heels   ☐ Men wearing skinny jeans
☐ Women wearing leggings   ☐ Men wearing boots

2

Talk about the following questions with your partner.

· Have you seen someone dressed terribly? Why did you think his or her clothes were terrible?

06 Ads & Announcements

A

Match each word with the correct definition.

1 an advertisement on television   •   • ⓐ lower

2 to change or influence something   •   • ⓑ leather

3 relating to a king or queen or their family   •   • ⓒ affect

4 to reduce something in value, number or amount   •   • ⓓ equipment

5 tools or machines that are used for a particular purpose   •   • ⓔ commercial

6 a material made of animal skin that is used for making bags •   • ⓕ royal

B

Choose the best sentence for each blank.

ⓐ It should describe the product in detail.   ⓑ Why did you decide to ban junk food ads on TV?   ⓒ Film directors place some products in movies on purpose.   ⓓ It hides what kind of product it is.   ⓔ What kinds of junk food will be affected by the law?   ⓕ The ad said it passed a skin allergy test.

1 M: Why did you buy the lotion?

   W: _____

2 M: What do you think makes a good advertisement?

   W: _____

3 M: _____

   W: We believe they're harmful for children.

1 What is the advertisement for?

① perfume

② lipstick

③ shampoo

④ vitamin pills

2 Write the floor that each person will visit.

① I want to look at famous paintings.

Tim

_____ floor

② I'd like to see the old-style dresses.

Katie

_____ floor

③ I'd like to know what kind of furniture kings used.

Andrew

_____ floor

3 Choose the wrong information.

Lost and Found Center   No.126

① Item: black leather bag

② Where: at ABC Sports Store

③ When: about 4:50 p.m.

④ What was in it: two books, a handkerchief

A - 1 Who is using Magic Solution?

①  ②  ③  ④

2 Choose the wrong information.

Magic Solution

① Try it twice a day!

② In just two weeks of use, you can feel the difference.

③ The special price in March is $100.

④ You can order by phone or online.

B - 1 What are they mainly talking about?

① The advantages of shopping online

② Cosmetics that passed allergy tests

③ Strategies for effective advertising

④ Advertisements that can't be trusted

2 What is the woman's tip for wise shopping?

① Buy brand-name products.

② Read product reviews.

③ Avoid buying cheap products.

④ Compare the prices of several brands.

C - 1   Which is true about BT 201?

    ① Its departure time has been changed.

    ② It's canceled due to weather conditions.

    ③ It's going to start boarding in a minute.

    ④ Its departure gate was changed to Gate 16.

2   Choose the destination and departure time of TX 1215.

	Destination	Departure Time
①	New York	11 a.m.
②	London	10 a.m.
③	New York	11:30 a.m.
④	London	10:30 a.m.

D - 1   What is a good point of teaser ads?

    ① They attract people's attention.

    ② They don't cost much money.

    ③ They give a positive brand image.

    ④ They give a lot of product information.

2   Choose a teaser ad.

①

②

③

A - 1 Which is NOT true about the Star Cruise trip?

① It's going to visit four islands in Greece.

② It takes seven days.

③ It features a magic show on Wednesday.

④ It provides various international foods.

2 What will the passengers do after this announcement?

① Have dinner

② Go on the deck

③ Watch fireworks

④ Put on life jackets

B - 1 Which ad is NOT banned on TV between 5 and 8 p.m.?

①  ②  ③  ④

2 Who has the same opinion as Mr. Williams?

① It's not fair to ban certain kinds of ads on TV.

② Junk food ads should be banned on TV all day long.

③ Children's health is more important than companies' profits.

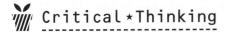 Critical ★ Thinking

Product Placement

1 **What are they mainly talking about?**

① Why do directors use product placement?

② Is it effective to use product placement?

③ Is it okay to use product placement in movies?

④ What are some bad points of using product placement?

2 **What is the man's opinion about product placement?**

① It shouldn't be allowed in movies.

② It shouldn't affect the quality of movies.

③ It is a very effective method for advertising.

④ It is not a good way of raising money for a movie.

What do you think?

1

Check [✓] if you have the same opinion. You can add your own opinion in the blank.

☐ Product placement often ruins the story, so it should not be used in movies.

☐ Without product placement, movies cannot be made because of a lack of money.

☐ Directors can use product placement, but it shouldn't lower the quality of movies.

_____

2

Talk about the following questions with your partner.

• Have you ever felt bothered by product placement in a movie? What product was it?

• Do you think product placement is effective in advertising products?

Technology

Auto Vac

A

Match each word with the correct definition.

1 to examine something in detail   ·   · ⓐ export
2 a typical quality of something   ·   · ⓑ consumer
3 a feeling, such as love or anger   ·   · ⓒ device
4 someone who buys products or services   ·   · ⓓ emotion
5 a machine invented to do a particular job   ·   · ⓔ analyze
6 the sale of goods or services to another country ·   · ⓕ characteristic

B

Choose the best sentence for each blank.

> ⓐ It turned out that productivity increased.   ⓑ Technology is used in every area of our lives.   ⓒ It was made by analyzing the sounds of many dogs.   ⓓ It can tell how your dog feels by the way it sounds.   ⓔ I'm pleased to show you our company's latest vehicle.   ⓕ It is not only stylish but also has several advanced functions.

1 M: How did that technology change the seeds?
   W: _____

2 M: Why do you recommend this car?
   W: _____

3 M: How was the dog translator invented?
   W: _____

1   Choose two ways that Kobian expresses its feelings.

① It says how it feels.

② It makes some gestures.

③ It makes various sounds.

④ It changes its facial expression.

2   What is the woman mainly talking about?

① How the Indian IT industry developed

② Why it is good to work in the IT industry

③ Which countries have a powerful IT industry

④ How the Indian government supported the IT industry

3   What are two advanced functions of Revolution?

① It doesn't work when you are drunk.

② It helps you stay awake while driving.

③ It helps you park easily.

④ It automatically stops you from speeding.

A - 1 What is the woman worried about?

① She lost her dog.

② Her dog is acting strange.

③ Her dog barks too often.

④ Her dog doesn't listen to her.

2 Check [✓] T for true or F for false about the dog translator.

	T	F
(1) It can identify six different feelings.	☐	☐
(2) It only shows your dogs' feelings on a monitor.	☐	☐
(3) It was made by researching the sounds of many dogs.	☐	☐

B - 1 Choose the picture of Spaceship 2.

①   ②   ③   ④

2 What makes the man prefer the Lynx?

① cost

② design

③ safety

④ travel time

C - 1   Choose the wrong information.

> JY Mobile Company
>
> ① *Join our 5th Annual Design Competition!*
>
> • Who can join: ② anyone over 18 years old
>
> • What will be judged: ③ consumer preference and creativity
>
> • What the winner will get: ④ $20,000 and the latest cell phone

2   Choose last year's winning design.

①  ②   ③  ④

D - 1   Why was the vending machine made?

① To reduce the number of old people who smoke

② To research the age of smokers

③ To get information about peoples' faces

④ To stop teenagers from buying cigarettes

2   What should you do to use the vending machine?

① Put your photo in it

② Enter your ID number

③ Show your fingerprints

④ Look at the digital camera

A - 1   Why does China send seeds to space?

① To make vegetables taste better

② To provide food to astronauts

③ To produce more food

④ To check if plants can survive in space

2   Which is NOT a change that the seeds from space showed?

① The taste of their vegetables got better.

② The weight of their vegetables increased.

③ Their productivity increased.

④ Their growth rate became faster.

B - 1   Which is likely to be covered in *Enjoy your Life*?

① How to get a job in the IT industry

② Ways to communicate with teenagers

③ Hobbies middle-aged men can enjoy

④ How to take photos using a digital camera

2   Why did the man start learning the latest devices?

① To get closer to his daughter

② To open an electronics store

③ To publish a book about them

④ To be a teacher at a community center

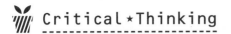
Technology in Sports

1 Check [✓] if each person is for or against getting help from technology in sports.

	For	Against
(1) Christina	☐	☐
(2) Chris	☐	☐
(3) Betty	☐	☐

2 Choose each person's opinion.

(1) Christina: _____   (2) Chris: _____   (3) Betty: _____

ⓐ Sports is about winning with only your body.

ⓑ Technology should be used in sports to break records.

ⓒ Using technology favors players from advanced countries.

ⓓ Getting the best result is not the most important thing in sports.

What do you think?

1

Check [✓] if you have the same opinion. You can add your own opinion in the blank.

☐ Winning with the help of technology is not truly winning.

☐ Using technology in sports makes competitions more interesting.

☐ For fair play, athletes should be encouraged not to use technology.

2

Talk about the following questions with your partner.

• Do you know any technology used in sports?

• How does technology affect athletes?

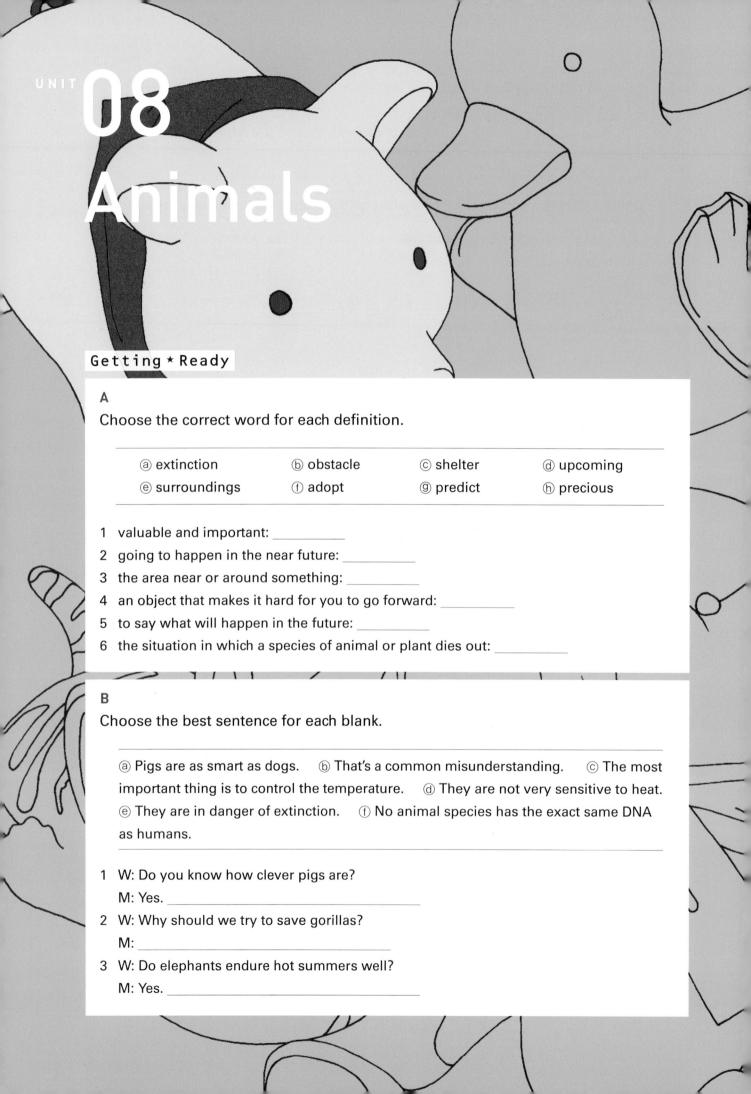

Animals

Getting ★ Ready

A

Choose the correct word for each definition.

ⓐ extinction	ⓑ obstacle	ⓒ shelter	ⓓ upcoming
ⓔ surroundings	ⓕ adopt	ⓖ predict	ⓗ precious

1 valuable and important: _____
2 going to happen in the near future: _____
3 the area near or around something: _____
4 an object that makes it hard for you to go forward: _____
5 to say what will happen in the future: _____
6 the situation in which a species of animal or plant dies out: _____

B

Choose the best sentence for each blank.

ⓐ Pigs are as smart as dogs.　ⓑ That's a common misunderstanding.　ⓒ The most important thing is to control the temperature.　ⓓ They are not very sensitive to heat. ⓔ They are in danger of extinction.　ⓕ No animal species has the exact same DNA as humans.

1 W: Do you know how clever pigs are?
   M: Yes. _____
2 W: Why should we try to save gorillas?
   M: _____
3 W: Do elephants endure hot summers well?
   M: Yes. _____

1   Choose the kind of dog that is described.

(1) _____   (2) _____

① 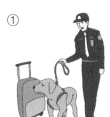   ②    ③    ④

2   According to the man, what is the sixth sense of animals?

① Sensing their death

② Hearing sounds far away

③ Predicting natural disasters

④ Sensing their enemies' approach

3   Which is NOT mentioned as a survival strategy of animals?

① Making their body bigger

② Pretending to be dead

③ Spraying smelly liquid

④ Changing their body color

A - 1 Why is the man NOT able to keep Betty anymore?

① He is going to study abroad.

② He is too busy to care for her.

③ He wants to get a different pet.

④ His family members don't like her.

2 What is important when taking care of Betty?

① Keeping her warm

② Feeding her insects

③ Not touching her often

④ Giving her enough water

B - 1 What would be the headline of the newspaper the man read?

① **How to Avoid a Shark Attack**

② **Why Sharks Attack People**

③ **Boy Survives Shark Attack**

④ **Are Sharks Really Dangerous?**

2 Which is NOT a way of avoiding a shark attack?

① Swimming in a group

② Not swimming at night

③ Wearing a dark-colored swimsuit

④ Remaining calm when you see a shark

C - 1 What are they mainly talking about?

   ① Tips for keeping a pet pig

   ② Misunderstandings about pigs

   ③ Reasons why pet pigs are popular

   ④ Things to consider when choosing a pet

2 Why do pigs roll in the mud?

   ① To find food to eat

   ② To make their bodies clean

   ③ To lower their body temperature

   ④ To protect their skin from the sun

D - 1 What is the man going to do this evening?

①    ②    ③    ④

2 When did the man learn about gorillas being in danger?

   ① After joining a gorilla tour in Africa

   ② After joining a campaign for wild animals

   ③ After reading a journal about wild animals

   ④ After watching a documentary about gorillas

A - 1   Match each animal with the way it deals with hot weather.

(1) Polar bears •   • ⓐ Getting their skin brushed

(2) Rhinoceros •   • ⓑ Eating frozen food in the water

(3) Elephants •   • ⓒ Taking a shower with cold water

2   What is the relationship between the speakers?

① tourist – tour guide

② reporter – zookeeper

③ customer – animal doctor

④ animal trainer – animal doctor

B - 1   Choose the wrong information.

No. 919

December 15th

① Where the dog was found: near the Union Square Theater

② Tags: Not found

③ Sex: Male

④ Condition: Broken leg

2   Write T for true or F for false about the Dog Center.

(1) It protects abandoned dogs for a month.   _____

(2) It is able to keep 100 dogs at a time.   _____

(3) It sells its dogs at a cheap price.   _____

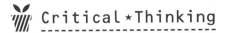 Critical ★ Thinking

Animal Testing

1 Check [✓] if each person is for or against animal testing.

	For	Against
(1) Mike	☐	☐
(2) Mary	☐	☐
(3) Bill	☐	☐

2 Match each person with their opinion.

(1) Mike • • ⓐ Animals are just as precious as human beings.

(2) Mary • • ⓑ Animal-tested medicines have saved a lot of people.

(3) Bill • • ⓒ Animal testing is not effective because humans and animals have different DNA.

What do you think?

1

Check [✓] if you have the same opinion. You can add your own opinion in the blank.

☐ Animal testing is very cruel, because animals can feel pain.

☐ We need to find other ways to test new drugs without animal testing.

☐ New drugs may have serious side effects, so they must be tested on animals.

_____

2

Talk about the following questions with your partner.

• Have you ever seen any TV programs about animal testing?

• What other methods do you think we could use to test new drugs?

09 Psychology

Getting ★ Ready

A

Choose the correct word for each definition.

ⓐ fake	ⓑ relieve	ⓒ appetite	ⓓ impression
ⓔ mental	ⓕ overcome	ⓖ praise	ⓗ crime

1 not real, but made to look real: _____
2 relating to the state of one's mind: _____
3 to reduce a pain or unpleasant feeling: _____
4 an action or activity that is against law: _____
5 to succeed in dealing with a problem or a feeling: _____
6 an opinion or a feeling that you have about someone: _____

B

Choose the best sentence for each blank.

ⓐ Married couples go through many things together. ⓑ It is the color that makes people feel calm. ⓒ That's why you look so depressed. ⓓ It would be the best color to use in a kitchen. ⓔ Married couples tend to resemble each other. ⓕ I lost my appetite after I broke up with my boyfriend.

1 M: Why aren't you eating much?
   W: _____

2 M: Why did you paint your room that color?
   W: _____

3 M: Look at my parents in this picture. Don't they look alike?
   W: Yes, they do. _____

1   What is the woman's point?

     ① Be kind to girls.

     ② Buy more stylish clothes.

     ③ Make a good first impression.

     ④ Don't judge others by their appearance.

2   Choose the right wallpaper color for each person.

ⓐ green	ⓑ blue	ⓒ orange	ⓓ pink

    (1) I want to lose weight.   _____

    (2) I want to focus on my writing.   _____

    (3) I feel uneasy, so I'd like to calm down.   _____

3   What are they mainly talking about?

     ① Why people get wrinkles

     ② Why married couples look alike

     ③ Why people like others who look like them

     ④ Why facial expressions are important

A - 1 What made Jeff change his attitude?

① Help from friends

② Concern and praise

③ A big enough reward

④ Proper punishment

2 What is the relationship between the speakers?

① teacher – parent

② teacher – teacher

③ teacher – student

④ teacher – principal

B - 1 Why did people NOT help the woman?

① They didn't know what to do.

② They were scared of the killer.

③ They didn't think it was an urgent situation.

④ They thought someone else would help her.

2 What would be the best way for someone in trouble to get help from others?

① Shout loudly

② Call for help in tears

③ Promise to give money

④ Ask a specific person for help

C - 1   What is the woman mainly talking about?

① Ways to buy products cheaply

② Reasons for using fake price tags

③ Difficulties in finding a real bargain

④ Pricing strategies to attract customers

2   Choose the two strategies that are described.

①	②
Every T-shirt $8.99	On Sale Today Only!

③	④
$80 → $40	3 T-shirts for $20

D - 1   What will the woman ask Peter to do?

① Watch her performance

② Change his presentation topic

③ Switch presentation times with her

④ Help her prepare for the performance

2   Who is following the man's advice?

① I'll buy Amy dinner before asking for a favor.

② I'll keep smiling while I ask for a favor.

③ I'll ask John for a favor when we're with other friends.

A - 1   Write T for true or F for false about people with Münchausen syndrome.

(1) They pretend they are sick.   _____

(2) They are afraid of getting hurt.   _____

(3) They have the syndrome because they want others' attention.   _____

2   What is Münchausen syndrome named after?

① A city in Germany

② The doctor who discovered the syndrome

③ A person who was famous for lying

④ A person who suffered from the disease

B - 1   Which book did the man probably read?

① *Changes in Fortune Telling*   ② *The Origins of Fortune Telling*   ③ *Various Forms of Fortune Telling*   ④ *Hidden Secrets of Fortune Telling*

2   What are the two tricks that fortune tellers use?

① Using difficult terms

② Telling a person positive things

③ Telling a person about common things

④ Guessing from the expressions on a person's face

 Critical ★ Thinking

Fighting Depression

1 What are they mainly talking about?

① Ways to feel better

② Benefits of working out

③ Reasons why people feel depressed

④ Things to do to improve one's appetite

2 What are the man's two explanations about human feelings?

① Exercising keeps you feeling good.

② Eating chocolate is helpful for depression.

③ Jogging is the best exercise to relieve stress.

④ Beta-endorphin makes people feel depressed.

What do you think?

1

Check [✓] the things you do when you want to feel better. You can add your own idea in the blank.

☐ Chatting with friends   ☐ Eating candy

☐ Doing outdoor activities   ☐ Going on a picnic

☐ Listening to music   ☐ Going shopping

_____

2

Talk about the following questions with your partner.

• Have you felt depressed lately?

• What did you do to feel better when you were depressed? Did it work?

10
Social Issues

A

Match each word with the correct definition.

1	relating to money	•	• ⓐ term
2	protection of yourself	•	• ⓑ local
3	connected with an area where you live	•	• ⓒ policy
4	a set of plans made by the government	•	• ⓓ financial
5	a good or useful quality that something has	•	• ⓔ advantage
6	a word or expression with a particular meaning	•	• ⓕ self-defense

B

Choose the best sentence for each blank.

> ⓐ It's due to an increase in double-income couples.   ⓑ At first, they were allowed to keep guns for self-defense.   ⓒ There are fewer side effects nowadays.   ⓓ They should be punished heavily.   ⓔ It's too early for children to face different cultures.   ⓕ It turned out to be a false bomb threat.

1   M: Why were people able to keep guns in the first place?
    W: _____

2   M: What do you think about studying abroad in elementary school?
    W: I'm against it. _____

3   M: Why is it difficult for families to eat together nowadays?
    W: _____

1   What is the man mainly talking about?

① How often children eat junk food

② Why people have fewer family meals

③ Why a family meal is important for children

④ What kind of meals children have nowadays

2   What does the man suggest to the woman?

① Use small grocery stores.

② Don't go shopping too often.

③ Work at a big discount store.

④ Go to a newly-opened store.

3   Check [✓] T for true or F for false about the "working poor."

	T	F
(1) They don't work hard to be rich.	☐	☐
(2) They have a job, but are paid low wages.	☐	☐
(3) Their number has grown rapidly since 2002.	☐	☐

A - 1   What are they mainly talking about?

① Ways to get self-confidence

② Why plastic surgery is popular

③ The danger of plastic surgery

④ Whether to get plastic surgery or not

2   Who has the same opinion as the man?

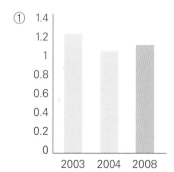

①

Have confidence in
yourself.

John

②

New medical
technology can be
trusted.

Kate

③

Consult with a doctor
before getting surgery.

Ted

B - 1   Which did the Singapore government NOT do to increase the birthrate?

① It made a wedding consulting agency.

② It provided wedding halls for free.

③ It helped colleges teach dating techniques.

④ It reduced taxes for families with children.

2   Choose the graph that shows Singapore's birthrate.

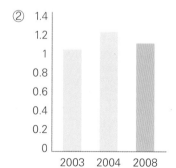
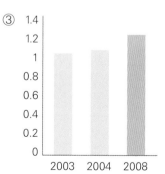

C - 1   Why was the woman's flight delayed?

① There was a terrible storm.

② There was a sick passenger.

③ It was searched for a bomb.

④ The plane's engine was out of order.

2   Which is the man's opinion?

① The airline should apologize for the delay.

② Airlines should be careful about flight accidents.

③ Heavy punishment for false bomb threats is needed.

④ The police should deal with bomb threats more quickly.

D - 1   Who are helicopter parents?

① We often give advice to our son, but he makes his own decisions.

John & Tina

② We always keep an eye on our son and worry about everything he does.

Joe & Cindy

③ We never worry about what our kid does.

Mike & Jill

2   Which describes children with helicopter parents?

① They are very responsible.

② They often make mistakes.

③ They find it hard to face failure.

④ They tend to succeed in society.

A - 1   What made the man start donating blood?

① His friend suggested that he do it.

② His doctor talked about a blood shortage.

③ His wife needed blood when getting surgery.

④ He saw a documentary about blood donation.

2   According to the man, what are two good points of blood donation?

① You can get healthier.

② You can help other people.

③ You can get blood when you need it.

④ You can get a medical checkup for free.

B - 1   Check [✓] T for true or F for false.   T   F

(1) About 30,000 people die from shootings every year in America.   ☐   ☐

(2) People over the age of 19 can keep a gun in America.   ☐   ☐

(3) An increase in the number of shootings can be related to   ☐   ☐

the economy.

2   According to the man, which is the main reason for teenage shootings?

① a bad economy

② illegal guns

③ easy access to guns

④ shooting scenes on screen

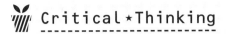 **Critical★Thinking**

Studying Abroad at an Early Age

1 Check [✓] if each person is for or against children studying abroad.

	For	Against
(1) Nick	☐	☐
(2) Anna	☐	☐
(3) Jay	☐	☐

2 Choose each person's opinion.

(1) Nick: _____   (2) Anna: _____   (3) Jay: _____

ⓐ Children without parents can be easily misguided.

ⓑ It takes a long time for children to get used to new culture.

ⓒ It's better to study abroad after establishing one's own identity.

ⓓ Learning foreign languages at an early age is helpful for their future careers.

What do you think?

1

Check [✓] if you have the same opinion. You can add your own opinion in the blank.

☐ It's better to learn foreign languages as early as possible.

☐ Children need to be with their parents while growing up.

☐ Studying abroad at an early age is good for developing a global mind.

2

Talk about the following questions with your partner.

• If you had been given the chance to study abroad when you were a child, what do you think it would have been like?

• Would you send your children to study abroad in the future? Why or why not?

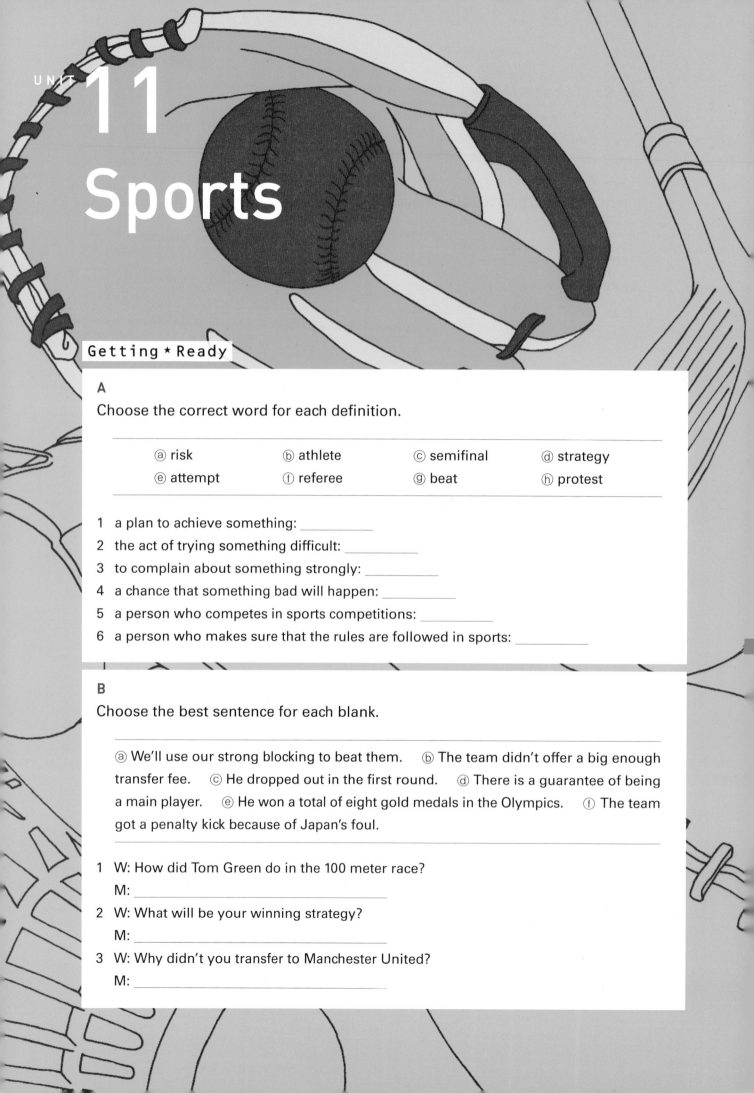

11
Sports

Getting ★ Ready

A

Choose the correct word for each definition.

ⓐ risk	ⓑ athlete	ⓒ semifinal	ⓓ strategy
ⓔ attempt	ⓕ referee	ⓖ beat	ⓗ protest

1 a plan to achieve something: _____
2 the act of trying something difficult: _____
3 to complain about something strongly: _____
4 a chance that something bad will happen: _____
5 a person who competes in sports competitions: _____
6 a person who makes sure that the rules are followed in sports: _____

B

Choose the best sentence for each blank.

ⓐ We'll use our strong blocking to beat them.   ⓑ The team didn't offer a big enough transfer fee.   ⓒ He dropped out in the first round.   ⓓ There is a guarantee of being a main player.   ⓔ He won a total of eight gold medals in the Olympics.   ⓕ The team got a penalty kick because of Japan's foul.

1 W: How did Tom Green do in the 100 meter race?
   M: _____

2 W: What will be your winning strategy?
   M: _____

3 W: Why didn't you transfer to Manchester United?
   M: _____

1   What happened to the woman?

     ① She fell down and broke her leg.

     ② Her car was damaged by a home run.

     ③ She hurt herself while playing baseball.

     ④ She got hit by a ball at a baseball stadium.

2   How will the man celebrate if he scores in the finals?

①    ②    ③    ④

3   Which is NOT true about Michael Phelps?

     ① He has won 14 Olympic gold medals.

     ② He broke seven world records in the 2008 Olympics.

     ③ He is much taller than other swimmers.

     ④ He has long arms and big feet.

A - 1   Choose the incorrect meaning of the uniform's number in soccer.

the best striker   the team's captain   the goalkeeper

2   How does the man feel now?

① excited

② worried

③ relieved

④ disappointed

70

B - 1   Write T for true or F for false about Usain Bolt.

(1) He became a runner because of his cricket coach's advice.   _____

(2) He won a silver medal in the Athens Olympics.   _____

(3) He won three gold medals in the Beijing Olympics.   _____

2   Why did Usain Bolt slow down during the 2008 Olympic 100 meter race?

① He hurt his leg.

② His shoelace was untied.

③ He was about to fall down.

④ He wanted to celebrate his victory.

C - 1   Which sport did the man watch yesterday?

①    ②    ③    ④

2   Who has the same opinion as the woman?

① Winning any Olympic medal is something to celebrate.

② The only goal for athletes is to win a gold medal.

③ For athletes, it's a great honor to take part in the Olympics.

D - 1   Why did David Adams transfer to the LA Galaxy?

① He respects their coach.

② They offered him a lot of money.

③ The Premier League teams didn't want him.

④ He has a better chance of being a main player.

2   What is the woman's attitude toward David Adam's decision?

① satisfied

② negative

③ favorable

④ indifferent

A - 1   What is the man's job?

① a sportscaster

② a volleyball player

③ a volleyball referee

④ a volleyball head coach

2   What is the team's winning strategy against Russia?

① quick speed

② powerful spikes

③ strong blocking

④ accurate serves

B - 1   What is the man mainly talking about?

① The most popular Olympic events

② The kinds of official Olympic events

③ Changes in the official Olympic events

④ Differences between the 2012 and 2016 Olympics

2   Which sport was selected for the 2012 Olympics?

①  ②  ③  ④

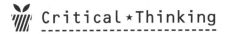 Critical ★ Thinking

Referees' Mistakes

1 **What are they mainly talking about?**

① Why referees often make a wrong decision

② How one soccer team cheated to win a game

③ Whether referees should correct their mistakes

④ How coaches can complain about referees' decisions

2 **Choose the woman's opinion.**

① When a referee makes the wrong decision, he should correct it.

② If a referee's decision doesn't change the result, it doesn't need to be changed.

③ Referees should not change their decisions in any situation.

73

What do you think?

1

Check [✓] if you have the same opinion. You can add your own opinion in the blank.

☐ Referees' mistakes can give an unfair advantage to one team.

☐ Referees should correct a wrong decision after seeing a close-up view.

☐ If referees change their decision whenever there are complaints, the game will never end.

2

Talk about the following questions with your partner.

• Do you remember any game in which a referee made a wrong decision?

• What should be done to reduce referees' mistakes?

12 Environment

Getting ★ Ready

A

Match each word with the correct definition.

1 making you feel angry   •

2 to use something again   •

3 to stay on the surface of water without sinking   •

4 something useful owned by a country or person   •

5 physical harm caused to someone or something   •

6 something that is thrown away because it's worthless   •

• ⓐ float

• ⓑ resource

• ⓒ recycle

• ⓓ damage

• ⓔ garbage

• ⓕ annoying

B

Choose the best sentence for each blank.

ⓐ The ice is melting and getting thinner.　　ⓑ How does recycling affect our environment?　　ⓒ Once they're buried, the chemicals last for a long time.　　ⓓ Why is the water polluted with black waste?　　ⓔ Animals will lose their homes and die out.　　ⓕ Will melting Arctic ice influence other areas?

1 M: _____
   W: We can save natural resources by doing it.

2 M: What environmental change is happening in the Arctic?
   W: _____

3 M: _____
   W: Factories threw away waste water.

1   What are they mainly talking about?

① The process of recycling

② How to save natural resources

③ The importance of separating waste

④ Environmental problems around the world

2   Choose the right situation for each country.

(1) Spain: _____   (2) France: _____   (3) America: _____

ⓐ Bears don't sleep during winter.

ⓑ There wasn't any snow at all during winter.

ⓒ The buds of chestnut trees come out earlier.

3   Check [✓] T for true or F for false.   T   F

(1) The reporter is at the International Airport now.   ☐   ☐

(2) Airplane noise can lower students' academic scores.   ☐   ☐

(3) The government is researching how serious the noise   ☐   ☐

near the airport is.

A - 1 Which is NOT an activity of the environment club?

① Selling recycled items

② Holding a variety of events

③ Leading campaigns for saving energy

④ Giving out guidebooks about environmental protection

2 What will they probably do next?

① Go to a bookstore

② Participate in a painting competition

③ Join the environment club at school

④ Watch a documentary about pollution

B - 1 What's the purpose of the contest?

① To inform students how to protect the earth

② To let students know how serious pollution is

③ To give students a chance to show their talent

④ To raise money for the environmental campaign

2 Choose the wrong information.

Join the Environmental Poster Painting Contest!

① Date: 6. 4 (Next Saturday)

② Time: from 9:00 a.m.

③ Location: at the school gym

④ How to apply: hand in an application form by this Friday

C - 1 What are they doing now?

① Looking up environmental sites

② Taking photos related to pollution

③ Searching for a photo for their homework

④ Looking at brochures about a photo exhibition

2 Choose the photo that Susan chose.

①  ②  ③  ④

D - 1 What is the woman mainly talking about?

① How to drive a hybrid car

② Why we should buy hybrid cars

③ How hybrid cars help the environment

④ Which power is usually used by hybrid cars

2 How are hybrid cars different from regular cars?

① They use gasoline.

② They use two power sources.

③ They don't produce harmful gas.

④ They can drive as fast as 200 kph.

A - 1   What are they mainly talking about?

① Ways to protect wildlife in the Arctic

② Why ice in the Arctic is melting fast

③ How the rising sea level will affect people

④ The effects of ice melting in the Arctic

2   According to Dr. J., what will happen if all the ice in the Arctic melts?

① Global warming will be more serious.

② The temperature of the Arctic will fall.

③ Some coastal areas will be underwater.

④ The number of animals in the Arctic will increase.

B - 1   How is the woman encouraging people to join the campaign?

① By mentioning the benefits of recycling

② By listing the chemicals in cell phones

③ By discussing the diseases caused by burying cell phones

④ By explaining harmful effects caused by cell phones

2   Choose the wrong information.

Save Earth!

① When: 6.1~7.31

② Where: ABC Service Center

③ Goal for this year: collecting 40,000 cell phones

④ Contact: 3142–0357

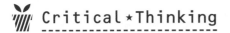

Critical ★ Thinking

Yellow Dust

1 **What are they mainly talking about?**

① Why should we reduce yellow dust?

② How does yellow dust affect people's lives?

③ What should China do to prevent yellow dust?

④ Should China be responsible for reducing yellow dust?

2 **Check [✓] T for true or F for false.**

	T	F
(1) Yellow dust is mostly from Chinese desert areas.	☐	☐
(2) The Chinese government strictly bans cutting down trees.	☐	☐
(3) Planting vegetables can be helpful in reducing yellow dust.	☐	☐

What do you think?

1

Check [✓] if you have the same opinion. You can add your own opinion in the blank.

☐ China is responsible for the damage caused by yellow dust.

☐ Other countries need to help China solve the yellow dust problem.

☐ China should pay money for the troubles caused by yellow dust.

2

Talk about the following questions with your partner.

• Have you ever had a problem because of yellow dust? What was it?

• What can the world do to prevent yellow dust?

Vocabulary ★ List

UNIT 01

camping
experience
totally
campfire
nature
set up
meal
relationship
report
horseback riding
rider
stay in shape
burn
calorie
relaxed
relieve
confident
rafting
safety guideline
shoelace
tighten
tie
life jacket
fit
tightly
take off
relax
float
struggle
sink
remain seated
trekking
scenery
trail
riverside
wildflower

forest
have ~ in mind
look up
even if
scuba diving
indoor
nearby
foreign
membership fee
overseas
experienced
beginner
be afraid of
basic
newcomer
soldier
divide
gun
shoot
get hit
starting point
flag
thrill
workout
strategy
hot-air balloon
basket
expect
rise
land
ground
pack up
on board
scary
take off
sunrise
be sure to-v
set

weather forecast
body temperature
get lost
wood
rescue
wonder
activity
participate in
outdoor
canoe
carry out
shallow
quality
limit
register
as though
breathe
trash
leave behind
hiker
awful
besides
throw
garbage
destroy
protect
entrance fee
realize
make an effort
put up
environmental

UNIT 02

mind
channel
perform
latest

for the first time
weird
schedule
get mixed up
be supposed to-v
broadcast
replace
related
wildlife
provide
food for thought
silly
joke
disappear
soap opera
necessity
brain
develop
calorie
chance
gain weight
negative
effect
relationship
triangle
miss
episode
tape
blank tape
get married
ending
in advance
rerun
patient
rent
would-be
reality show
idol

competition

competitor

compete

remain

debut

come true

judge

honor

failure

participate in

be sick of

variety show

entertainer

promote

concept

copy

broadcasting company

protest

create

effective

raise one's voice

viewer

million

air

release

recently

inform A of B

box office

specialist

make one's debut
—
cartoon

niece

nephew

article

violence

violent

scene

character

influence

station

be to blame

monitor

educational

pleased

award

category

announce

so far

nominate

witch

performance

unforgettable

plot

take place

special effect

real

envelope

host

camerawork

sound effect
—
detail

private

privacy

general public

respect

paparazzo

gossip

the media

satisfy

curiosity

be responsible for

deliver

regular customer

additional

order

rush

delivery

delay

bite

be short of hands

chef

excuse

complain

take care of

reputation

professional

packaging

technique

provide

overseas

pack

unpack

arrange

schedule an appointment

have one's hair done

get a perm

curly

curl

edge

give it a try

dye

damaged

at the same time

condition

hair treatment
—
transportation

wallet

describe

lost and found

identification

unfortunately

stripe

as soon as possible

passenger

develop

customer

trend

comment

extra

be affected by

electromagnetic wave

be aware of

flow

electronic

goods

at least

water content

absorb

antenna

device

turn off

make sure to-v

unplug

subscribe

issue

discount

since

annual

subscription

credit card

prefer

bank transfer
—
billing address

social security number

consider

sign up for

e-billing service

benefit

gasoline

annual fee

soak

salt

sneakers

toothpaste

dress shirt

collar

rub

washing machine

dirt

remove

extend

weekday

business hours

unfair

force A to-v

convenience

have a hard time v-ing

branch

region

clerk

rotate

overtime work

UNIT 04

dish

vegetable

sliced

beef

boiling

dip

sauce

traditional

bowl

contain

carrot

cucumber

mushroom

spinach

red pepper paste

appetizer

honey

mustard

dressing

recommend

well-done

rare

offer

recent

research

destroy

nutrient

avoid

element

prevent A from v-ing

take in

iron

besides

reduce

cholesterol level

not to mention

corn

calorie

burn off

in the first place

store

fridge

cloudy

cabinet

even though

reservation

put up with

inconvenience

apologize for

rib

tough

chef

appetite

charge

tasty

Spanish

be surrounded by

seafood

paella

spice

saffron

flamenco

performance

midnight

cabbage

medical

benefit

in particular

stomach

effect

stand

bitter

as soon as possible

boil

owner

run

raw

nonsense

create

appeal

come up with

apart from

recognize

Eastern

decorate

negative

favorable

indifferent

ingredient

food tasting event

calm down

evaluate

based on

publish

tire

version

honored

complain

annoyed

depressed

embarrassed

canned

genetically

modified

price tag

GM(genetically modified)

guarantee

in the long run

shortage

beneficial

UNIT 05

trend

keep in mind

basic

colorful

accessory

stay away from

beige

necklace

fashionable

monitor

worst dresser

festival

sweep

attractive

unfortunately

go well with

tone

slim

count

editor

article

fancy

manage

related to

shoot

cover

concept

sponsor

monitor

makeup

up-to-date

career

silhouette

practical

talented

casual

finale

responsibility

profit

facility

the disabled

refuse

cause

fitting

raise money

advisor

match

top

bottom

stripe

vertical

chest

upper body

latest

survey

positively

recently

collection

shocking

encourage

praise

courage

popularity

designer brand

stylish

suddenly

have a crush on

overnight

consider

shape

skinny jean

smart

be based on

reflect

material

environmentally-friendly

unsold

trash

outdated

garbage

purchase

negative

indifferent

childhood

look

labeled

hire

solo exhibition

icon

pants suit

freedom

status

retire

work of art

protest

right

expression

personal

preference

bracelet

double standard

in the world

embarrassing

underwear

current

UNIT 06

velvet

material

contain

heal

damaged

shiny

smooth

blueberry

perfume

vitamin pill

theme

present

collection

traditional

costume

exhibition

royal

jewelry

furniture

gallery

Lost and Found

leather

handle

marketing

handkerchief

be located

slim

work out

solution

equipment

lose weight

lift

switch on

shake

notice

original

offer

dial

cosmetics

sensitive skin

allergy

ad

government

advantage

strategy

effective

trust

brand-name

compare

announcement

passenger

departure

delay

repair

ground crew

currently

gate

board

apologize for

inconvenience

cancel

due to

destination

commercial

advertise

have to do with

teaser advertisement

in detail

attention

attract

positive

on board

cruise

scenery

firework

performance

taste

sauna

duty free shop

safety lesson

gather

life jacket

staff

feature

deck

issue

junk food

government

appear

particular

harmful

ban

affect

soda

disagree with

fair

profit

main actress

scene

product placement

film director

on purpose

annoying

unnecessary

lower

properly

UNIT 07

robot

human

emotion

sadness

position

eyelid

eyebrow

make a gesture

lift

purpose

facial expression

IT(information technology)

industry

effort

encourage

export

software company

although

technical

labor cost

developed country

hire

follow up

latest

vehicle

revolution

stylish

advanced

function

fall asleep

drunk driving

sensor

alarm

parking

wheel

forward

backward

automatically

upset

pet

not ~ an inch

totally

translator

technology

analyze

bark

identify

gather

tourist

spaceship

space shuttle

side by side

regular

take part in

competition

participate

judge

favorable

consumer

creativity

count

wrist

wireless

annual

preference

unique

cigarette

vending machine

prevent A from v-ing

in order to-v

stare

digital camera

wrinkle

bone structure

compare A with B

set

reject

driver's license

fingerprint

seed

huge

shortage

genetic

characteristic

turn out

productivity

increase

cucumber

taste

weight

green pepper

astronaut

author

middle-aged

high-tech

device

community center

recommend

electronics store

publish

result

challenge

limit

spirit

swimsuit

athlete

performance

break a record

scientific

make sense

equal

advantage

technically

take the lead

favor

highly

sensitive

sight

hunter

shoot

guide

blind

deal with

obstacle

crosswalk

order

forward

sixth sense

touch

tsunami

occur

Indian Ocean

sense

upcoming

natural disaster

predict

earthquake

volcano

enemy

approach

strategy

protect

gray tree frog

depending on

surrounding

blowfish

blow up

scare away

skunk

liquid

survival

pretend

spray

smelly

hand over

give away

go abroad

particularly

control

temperature

chameleon

active

shady

care for

feed

headline

attack

shark

surf

fortunately

seriously

bite

off the coast

calm

sudden

attract

attention

survive

remain

common

misunderstanding

roll

mud

by oneself

unbelievable

greedy

lower

costume

gorilla

raise money

save

extinction

be supposed to-v

dress up

decrease

campaign

journal

documentary

viewer

endure

polar bear

frozen

cube

beat

heat

rhinoceros

brush

make sense

effort

zookeeper

abandon

name tag

female

shelter

adopt

put to sleep

adoption

fee

male

animal testing

necessary

process

medicine

test

drug

possible

side effect

develop

experiment

disease

pain

precious

cruel

creature

species

exact

effective

blind date

type

far from

stylish

well-dressed

impression

judge

pay attention to

appearance

wallpaper

concentrate

reduce

appetite

on the other hand

improve

prison

violence

uneasy

calm down

look alike

tend to-v

resemble

scientifically

prove

go through

share

facial

wrinkle

notice

troublemaker

react

behavior

punish

approach

praise

embarrassed

make an effort

attitude

concern

reward

proper

principal

crime

scene

instead of

responsible

face

situation

specific

shout

be scared of

urgent

loudly

call for

tear

seller

strategy

product

fake

suppose

bargain

preparation

presentation

at the same time

switch

favor

owe

be likely to-v

refuse

request

exactly

syndrome

mental

illness

pretend

patient

attention

German

discover

liar

lie

symptom

suffer from

fortune teller

lonely

completely

general

from time to time

make sense

trick

trust

waste

origin

form

term

break up with

move on

depressed

research

overcome

depression

jog

work out

mood

produce

material

beta-endorphin

relieve

UNIT 10

meal

due to

double-income couple

advantage

rather than

junk food

moreover

take part in

regular

alcohol

drug

grocery

large discount store

go out of business

selection

shut down

affect

local

economy

in the long run

own

survive

lately

term

mid

refer to

remain

income

directly

class

full-time job

decrease

part-time job

travel abroad

be satisfied with

plastic surgery

side effect

self-confidence

persuade

concern

medical

consult with

birthrate

policy

found

wedding consulting agency

riverboat

encourage

technique

average

drop

financial

tax

reach

departure

bomb

passenger

on board

search

turn out

false

threat

behavior

no longer

punish heavily

storm

out of order

apologize for

deal with

care

frequently

adult

insist on v-ing

when it comes to

marriage

fail

problem solving ability

have a hard time v-ing

failure

as a result
successful
keep an eye on
responsible
donate
shortage
surgery
blood donation
benefit
pay attention to
work out
healthy diet
medical checkup
gun control
professor
shooting
identification
self-defense
what's more
sudden
carry out
teenager
copy
be related to
illegal
access
lately
guide
direction
get used to
environment
confused
identity
establish
misguide

UNIT 11

fall down
stadium

foul ball
right away
bill
responsibility
avoid
fair
parked
damage
victory
second half
score
celebration
final
coach
look forward to v-ing
celebrate
medal
hero
set
record
achieve
suitable
length
soccer
uniform
be anxious to-v
represent
striker
whatever
symbolic
goalkeeper
captain
relieved
disappointed
Jamaica
cricket
runner
drop out
first round
injury

ability
event
slow down
finish line
shoelace
untied
team relay
be about to-v
fencing
semifinal
match
weightlifting
result
attempt
athlete
second best
achievement
bronze
transfer
offer
transfer fee
reject
the Premier League
guarantee
main player
left-wing
position
risk
gain
opportunity
decision
eventually
respect
attitude
favorable
indifferent
tight
make the finals
strategy
blocking

powerful
spiker
quickness
beat
sportscaster
volleyball
referee
head coach
spike
accurate
serve
official
International Olympic Committee
mixed
doubles
ping pong
remove
hurdle
marathon
add
softball
on the other hand
karate
rugby
penalty kick
foul
obviously
appeal
complain
protest
correct
cheat
situation

UNIT 12

garbage
trash bin
separate

87

annoying

environment

affect

resource

recycle

reduce

waste

bench

process

environmental

global warming

unusual

area

awake

Alps

bud

chestnut

reporter

overhead

cause

hearing ability

furthermore

academic achievement

government

immediately

lower

pollution

guidebook

protect

hand out

recycled product[item]

contest

based on

apply

drop by

campaign

protection

participate in

poster

purpose

exhibit

local

art gallery

application form

hand in

inform

due

search for

float

dead

alive

black

waste water

pour

brochure

exhibition

hybrid car

power source

driving power

gasoline

engine

electric

motor

speed up

turn off

effectively

harmful

kph(kilometer per hour)

guest

expert

Arctic

average

rise

melt

trend

die out

influence

entire

sea level

coastal

island

tragic

wildlife

underwater

increase

dangerous

chemical

bury

pollute

last

conduct

donate

benefit

yellow dust

hold ~ responsible for

damage

as long as

desert

cut down

worsen

plant

mostly

strictly

ban

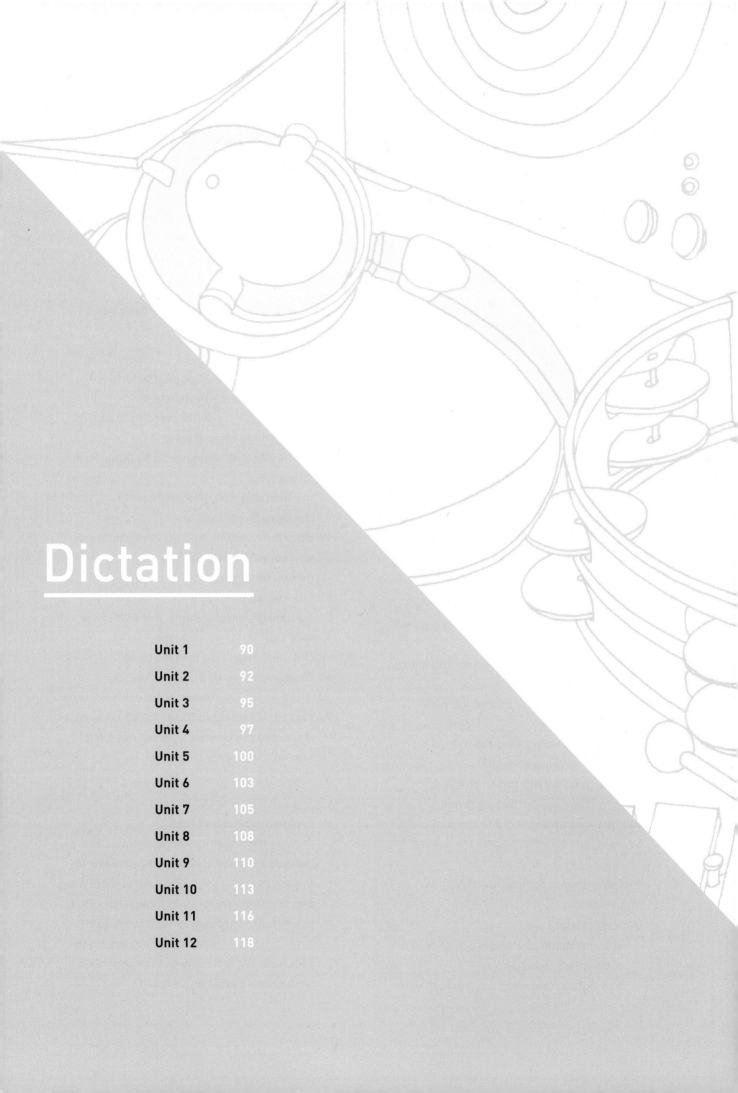

Dictation

UNIT 01 Outdoor Activities

Listening ★ Start   Answers p. 2

1

M: When my dad first suggested _____ _____, I didn't want to go because I thought a camping trip would be uncomfortable. But the camping experience totally _____ _____ _____. It's fun to play in the water, catch fish, and have a campfire in the evening. And of course, I can enjoy beautiful nature. But _____ _____ _____, it's a great way to become closer with family members. When camping, we have to work together to _____ _____ _____ _____ or cook a meal. While doing those jobs, we can talk and laugh a lot.

2

M: This is Alex Kim reporting for NTV. These days, many people _____ _____ _____. Let's hear from riders why they do it. Hello.

W: Hello.

M: How long have you been riding horses?

W: It's been _____ _____.

M: Was there any special reason you started horseback riding?

W: I just wanted to do something with animals. _____ _____ I started horseback riding, I started to love it.

M: What's so good about it?

W: It's a good way to stay in shape. It _____ _____ _____ than swimming.

M: That's surprising. I didn't know that.

W: Also, as I spend time with the horses, I _____ _____ _____.

M: I see. Thanks for the interview.

3

W: Hello. Before we _____ _____, I'll tell you the safety guidelines you should follow. First, wear shoes _____ _____ and tighten them. It is easy to lose your shoes if they aren't tied. The second guideline is about helmets and life jackets. _____ _____ they fit tightly. Never take them off. Next, once we start rafting, don't stand. _____ _____ inside the boat is dangerous. Lastly, if you fall into the water, just relax. That will help you float. If you struggle, _____ _____.

Listening ★ Practice   Answers p. 2

A [1-2]

M: Maria, let's _____ _____ tomorrow.

W: Trekking? I've never done it before.

M: Then you should try it! You can _____ _____ _____ while walking in nature.

W: Okay. Where should we go?

M: I'm thinking of Yellowwood National Park. There are _____ _____ _____ there: the riverside trail, the wildflower trail, and the deep forest trail.

W: Both the riverside trail and the wildflower trail sound wonderful. _____ _____ do you have in mind?

M: I looked up photos of each trail on the homepage, and I thought the wildflower trail was _____ _____ _____.

W: Did you? Then let's take that one.

M: Or, if you want, you can decide after _____ _____ those photos.

W: Well, it will be too difficult to decide even if I do see the photos. Just tell me what I should prepare for tomorrow.

M: Okay.

B [1-2]

W: Dream Scuba Diving Club _____ _____ _____ new members. We practice every Saturday in indoor swimming pools or in the sea at _____ _____. Also, there are two scuba diving tours to foreign countries every year. Our membership fee is $50 _____ _____, not including overseas tour fees. We welcome both experienced scuba divers and beginners. If _____

_____ _____ trying scuba diving, please come to the California University school pool this Saturday. You can learn some of _____ _____ _____ _____ for free. Experience it for yourself and decide if you want to join us.

C [1-2]

M: Wow, look at you in this picture. You're _____ _____ a soldier and covered in paint!

W: Oh, yes. That picture was taken after a paintball game.

M: A paintball game?

W: It's a kind of _____ _____. Players are divided into two teams and fight each other with paintball guns.

M: They try to _____ _____ of the other team, right?

W: Yes. A person who gets hit by a paintball is out of the game.

M: Does one team need to shoot all the other team's members to _____ _____ _____?

W: No, the game ends when one team comes back to the starting point after catching _____ _____ _____ _____.

M: It sounds so exciting. I guess it's important to think of a good plan to catch the flag quickly.

W: Exactly. That's the most interesting part and _____ _____ I love paintball.

D [1-2]

M: This morning, I went on a hot-air balloon ride with my friend. We paid _____ _____ for a 30-minute ride. The basket under the balloon was large enough to _____ _____ _____, and it was almost full. At first, I thought it would be boring to look at the city _____ _____ _____. But watching the city and nearby forests was more amazing than I expected. I also watched the sun rise, and it was the most beautiful thing _____ _____ _____. Thirty minutes in the

air felt really short. After landing on the ground, we packed up the air balloon with the other people _____ _____.

Listening * Challenge Answers p. 2

A [1-2]

W: Dad, I'm _____ _____ in the mountains with my friends this Saturday.

M: Only with your friends? Don't you know how dangerous the mountains are _____ _____?

W: Well, they're not high mountains, so we'll be okay.

M: Even so, be sure to come down before it _____ _____. The sun sets early these days.

W: Okay. Dad, what clothes should I wear? The weather forecast says it'll be _____ _____.

M: Put on many thin items of clothing under a warm winter coat. That'll help you control your _____ _____.

W: I see.

M: And eat some chocolate or candy while you're climbing. You'll _____ _____ if you get hungry.

W: Okay. I'll buy some tomorrow.

M: One more thing! If you _____ _____ in the woods, don't move around. Stay where you are and wait for rescue.

W: I don't think _____ _____ _____ we will get lost.

M: Oh, I can't relax. Maybe I should go with you.

W: Dad!

B [1-2]

(Telephone rings.)

M: Pine Camp office, how may I help you?

W: Hello. _____ _____ _____ _____ about the summer camp program at Bear Lake that starts on July 7th.

M: Sure.

W: I'm wondering _____ _____ are

91

included in the program.

M: For 5 days, children will participate in basic camp activities like hiking and _____ _____. Plus, there'll be special programs including swimming and canoeing.

W: My younger daughter is afraid of deep water. Will she be okay?

M: Water activities will be _____ _____ in shallow water, so don't worry about it.

W: Great. How much is it?

M: It is $400 per child. It's more expensive than other camps, but the quality is _____ _____.

W: Okay. I want to send my two daughters. They're 10 and 6 years old.

M: Ma'am, I'm sorry but this camp is _____ _____ ages 8 to 12.

W: Really? I didn't even think about the age limit.

M: Would you like to _____ _____ _____ _____ only?

W: Well... yes, please.

Critical ★ Thinking   Answers p. 2

M: Sally, I'm glad I came here to hike. I feel _____ _____ I can breathe better in this fresh air.

W: Me, too. Anyway, shall we set up a tent over there?

M: Okay. Oh, no! Look at all that trash _____ _____ by hikers!

W: That's awful!

M: You know what? Besides throwing garbage on the ground, I heard many hikers are _____ _____ by cutting them down for fires. I don't know why they don't care more about nature.

W: You're right. If they want to _____ _____, they should try to protect it.

M: It might be better if national parks weren't open to hikers.

W: But it would be hard to _____ _____ without visitors' entrance fees. Instead, I

think hikers should realize the importance of _____ _____.

M: I agree. Then, why don't we make a little effort first? Let's clean up the trash before _____ _____ our tent.

W: Good idea.

UNIT 02 Entertainment

Listening ★ Start   Answers p. 2

1

M: Jane, _____ _____ _____ turning to Channel 11?

W: No, I don't mind. Is there a special program on?

M: Yes. *ABC Music* is on now. My favorite singer, Christina, will be performing _____ _____ _____ for the first time.

W: Wow, let's watch it together... well, that's weird. The evening news is on Channel 11 now.

M: Really? Maybe it's _____ _____ _____. Check some other channels.

W: I don't see any music programs on the other channels, either. _____ _____ _____ about the time?

M: Let me check the TV schedule... uh-oh. It looks like I got mixed up.

W: What does the schedule say?

M: _____ _____ _____ be broadcast tomorrow.

2

M1: I'm Adam. I like watching programs _____ _____ animals, especially the lives of animals in Africa. Last week, I watched one about the wildlife of southern Africa. It was _____ _____.

W: I'm Betty. I'm curious about what is happening around the world. So I like programs that provide _____ _____ _____ _____. TV shows about events around the world give me a lot of food for thought.

M2: I'm Chris. I hate _____ _____
_____. So I watch shows full of silly
jokes. The day's stress disappears when I

_____ _____.

3

W: TV has _____ _____ _____ we can't
live without. Some people say that TV can
help us in many ways. But I believe
_____ _____ not to watch too much
TV. Why? As you know, our brains don't
do any work while we're _____ _____,
because we're only receiving TV images.
It's especially bad for children whose
brains are not _____ _____. Also,
people don't burn calories while sitting
watching TV. A study showed that people
who watch a lot of TV have a higher
chance of _____ _____.

Listening * Practice   Answers p. 3

A [1-2]

M: Did you watch *Love Triangle* yesterday?

W: Of course. You know I always watch it on

_____ _____.

M: I missed yesterday's episode.

W: Why did you miss it? Did you go to bed
early?

M: No, I had a lot of _____ _____, so I
had to work on it all night.

W: What a pity! You shouldn't have missed
yesterday's episode.

M: You _____ _____ _____, right? Can
you lend it to me?

W: Sorry, but I couldn't tape the last episode
because I didn't have a _____ _____.

M: Oh, that's too bad.

W: I can tell you what happened, though.
Sophie and James finally _____
_____ and...

M: Stop it! I don't want to know the ending
in advance. I'm going to _____ _____
_____.

W: Are you going to watch the rerun?

M: I'm not patient enough to wait that long. I'll
just download it _____ _____ _____.

W: (*laughs*) All right.

B [1-2]

M: Did you hear that KBC is looking for
_____ _____ for its new reality show?

W: Is it like *American Idol*?

M: Yes. The program is called *Star*. It's a
_____ _____ for you.

W: How does the competition work?

M: There are 12 competitors and two of them
compete each week. The person who
remains _____ _____ _____ is the
winner.

W: But what if I fail?

M: How do you know what will happen
without trying? The winner gets the
chance to _____ _____ _____
_____ and win $10,000.

W: I don't know...

M: Being a singer is your dream, right? If you
don't try, it'll never _____ _____.

W: Do you know who the judges are?

M: Famous singers like Madonna and Sting.

W: Wow. _____ _____ _____ _____
just to sing in front of them.

M: So try it. Don't be afraid of failure.

C [1-2]

M: I'm so _____ _____ variety shows
these days.

W: What's wrong with them?

M: The same entertainers are on every
channel. They're only there to _____
_____ _____ or songs.

W: That's true.

M: And it's not just that. The programs all
follow the same concept, which is all
about _____ _____.

W: I think the bigger problem is copying
other countries' entertainment shows. It's
like watching the same program _____
_____ _____ _____.

M: I agree. There's a lot to be changed.

93

W: How about making our opinions heard? We could call the broadcasting companies to protest or _____ _____ with others who have the same opinion.

M: Why don't we create an online community? It will be more effective if we raise our voices _____ _____ _____.

W: Good idea. Let's start one right now.

D [1-2]

M: Here's tonight's Fun TV schedule. _____ _____ _____, *Focus* will be broadcast. Competitors answer ten questions, and the winner of the final round takes home _____ _____ _____! *Jimmy's Show* is going to air at 8:30 p.m. Usher and Britney, who released new albums recently, will sing _____ _____ _____. *With Anne* is scheduled at 10 p.m. We'll inform you of what's been going on in Hollywood this week, _____ _____ who's dating and what's new at the box office. At 11 p.m., famous drama writer Jason Smith's *Specialists, Season 1*, will _____ _____ _____. Come check out what's happening at the hospital.

Listening ★ Challenge   Answers p. 3

A [1-2]

W: Have you watched cartoons on TV recently?

M: No. But _____ _____ _____ and nephews watch them every day.

W: If I were you, I would be worried about them. I saw an article _____ _____ _____ saying that violence in cartoons is a serious problem.

M: Are there many violent scenes?

W: Yes. Characters fight or _____ _____ _____ in many scenes.

M: I can't believe it. That could be a bad influence on little kids.

W: I know. I think the TV stations _____ _____ _____. They show these kinds of cartoons in the early evening when kids

watch TV the most.

M: I think parents also _____ _____ _____ what their children are watching and not allow them to watch violent shows. Usually, parents don't think cartoons could be _____ _____ _____ _____.

W: But I think TV stations should do something first. They should select educational cartoons that are good for _____ _____.

B [1-2]

W: Good evening. I'm Amy Jones. _____ _____ to be part of the Best TV Drama Awards.

M: Good evening. I'm Justin Watson. Awards in _____ _____ have been announced so far. Now, I'm curious about the Best Drama of the Year.

W: Me, too. Three dramas _____ _____ _____ for this award.

M: Yes. Let's check them out one by one.

W: Okay. First, we have *Witches*. Wonderful performances by _____ _____ made this drama unforgettable.

M: And here's another strong one, *The Boys*. The exciting plot made this series _____ _____ _____ _____ of the year.

W: And lastly, there's *Dream*. This show takes place 100 years in the future. Amazing special effects made the future _____ _____.

M: What a difficult choice to make!

W: All right, Justin. We can't wait any longer. Could you please _____ _____ _____?

M: Okay. I think it's time to find out.

Critical ★ Thinking   Answers p. 3

M: I'm Ted. Entertainment news on TV gives _____ _____ _____ about stars' private lives. But stars also need their privacy. Although the general public wants to know every single detail of the

94

_____ _____, the privacy of these people should be respected. How would you feel if the paparazzi were around you _____ _____ _____ _____ and your mistakes were all over the news?

W: I'm Nell. Entertainers already knew their lives would be other _____ _____ when they joined the entertainment business. Also, some entertainers make their lives open to the media to _____ _____ _____. It's natural for the general public to be interested in entertainers. News about their _____ _____ satisfies people's curiosity. It's good for not only the entertainment business and the public, but also the _____ _____.

UNIT 03 Daily Life

Listening ⋆ Start Answers p. 3

1

(*Telephone rings.*)

W: Hello, Grand Chinese Restaurant.

M: Yes. My address is 603 Main Street and I _____ _____ _____ _____ about an hour ago.

W: I remember. You're one of my regular customers. Do you want to _____ _____ _____ _____?

M: That's not the reason I called. My food was cold when it arrived.

W: I'm sorry. We had a rush of orders, so your delivery may have been delayed.

M: That's not all. It was _____ _____ _____ I couldn't have more than one bite.

W: Was it? We are really short of hands, so maybe our chef made a mistake.

M: I understand that you're busy, but _____ _____ _____ for bad food.

W: I'm so sorry.

2

M: Are you planning to move soon? If so, one call to Speed Movers will _____ _____ _____ all your moving needs. With 20 years of experience, we have maintained a great reputation. Using our _____ _____ and packaging techniques, we provide moving services to any place, even overseas. Our main services are _____ _____: packing, moving, new house cleaning, unpacking, and arranging unpacked items. We are here for you _____ _____ _____ _____ from 9 a.m. to 7 p.m. Please call 143–9012 to schedule an appointment.

3

M: How would you like to _____ _____ _____ _____ today?

W: I can't decide between cutting it short and getting a perm.

M: In my opinion, you'll look prettier _____ _____ _____. How about some curls just on the edge?

W: Well... I've never thought about that kind of style.

M: Try it. I'm sure it'll _____ _____ on you.

W: If you say so, I'll give it a try. Plus, I want to dye my hair light brown.

M: Well, your hair is _____ _____ now. I don't think it's a good idea to do both at the same time.

W: Oh, I see. I didn't know the condition of my hair was that bad.

M: Why don't you _____ _____ _____ _____ instead?

W: Okay.

Listening ⋆ Practice Answers p. 3

A [1-2]

(*Telephone rings.*)

M: BG transportation company.

W: Hello. I rode one of your buses this morning and _____ _____ _____

95

on it. Do you happen to have it?

M: Let me check. Do you remember the
_____ _____?

W: It was 14.

M: Okay. Could you describe the wallet? I'm
looking up the lost and found list on the
computer.

W: It's a _____ _____ wallet. Please check
carefully. I have to find it.

M: Hmm... we have several brown wallets. Is
there _____ _____ inside?

W: Unfortunately, no. But my wallet has light
yellow stripes on it.

M: I'm sorry but we don't have a wallet with
_____ _____. Are you sure you left it
on the bus?

W: Yes. As soon as I got off the bus, I realized
I lost it.

M: _____ _____ that one of the other
passengers took it.

W: Oh, no! I hoped I would find it.

B [1-2]

M: What can I do for you?

W: I'd like to get the photos _____ _____
_____ developed.

M: What size would you like, three by five or
four by six?

W: _____ _____ _____, please.

M: Would you write down your name and
phone number here?

W: Okay... oh, what a nice photo album. Do
you make these _____ _____?

M: Yes. It's a hot trend among young couples
these days.

W: I was thinking of making one for my
boyfriend. _____ _____ does it cost?

M: The album you saw is $60. It has 30
pages with two photos per page. Putting
comments costs an _____ _____.

W: I want to order one with comments. But
can I just put one big picture per page?

M: Sure. The price is _____ _____.

C [1-2]

M: In our daily lives, _____ _____ _____
lots of electromagnetic waves but aren't
aware of them. They flow in the air when
we use _____ _____ such as TVs and
cell phones. Therefore, keep at least two
meters away from the TV when watching
it. _____ _____ produce more
electromagnetic waves, so always watch
them from far away. Plants with _____
_____ or high water content absorb the
waves, so put some near your TV. When
using your cell phone, don't touch the
antenna. Lots of electromagnetic waves
_____ _____ _____ _____. And
even if you turn electronic devices off,
make sure to unplug them. Otherwise, the
electromagnetic waves _____ _____.

D [1-2]

(Telephone rings.)

W: Top Magazine.

M: Hello. I want to _____ _____ your
magazine for six months. How much will
that be?

W: That's $27. One issue is $5, so it's a _____
_____.

M: Well, the discount isn't as big as I expected.

W: If you subscribe for a year, there's a 20%
discount.

M: Really? Since the _____ _____ is $60,
that means I can save $12. I'll go with an
annual subscription.

W: Great. Do you want to _____ _____
this month?

M: I already bought this month's issue. So
I'd like my subscription to start _____
_____.

W: All right. What's your name and address?

M: It's James Pitt and my address is 160
Clinton Street.

W: All right. Will you pay with _____
_____ _____?

M: No, I'd prefer to pay by bank transfer.

W: All right.

Listening ★ Challenge Answers p. 3

A [1-2]

(*Telephone rings.*)

W: BT Credit Card. How may I help you?

M: I called to change my _____ _____.

W: Could you tell me your name and social security number?

M: I'm Tom Wilson, and my number is 555–21–0707.

W: Have you considered _____ _____ _____ e-billing service? You wouldn't need to change your address with e-billing.

M: No, thanks. I don't use email _____ _____.

W: Okay. What's your new address?

M: 97 Victoria Street.

W: It's done. But your card is old and has _____ _____. Why don't you change it to a new card?

M: Well, I don't know.

W: We have a new card called the "Green Card." You can _____ _____ _____ _____ on hotels and a 15% discount in most family restaurants.

M: Is there a discount for gasoline?

W: I'm sorry but there isn't.

M: Wouldn't it have a _____ _____ _____?

W: We don't charge an annual fee.

M: Great. Then I'll get the new card.

B [1-2]

W: Hello. _____ _____ Janet from *Guess What*. Today, I'll give you clear answers about the questions you asked about _____ _____. First, white socks are easy to get dirty and hard to get clean. But if you wash them after soaking them in water with _____ _____ and salt for a while, they'll be as good as new. If your sneakers are still dirty after washing them, _____ _____ _____ on the dirty parts and dry it. When a dress shirt collar is dirty, rub shampoo on it before running

it _____ _____ _____ _____.

Then the dirt will go away. Next week, I'll tell you about cleaning techniques for kitchens and bathrooms, _____ _____ _____ how to remove bad smells from your house. Please join us next week.

Critical ★ Thinking Answers p. 3

W1: I'm Eve. It's difficult to find time to _____ _____ _____ _____, because they are closed when I finish work. I think if they can't extend their weekday _____ _____, banks should open on the weekends.

M: I'm Tom. I have a different opinion. Wouldn't it be unfair to _____ _____ _____ on weekends? We can't force them to work more days just for our convenience. They also need _____ _____ _____ and rest.

W2: I'm Janet. It's true that many workers have a hard time using banks. But I don't think all banks need to open _____ _____. Opening a few branches in each region will be enough. Bank clerks could rotate their schedules and _____ _____ _____ weekend overtime work.

UNIT 04 Food

Listening ★ Start Answers p. 4

1

M: (1) This is a _____ _____ which includes various vegetables and sliced beef. I lightly cook them by putting them in _____ _____ for a while. Then I dip them in a delicious sauce and eat them.

W: (2) This is a _____ _____ _____. It is served in a large bowl. It contains rice, vegetables _____ _____ carrot, cucumber, mushroom and spinach, and an egg. I mix them together with red pepper paste. This food is _____ _____ delicious _____ _____ healthy.

2

M: Can I take your order?

W: Yes. I'd like to have _____ _____ _____ as an appetizer.

M: All right. We have Thousand Island, honey mustard, and French dressing.

W: _____ _____ _____ French dressing, so I want to try it this time. Can you recommend a steak?

M: Our rib-eye steak and New York steak are _____ _____ _____.

W: Why is there such price difference between them?

M: The New York steak is _____ _____ the rib-eye steak.

W: I see. Then we'll have two rib-eye steaks, _____ _____ and the other rare.

M: Okay. Would you like to have some wine? It's offered at a 20% discount when you _____ _____ _____.

W: Yes. One glass of red wine, please.

M: Okay.

3

W: Recent research has shown that certain foods _____ _____ _____ together. It's because some foods destroy the nutrients in other food. Let me give you _____ _____. When you make a salad, you should avoid using cucumbers and carrots together. An element in carrots _____ _____ _____ _____ in cucumbers. Here's another example. Some people eat tomatoes with sugar on them. But that's not a good idea because sugar _____ _____ _____ _____ in vitamin B from the tomatoes. Also, putting honey in black tea makes it hard for our bodies to _____ _____ iron.

Listening ∗ **Practice**   Answers p. 4

A [1-2]

M: Julie, _____ _____ _____. Help me choose a cooking oil.

W: There's no need to think it over. Pick the olive oil.

M: What makes you _____ _____?

W: I think food tastes better with olive oil. Besides, it's helpful in reducing cholesterol levels, _____ _____ _____ good for your heart.

M: Well... it's more expensive than corn oil.

W: But the calories in olive oil are easier to _____ _____ than those in other oils. That's why olive oil is widely used in diet programs.

M: _____ _____ _____, I should buy it! Why didn't you say that in the first place?

W: (laughs) Don't forget to store it in a cool, _____ _____.

M: Okay, I'll put it in the fridge.

W: No, that'll make the oil turn cloudy and thick. Just put it _____ _____ _____.

B [1-2]

M: Would you like something else to drink?

W: No, thanks. I'd like to _____ _____ _____ _____.

M: Oh. Is there some kind of problem?

W: Yes. Today, I waited for an hour to be seated even though I _____ _____ _____. But I put up with the inconvenience in order to enjoy your delicious food.

M: I _____ _____ that. We have too many customers tonight.

W: Well, what's worse is that my chicken salad is _____ _____ and these ribs are tough.

M: I'm sorry to hear that. I'll serve you the food again after talking about it with the chef.

W: No, thanks. I've already _____ _____ _____.

M: Let me bring you today's special steak. I'm sure you'll like it. And there'll be no charge.

W: Hmm... okay, that _____ _____.

C [1-2]

W: This Friday is Dan's birthday. Can you suggest a good restaurant?

M: _____ _____ El Cruce? The chef is from Spain, so the food is really great.

W: I haven't tried Spanish food. _____ _____ _____?

M: Sure. Garlic and red pepper are usually used in Spanish food, so you will like the taste.

W: _____ _____ _____ _____ do the Spanish enjoy eating?

M: Since Spain is surrounded by the sea, seafood is pretty popular.

W: Great. Dan _____ _____.

M: Also, many Spanish dishes use rice. One of the nicest dishes is paella, which is a _____ _____ that contains an Indian spice called saffron.

W: Sounds good. I'll make a reservation.

M: _____ _____ hurry. That restaurant has been popular since it opened twelve years ago.

W: When does it close?

M: At 11 p.m. Oh, and you can watch a flamenco performance there _____ _____.

D [1-2]

M: _____ _____! It's time for *All about Super Foods*! Today's super food is cabbage. Its medical benefits are _____ _____ _____ _____ it's called "the doctor of the poor." In particular, cabbage is good for the stomach. Its effect increases when you drink it _____ _____ _____. If you can't stand the bitter taste of cabbage, mix it with lemon or orange. Make sure you drink cabbage juice _____ _____ _____ _____ because its nutrients are quickly destroyed. If you want to eat cabbage by boiling it, _____ _____ to drink the boiled water too, because many of the nutrients go into the water.

Listening ∗ **Challenge** Answers p. 4

A [1-2]

W: Good morning, viewers. Today I'm visiting a famous _____ _____. The owner of this restaurant, Michael Taka, is here. Hello, Mr. Taka.

M: Hello. Welcome to Taka Sushi Bar.

W: How long have you been _____ _____ _____?

M: It's been 20 years.

W: I heard that more than 200 customers visit here each day. Was this place popular _____ _____ _____?

M: Not at all. At first, Americans thought eating raw fish was nonsense.

W: How did you _____ _____ _____?

M: I created a new kind of sushi to appeal to American tastes. You can't imagine how hard I worked to _____ _____ these delicious sushi rolls.

W: What do you think was the key to your success, apart from that?

M: I recognized that many Americans _____ _____ _____ Eastern culture. So I decorated my restaurant with Japanese items so that customers would feel as though they were in Japan.

B [1-2]

M: We finally _____ _____ _____.

W: I can't believe this! We've waited almost for an hour. I feel like we've wasted our time.

M: _____ _____. This restaurant got two stars in the Red Guide.

W: What's the Red Guide?

M: It's a restaurant guidebook. It evaluates restaurants _____ _____ food, service and interior design. André Michelin from France first published it.

W: Oh, he was the owner of a _____ _____, right? Isn't that book called the Michelin Guide?

M: Yes. But it's also known as the Red Guide _____ _____ the color of its cover.

W: I thought it was a guidebook only for restaurants in France.

M: At first, but then versions for countries _____ _____ the US, the UK, and Japan were also published.

W: Oh, now I feel honored to be served in a two-star restaurant from the Michelin Guide.

M: (_laughs_) You should _____ _____ for bringing you here.

W: Thanks. I'm sorry for complaining earlier.

W: What are we going to buy next?

M: We need some _____ _____. Oh, there it is.

W: Hmm... how about choosing some other brand? This one says it's a _____

    _____ _____.

M: Can't you see the price tag? It's much cheaper.

W: But this corn was genetically changed by humans. I don't want to eat _____

    _____.

M: Look! It says it contains more vitamins. GM technology made that possible. It's

    _____ _____ _____ _____.

W: No way! I would eat GM food if it guaranteed our health in the long run. But nobody can be sure about _____

    _____ _____ in the future if we keep eating it.

M: I've only heard about the benefits of GM food.

W: And I bet you've heard that GM food can solve the world _____ _____ _____.

M: That's right. We can produce more food with GM technology.

W: Yes, but I think it's useless if it can harm our health.

UNIT 05 Fashion

1

W: Hello, all. Welcome to _Fashion World_. Today, let's learn about _____ _____

    _____. There are two key points you should keep in mind, "back to basics" and "_____ _____." This season is about simple designs which show the lines of your body. _____ _____ from bright colors like yellow and pink or large prints. Choose black, white, and beige clothes. And don't forget to wear _____ _____

    _____. A brightly colored hat, scarf, tie, or large necklace will make you _____

    _____ _____.

2

W: Let's look at the monitor and talk about

    _____ _____ _____ at the Cannes Film Festival. Let's discuss Jane Stewart first.

M: Oh, my goodness. Her dress is too long for _____ _____ _____ _____.

W: It looks like she's sweeping the red carpet with it.

M: Next is Susan Morris, wearing a yellow dress.

W: That is an _____ _____, but unfortunately, it doesn't go well with her skin tone.

M: You're right. I like the slim line, though.

W: Finally, it's Kate Smith. She's wearing an

    _____ _____ _____.

M: I think it looks great.

W: The problem is not the dress, but the accessories. I can't count _____ _____ she's wearing.

M: Wearing just one necklace would've been better.

3

M: Fashion editors are people who _____

    _____ about fashion in magazines. It

may seem like a fancy job, but they do a lot of _____ _____. They visit fashion shows, watch fashion trends, and interview fashion people. _____ _____ _____. They manage all the things related to photo shoots. They think of the _____ _____ and get clothing sponsors. On the day of a photo shoot, they _____ _____ _____ models' hair, makeup, and clothes. And fashion editors sometimes take trips to other countries to keep up-to-date with the _____ _____ _____.

Listening * Practice   Answers p. 5

A [1-2]

M: Sarah, welcome. _____ _____ _____ _____.

W: Yes. It's been two years since I last worked with you.

M: Wow! _____ _____. So did you see the clothes you'll be wearing? How do they look?

W: The silhouettes are pretty. They're _____ _____ _____. You really are talented.

M: You're so kind. The hairstyle and makeup will be natural.

W: Okay. Then, walking should be casual, right?

M: Yes. You are _____ _____ _____, so you have a big responsibility.

W: I'll do my best.

M: Thank you again for doing my show for free. It _____ _____ _____ to me.

W: Well, all the profits go to a facility for the disabled. How could I refuse to do something for a _____ _____?

M: You really have a good heart. Okay. Let's do the fitting.

B [1-2]

W: Hello. I'm your fashion advisor, Christina. Many viewers asked about how to _____ _____ and thinner. There are several ways. Follow these rules and you'll look

tall and thin, _____ _____ while wearing clothes! First, match the top and bottom in similar tones. But don't dress in the same color _____ _____ _____ _____. Also, dark colored clothes will make you look slim. If you want to wear stripes, choose vertical ones, which make the body _____ _____. Lastly, wear your accessories above the chest. That way, other people will _____ _____ your upper body and you'll look taller.

C [1-2]

M: Hello. I'm Tommy, helping you with the _____ _____ _____. I'm on Tokyo's fashion street, Harajuku. Here, you can easily find men wearing skirts. _____ _____ one Japanese survey, 40% of men answered positively about wearing skirts. Recently, world famous designers like Mark Jacobs showed men's skirts _____ _____ _____. It might be shocking to many viewers, but some of the men think skirts aren't just for ladies _____ _____. They especially love skirts during hot weather because they are cooler than pants. I think this kind of new fashion is _____ _____ _____. I really want to praise their courage.

D [1-2]

M: Amy, I want to be _____ _____, but don't know where to start.

W: Why do you suddenly feel this way?

M: There's a girl I _____ _____ _____ _____. But she told me that she didn't like how I dress. I was so disappointed.

W: You can't be fashionable overnight. It requires _____ _____ _____ _____.

M: What am I doing wrong?

W: In my opinion, you never consider your shape when _____ _____.

M: What do you mean?

W: Well, you always wear skinny jeans with dark T-shirts. But they make you look even

101

thinner.

M: I should _____ _____ _____ right now! What else should I do?

W: Reading fashion magazines can help you _____ _____.

M: What else?

W: Smart dressers always match accessories, shoes or bags nicely with their clothes.

M: _____ _____. Will you help me?

W: You bet.

Listening ★ Challenge Answers p. 5

A [1-2]

W: Let's go to the Pineapple Store. They have various clothes _____ _____ _____.

M: Do you go there often?

W: Yes. They carry up-to-date designs.

M: Well, I don't think you should go there. That store is _____ _____ fast fashion.

W: Fast fashion?

M: It means clothing collections which reflect the latest fashion trends. The designs change almost every two weeks. It doesn't focus on materials, so it's very cheap.

W: _____ _____ _____ with it?

M: The problem is that it's not an environmentally-friendly store.

W: How come?

M: They produce _____ _____ _____ _____ to reflect the latest fashions. Their unsold clothes become trash.

W: That isn't a good thing.

M: Also, do you _____ _____ from the Pineapple Store for a long time?

W: No. I don't wear them for long because they become _____ _____.

M: Exactly. That means more garbage. We need to protect our environment.

W: Good point. _____ _____ _____, I'll consider the environment more before purchasing new clothes.

B [1-2]

W: Yves Saint Laurent was a _____ _____ _____ who was born in 1936. Since childhood, he had great fashion sense, and created various looks _____ _____ _____ _____ of his designing career. He was the one who introduced "the safari look" and designer labeled _____ _____ to the world. He was also the first person to hire black models for his shows. He even _____ _____ _____ _____ in the Metropolitan Museum of Art. But there's another reason why he is known as a fashion icon. He is considered to have _____ _____ _____ through fashion by introducing pants suits for women. Pants suits gave freedom to women and _____ _____ _____ in society. This great designer retired in 2002 and died in June 2008.

Critical ★ Thinking Answers p. 5

W: Today, I saw a guy _____ _____ _____ _____ on the street.

M: What's wrong with that? It's just an expression of personal preference.

W: You _____ _____ _____ _____. He was wearing several gold bracelets and necklaces, along with two big earrings. They were _____ _____ than the kinds of earrings women usually wear.

M: What about rock stars? They wear many accessories.

W: _____ _____, because they look great whatever they do.

M: That's a double standard. Actually, there's something _____ _____ _____ about women.

W: Yes? Go on.

M: Why in the world do they wear _____ _____ _____?

W: I think miniskirts look cute. Don't men love women wearing miniskirts?

M: Maybe. But some women _____ _____ that are too short. I don't know where to look when I meet them on the street! _____ _____ _____ _____ is that I sometimes see their underwear when they walk up the stairs.

UNIT 06 Ads & Announcements

Listening * Start   Answers p. 5

1
W: All my friends say I _____ _____ these days. What's my secret? I've started using Shining Velvet.
M1: Shining Velvet is made with _____ _____ _____. It contains vitamins B and E. It heals your dry, damaged hair. With Shining Velvet, you can _____ _____ _____ in just three weeks.
W: Have a look! My hair is really shiny and feels _____ _____ _____ velvet. Also, it has the sweet smell of blueberries! You don't need to use any perfume when you use Shining Velvet.
M2: Hey, Vivian. You look great today.
W: See? Shining Velvet, it's my _____ _____.

2
M: Thank you for visiting the Museum of Art and History. We have a _____ _____ on each floor. On the first floor, we present a large collection of _____ _____. It's a good place to learn about clothes in the old days. On the second floor, we have an exhibition of _____ _____ _____, such as jewelry, furniture, and books. In the gallery on the third floor, you can see _____ _____ of the 18th century. The collection includes more than 300 paintings. We hope you _____ _____ _____.

3
W: Attention, please. This is the Lost and Found Center. We just received _____ _____ _____, which is made of black leather. It has a front pocket and a short handle. It was found at ABC Sports Store _____ _____ _____ _____ at around 4:15. There are two books about marketing and a red handkerchief in the bag. If you think _____ _____, please come to the Lost and Found Center. It is located on the 6th floor and _____ _____ 8:45. Thank you very much.

Listening * Practice   Answers p. 5

A [1-2]
M: Do you want to be slim, but don't have much time to _____ _____? Then you should try Magic Solution! Magic Solution looks like a chair, but it is a special piece of _____ _____. It helps you lose weight easily. You don't have to run or lift anything. All you have to do is to _____ _____ _____ _____. When you switch the power on, it will shake your whole body. Try it twice a day _____ _____ _____ and after two weeks, you will notice your body change. Its _____ _____ is $200, but we're offering a 40% discount during March only. Order now _____ _____ _____, or dial 1–800–1234.

B [1-2]
W: _____ _____ _____ _____?
M: I went to a cosmetics store. I bought some Venus Best lotion for my sensitive skin.
W: Oh, no! You shouldn't use it.
M: _____ _____?
W: I read some reviews on the Internet. People with allergies had _____ _____ _____ after using it.
M: Really? But the ad said it passed a skin allergy test.
W: Yes, but I don't think they're _____ _____ _____.

103

M: That's so wrong. I'll never buy another product from the Venus Company.

W: It's not only the Venus Company. I _____ _____ _____ which said that the government made over twenty companies change their ads.

M: Did they also _____ _____ _____ in their ads?

W: Right. We shouldn't always believe advertisements. So before I shop, I read _____ _____ to get information.

C [1-2]

W: _____, _____. This is an announcement for passengers on flight BT 201 to New York. The departure of the flight _____ _____ _____ because of repair problems. The ground crew is currently working on it, but the departure time has been changed to _____ _____. The departure gate may also be changed, so please check before boarding the plane. And there's _____ _____ _____. The departure gate of flight TX 1215 to London, leaving at 10:30 a.m., has been changed from Gate 2 to _____ _____. The passengers for this flight should arrive at Gate 16 by 10 a.m. We apologize for the inconvenience.

D [1-2]

M: Hey, look at this TV commercial. I have no idea _____ _____ _____ _____.

W: I heard that's a new car ad.

M: But it only shows a girl swimming in the sea! What does it _____ _____ _____ _____ a car?

W: It's a teaser advertisement. It's common these days.

M: A teaser advertisement?

W: Yes. It doesn't give _____ _____. It even hides what kind of product it is.

M: That's not good. An advertisement should describe the product _____ _____ so that people want it.

W: In most cases, you're right. But teaser ads can make people _____ _____ about the product.

M: I see. As you said, it seems to be good for _____ _____.

W: Yes, that's why teaser ads are often used for new products.

Listening ∗ **Challenge**   Answers p. 5

A [1-2]

M: Ladies and gentlemen, welcome _____ _____ Star Cruise. Star Cruise is going to travel to four beautiful Greek islands in seven days. _____ _____ _____, you will get to enjoy some beautiful scenery. Fireworks on Monday evening, a special dance performance _____ _____, and a magic show on Friday — all of these are waiting for you. And if you want to _____ _____ _____ from all around the world, just walk down to the Lux Restaurant! You can also visit our sauna, sports center, bar, and _____ _____ _____ anytime you want. In ten minutes, however, our safety lesson will start. I'd like you to _____ _____ in the main hall with your life jackets on. If you have any problems, please let our staff know. Thank you.

B [1-2]

W: Welcome to *Issues of the Day*. We're going to discuss _____ _____ _____ tonight. We have Mr. Williams from the government here. Hello.

M: Hello, Ms. O'Brien.

W: I heard that _____ _____ a new law, some junk food ads will not be allowed to appear on TV at a particular time of day. Can you explain _____ _____ _____?

M: We believe junk food is harmful for children. So we've decided to _____ _____ _____ when most kids watch TV.

W: Could you explain when that is?

M: It's for three hours, from _____ _____

_____ p.m.

W: What kinds of junk food will be affected by the law?

M: Ads for hamburgers, pizza, chocolate, chips, and soda will be affected.

W: I guess the _____ _____ _____ might disagree with the law.

M: You're right. However, I believe children's health should _____ _____. I hope companies understand this and make their food healthier.

W: I see. _____ _____ _____ _____ today.

Critical★Thinking Answers p. 6

W: Did you like the movie?

M: _____ _____ _____. The only thing I can remember is the main actress's cell phone.

W: Yeah, it appeared in so many scenes. _____ _____ _____ was when the actress suddenly explained how good her phone was.

M: That's product placement. Film directors _____ _____ _____ in movies on purpose, after they receive money from the companies.

W: I know. But I don't think _____ _____ should be used in movies. It is very annoying.

M: But I understand the film directors. To _____ _____ _____ _____, they need a large amount of money.

W: So, do you think _____ _____ even when there are many unnecessary product placement scenes in movies?

M: No. I don't think product placement should ever _____ _____ _____ of the movie. But I think it's okay for directors to use product placement properly.

UNIT 07 Technology

Listening ★ Start Answers p. 6

1

M: Robots are becoming more and more _____ _____. Have you heard about the robot called Kobian?

W: No. Is it very similar to a human?

M: Yes. It _____ _____ just like humans do. It shows seven emotions, including happiness and sadness.

W: Wow, how does it do that?

M: Kobian can _____ _____ _____ of its lips, eyelids and eyebrows, as well as make gestures.

W: How interesting!

M: So, when happy, it _____ _____ _____ and mouth widely, lifting its arms above its head. When sad, it drops its head and _____ _____ _____.

W: Wow, I want to see it. What's the purpose of this robot?

M: It's going to be used to _____ _____ for old people.

2

W: India is a country with a powerful _____ _____. How did it create such an industry? First of all, there was the effort of the government. The government encouraged _____ _____ and cut taxes for software companies. Also, although Indian workers have good English and technical skills, _____ _____ are cheap. Therefore, developed countries began to hire them. The final reason is the _____ _____ _____ between India and the world's IT center, the U.S. Indian workers can follow up on projects from U.S. workers _____ _____ _____, allowing IT companies to work 24 hours a day.

3

M: Hello. I'm the CEO of IB Motors. I'm _____ _____ _____ you our

105

company's latest vehicle, the Revolution. The Revolution is not only stylish but also has several advanced functions. You may have heard that _____ _____ while driving is more dangerous than drunk driving. Well, the Revolution's mirrors have sensors that watch the movement of the _____ _____. If the driver's eyes stop moving, an alarm sounds. There's also a special function for _____ _____. The computer screen in the car lets you know which way to turn the wheel and whether to _____ _____ or backward.

Listening ★ Practice   Answers p. 6

A [1-2]

M: Kate, _____ _____ _____ about something?

W: Yes. It's my pet dog. He doesn't move an inch or eat anything these days. And he sometimes _____ _____ _____ _____.

M: Maybe he's sick. Have you taken him to an animal hospital?

W: Yes, but the doctor said he's _____ _____. I don't know how to find out what's wrong.

M: How about using a dog translator, then?

W: A dog translator?

M: Yes. It can tell _____ _____ _____ _____ by the way it sounds. It knows six different feelings, such as happy or sad.

W: Amazing! Does it show you _____ _____ _____ or something?

M: Yes. But it can also tell you with a human voice.

W: How was this technology developed?

M: It was made by _____ _____ _____ of many different kinds of dogs.

W: Maybe I should buy one today.

B [1-2]

M: An American company is _____ _____ for its new spaceship, the Lynx. Did you hear about it?

W: No. But I heard some companies have been developing _____ _____ for a space trip. Spaceship 2 is one of them.

M: Spaceship 2? What does it look like?

W: It _____ _____ three planes put side by side, and it can hold eight people.

M: Wow. I guess it's larger than the Lynx. The Lynx looks like _____ _____ _____, but smaller.

W: How much do tourists have to pay for a space trip on the Lynx?

M: It's $95,000 _____ _____ _____.

W: Thirty minutes seems too short. You can travel through space for two hours if you take Spaceship 2.

M: That's _____ _____ _____ _____, but I guess it's more expensive.

W: Right. It costs $200,000.

M: In that case, _____ _____ _____ the Lynx.

C [1-2]

M: Why don't we _____ _____ _____ this year's design competition held by JY Mobile Company?

W: What kind of competition is it?

M: It's a competition to design _____ _____ _____. This is the 3rd year of the competition and the winner gets $20,000 plus the latest cell phone.

W: _____ _____. Tell me more about the competition.

M: Well, anyone over the age of 18 can participate. The judges mostly consider whether it will be _____ _____ _____.

W: What else?

M: Well, creativity also counts.

W: Did you see last year's _____ _____?

M: Yes. It was a cell phone which was worn around the wrist. It could be used as an accessory, too.

W: Wow, _____ _____ _____ _____.

M: But I liked another one more. It looked like a regular cell phone, but it could _____ _____ wireless headphones.

W: Wow, that's amazing.

D [1-2]

W: There's a very unique cigarette _____ _____ in Japan. This smart machine can identify a person's age. It was made to prevent teenagers from _____ _____ from vending machines. In order to use this machine, the person must _____ _____ a digital camera set in the machine. The machine then takes a photo. From this photo, it _____ _____ _____ _____ by the number of wrinkles, skin condition and bone structure. It then compares the face with 100,000 sets of _____ _____ saved in the machine. Adults who get rejected because of a younger looking face can put their _____ _____ into the machine to be checked.

Listening ★ Challenge   Answers p. 6

A [1-2]

M: China has been _____ _____ _____ into space since the 1980s. For China, where the number of people is huge, this is one way to solve the _____ _____ _____. You might wonder why they're sending seeds into space. It's because scientists found that _____ _____ _____ were changed after a trip to space. When the seeds were planted, it turned out that productivity increased. _____ _____, wheat grew up to 9% more. For tomatoes and cucumbers, both productivity and taste improved. The weight of _____ _____ _____ even went up to nearly 750 g. The Chinese scientists are not sure why these changes happen. But if this study _____ _____, food shortages

won't be a problem in China in the future.

B [1-2]

W: Good morning. On today's *Book Club*, we have Peter Adams, the author of *Enjoy Your Life*, _____ _____ _____.

M: Thank you for having me here.

W: Could you introduce your book first?

M: Of course. This book helps _____ _____ learn how to enjoy high-tech devices like cell phones, digital cameras, PMPs and MP3 players just like teenagers do.

W: I _____ _____ to learn that you didn't even know how to turn on a computer three years ago. What made you change?

M: It was _____ _____. She would play with her computer and cell phone for hours. But I didn't know anything about these devices, so we had _____ _____ _____ to talk about.

W: So how did you learn about them?

M: I started by learning how to use a computer. I _____ _____ _____ _____ at a community center. I strongly recommend these classes to readers of my book.

Critical ★ Thinking   Answers p. 6

W1: I'm Christina. Getting _____ _____ _____ by challenging your body's limits is the true spirit of sports. But now, wearing a _____ _____ or running shoes can improve an athletes' performance. Some athletes are even breaking records with _____ _____ _____ _____. This is only the competition of scientific technology, not of sports.

M: I'm Chris. Technology is used in every area of our lives. Therefore it _____ _____ _____ not to use it in sports. There's no reason we shouldn't use technology in sports if it helps athletes get _____ _____ _____.

W2: I'm Betty. Fair play is the most important

part of sports. That means all players should _____ _____ _____ _____. But players who get help from technology have an advantage over those who don't. This means that only players from _____ _____ _____ will be able to take the lead.

UNIT 08 Animals

Listening ★ Start Answers p. 7

1

W: (1) This kind of dog is highly _____ _____ _____ and has good sight, so it can easily find rabbits or foxes which are hiding. When a hunter shoots a bird, causing it to _____ _____ _____ _____, this kind of dog quickly goes and gets it.

M: (2) This kind of dog is trained to guide _____ _____ in the streets. It knows how to deal with many obstacles on the road. At a corner or crosswalk, this kind of dog stops and _____ _____ _____ _____ such as "forward," "stop," "right," or "left."

2

M: Have you heard that animals have _____ _____ _____?

W: No, what's that?

M: Humans have five senses, which are sight, hearing, taste, touch and smell. But _____ _____ animals have an extra sense.

W: Really?

M: Yes. Do you remember the tsunami that occurred in the _____ _____ in 2004?

W: Of course. Many people were killed by it.

M: At that time, more than 200 people died in a national park in Sri Lanka. However, _____ _____ _____ _____ living there died.

W: How come?

M: Well, they seemed to sense the upcoming natural disaster using a sixth sense, and then moved to _____ _____.

W: I find that hard to believe.

M: There are many similar cases in which animals seemed to _____ _____ or volcanoes.

W: How surprising.

3

M: Animals have various strategies to _____ _____ from enemies. Some animals change their body color so as not to be seen. For example, gray tree frogs can _____ _____, green, or brown, depending on their surroundings. Animals like the blowfish blow up their bodies when they are _____ _____. It makes them look bigger and stronger, so they can scare away their enemies. Lastly, skunks _____ _____ _____ shooting a liquid at their enemies. The liquid smells so terrible that it makes their enemies run away.

Listening ★ Practice Answers p. 7

A [1-2]

M: Excuse me. Are you Melrose Brown? I'm Sam Jackson.

W: Oh, yes. We _____ _____ _____ _____.

M: Nice to meet you. Well, this is my pet, Betty. I'll hand her over to you.

W: Wow, she looks _____ _____ than in the pictures.

M: She really is a lovely pet. Please take good care of her.

W: May I ask the reason why you're _____ _____ _____?

M: I'm going abroad to study, and I can't take her. And everyone in my family is too busy to _____ _____ _____ her.

W: That's too bad. Is there anything that I should be particularly careful about?

M: The most important thing is to _____

_____ _____. A chameleon isn't active
if it's cold or shady.

W: Okay. I'll keep her somewhere sunny.

B [1-2]

W: Jason, let's _____ _____ _____
_____ to swim.

M: Didn't you see the headline in today's
newspaper? A boy was attacked by a
shark _____ _____.

W: Oh, my god! Is he okay?

M: Fortunately, he didn't get seriously hurt,
though he was bitten _____ _____
_____.

W: What a relief.

M: The news said this is the time when
sharks often appear _____ _____
_____.

W: We should be careful, then. But is there
any way to avoid a shark attack?

M: The most important thing is not to _____
_____. Also, sharks are most active at
night, so it's better to swim during the day.

W: Okay. Do you know what we should do if
we _____ _____ _____?

M: We should stay calm, as sudden
movements may attract its attention.

W: That could be very difficult!

C [1-2]

M: I'm considering _____ _____ _____,
but I can't decide what kind.

W: Why don't you get a pet pig? I have one,
and he's really cute.

M: You're _____ _____ _____ in your
house? Aren't pigs dirty animals?

W: Not at all. That's a _____ _____.

M: But I've seen pigs rolling in mud many
times.

W: That's because they can't control their
body temperature _____ _____. They
keep themselves cool by rolling in mud.

M: I see. But I want a smart animal like a dog.

W: Well, you know what? Pigs are just
_____ _____ _____ dogs.

M: Really? That's unbelievable.

W: Besides, pigs are not greedy about food.
They eat just _____ _____ _____
_____ that their bodies need.

M: Wow, I'm learning many things about pigs.

D [1-2]

W: What are you doing? What is that _____
_____?

M: This is a gorilla costume that I'll wear for
the "Great Gorilla Run" this evening.

W: What's that?

M: It's an event to _____ _____ to save
gorillas. They are in danger of extinction
now.

W: What do you do in the event?

M: We're _____ _____ _____ or run
7 km, dressed up like a gorilla.

W: That sounds very funny. How did you
find out about _____ _____ _____
_____?

M: When I went to Africa last year, I joined
a tour to watch gorillas. During the tour,
I learned that their numbers are _____
_____.

W: So you wanted to do something for them.

M: Right. And I found out about this event
online.

W: _____ _____ _____ _____ I go to
watch you?

M: Of course not.

W: Great. I'll take pictures.

Listening ⋆ Challenge   Answers p. 7

A [1-2]

W: Hello, viewers. This is Cindy Simpson at
California Zoo. Today, I'll explain how
animals endure the _____ _____
_____. Hello.

M: Hello. I'm Samuel Wilford.

W: What are you doing?

M: I'm _____ _____ for polar bears. It's
frozen fruit and fish.

W: It looks like a big ice cube. _____
_____ they like it.

M: Sure. They spend time eating these delicious ice cubes in the pool.

W: I see. How do other animals beat the heat?

M: Rhinoceros don't feel the summer heat when somebody brushes their skin. So we brush them _____ _____ _____ _____ every day.

W: That's very interesting.

M: In the case of elephants, they are not very sensitive to heat, because they _____ _____ hot countries.

W: That makes sense.

M: However, when it's very hot during the day, we _____ _____ _____ on them.

W: That's great. Thanks to your efforts, animals can keep cool.

B [1-2]

M: May I help you?

W: I found this dog near the Union Square Theater. It _____ _____ _____ _____.

M: Does it have a name tag?

W: No, it doesn't.

M: Let me see. It looks like _____ _____ _____. What happened to its legs?

W: She was not walking well when I found her. It seems like she _____ _____ _____.

M: Okay. This Dog Center will provide a shelter for her for a month.

W: What will happen _____ _____ _____?

M: If we can't find her owner and she is not adopted during the period, we'll have her _____ _____ _____.

W: Are you saying she'll be killed? No way!

M: We can't help it. Our center can only _____ _____ _____. But more dogs than that are brought in.

W: Oh, no. Well, I'll try to find a person who can adopt her. Is there an _____ _____?

M: No, it's free. You can show people the dog's picture on our website.

W: Great.

M1: I'm Mike. _____ _____ is a necessary process when making new medicines. We can't test new drugs on people when _____ _____ _____ about their possible side effects. Many drugs have been developed after experiments on animals, and these drugs have _____ _____ _____ _____ from diseases.

W: I'm Mary. Animals are living things just like humans. They can _____ _____ and have feelings. Who can decide that animals are less precious than humans? We have to _____ _____ _____ using living creatures.

M2: I'm Bill. No animal species has the exact same DNA as humans. _____ _____ a new drug doesn't harm an animal, this doesn't mean that it is safe for humans. That means that animals are killed _____ _____. So we have to develop another way to test new drugs.

UNIT 09 Psychology

1

W: How was your _____ _____ yesterday?

M: It didn't go well. She said I wasn't her type.

W: What did you wear on the date?

M: The yellow T-shirt and _____ _____ that I often wear. Is something wrong?

W: You should've dressed carefully. You look _____ _____ _____ when you wear those clothes.

M: You mean the girl didn't like me because I wasn't well-dressed?

W: I'm saying that clothes are important for making a _____ _____ _____. She didn't know about you, so she might have judged you on a first impression.

M: _____ _____.

W: And once a first impression is made, it's difficult to change it.

M: Okay. I'll _____ _____ _____ to my clothes from now on.

2

M: When you _____ _____ for your house, it's important to choose the right color. For example, green can _____ _____ _____. Students can focus on their studying better in a green room. Blue is used to _____ _____ and appetite. On the other hand, orange improves appetite. It would be the best color to use _____ _____ _____. Pink is the color that makes people feel calm. After a prison in the US painted its walls pink, there was _____ _____.

3

W: Who are the people in this picture? Are they _____ _____?

M: Yes. This is when my family went to France.

W: Wow, your mother and father _____ _____ _____ _____. It might be true that married couples tend to resemble each other.

M: That's been scientifically proven. I've read _____ _____ about it.

W: Really? Why does it happen?

M: Married couples go through many things together, both _____ _____ _____, don't they?

W: Of course.

M: Because they share the same experiences, they begin to have _____ _____ _____. This makes them have similar wrinkles on their faces.

W: I see.

M: Also, people tend to like others who _____ _____ themselves. Maybe that's another reason.

A [1-2]

M: Ms. Smith, have you noticed that Jeff is _____ _____ these days?

W: Oh, yes. He was a troublemaker, but he changed a lot. What happened to him?

M: Well, I _____ _____ _____ I reacted to his bad behavior.

W: Tell me more.

M: I used to punish him in class when he did _____ _____. But it didn't help.

W: You're right. I had the same experience.

M: So I decided to change my approach. I tried to show _____ _____ _____ _____ in him. And I praised him whenever he did something good.

W: So did that work?

M: At first, he _____ _____. But soon he started making an effort to be praised.

W: That's amazing. I'll try that with my class, too.

B [1-2]

M: One day in 1964, a woman was killed _____ _____ _____ in New York. There were about 30 people at the crime scene, but nobody helped her. Why did it happen? When people _____ _____ help someone, they consider whether there are other people around or not. If there are other people _____ _____, they might think someone else can do something instead of them. However, if there's nobody else around, people _____ _____ _____ more responsible and try to help. Now what should you do to get help when you face a dangerous situation? You should _____ _____ _____ _____ to ask for help. For example, you can shout "You in the blue T-shirt! Please help me!"

C [1-2]

W: Sellers use many _____ _____ to sell their products. One of the most common

111

strategies is having prices end _____
_____ _____. Most people feel that a
$9.99 T-shirt is much cheaper than a $10
T-shirt, even though it's only a _____
_____ _____. Another common
strategy is using fake prices. Suppose there
is a $70 bag. Sellers put a _____
_____ _____ on it that says it's $100,
not $70. Then, they tell customers it's on
sale at 30% off. Customers pay $70 for the
bag, which is its _____ _____.
However, because they think it used to
cost $100, they feel that they have found a
bargain.

D [1-2]

M: How's your preparation for the
performance going? It's _____ _____
_____, right?

W: Yes. But there is a problem. I have to give
a presentation in science class next Friday.

M: That's too bad. You have to _____
_____ _____ two things at the same
time.

W: Right. So I'm considering asking Peter to
_____ _____ _____ with me.

M: That's a good idea.

W: But I'm afraid he might say no.

M: I'll let you know how you should do it.
Before _____ _____ _____ _____,
do something nice first.

W: I don't get it.

M: For example, buy him a Coke or _____
_____ _____ his homework. It will
make him feel like he owes you something.

W: I see. Then he is less likely to refuse my
request for a favor, because he thinks
_____ _____ _____ one.

M: Exactly!

Listening ∗ Challenge Answers p. 8

A [1-2]

M: Susan, you _____ _____ today. What's
the matter?

W: I stayed up all night reading a very
interesting book.

M: _____ _____ _____ _____?

W: It was a book about Münchausen
syndrome.

M: What's that? I've never heard about it.

W: It's _____ _____ _____ mental
illness. People pretend to have an illness
although they're actually fine.

M: That sounds really strange.

W: The patients even _____ _____ to
make others believe they're sick.

M: Really? Why do people act like that?

W: It's because they want love and attention.
You know, we _____ _____ _____
_____ sick people.

M: I see. By the way, why is it called
Münchausen syndrome?

W: It's _____ _____ a German who lived
in the 18th century.

M: Is he the one who discovered the illness?

W: No. He was a great liar. Because lying is
the _____ _____ of the syndrome, it
was given his name.

B [1-2]

W: I _____ _____ _____ _____ today.
I was so surprised because she knew so
many things about me.

M: What did she say?

W: She said I'm _____ _____ something
now. And I've had a hard time because of
love.

M: Um... what else?

W: She also said I sometimes _____
_____. Isn't that amazing?

M: Do you really believe her?

W: Why not? What she said about me was
_____ _____.

M: She only talked about general things. Who
doesn't worry about something? Who
doesn't feel lonely from time to time?

W: Oh... _____ _____ _____.

M: I read a book about fortune tellers' tricks.
It said that when people are told a fact

that everybody shares, they often believe
it's _____ _____ _____.
W: Just like me.
M: That's right. Also, if people are told good
things about them, they _____ _____
_____ them.
W: I didn't know that. I won't waste my time
and money again.

Answers p. 8

M: Why have you stopped eating? Have
some more.
W: I _____ _____ _____ after I broke
up with Mark. I want to forget him and
move on, but it's difficult.
M: That's why you _____ _____ _____.
Cheer up. How about eating some
chocolate?
W: No, I don't want any.
M: Hey, just try it. Chocolate can make us
_____ _____. Research has shown
that eating chocolate for a couple of
months is good for _____ _____.
W: Sorry, but I don't feel like eating anything.
M: Then let's go jogging or bike riding. It's
also proven that working out helps

_____ _____ _____.

W: Really? Does it need to be for a long time?
M: Just move your body for 20 minutes. Then
you'll feel much better for the _____

_____ _____.

W: How come?
M: While we're working out, our brains
produce a material called beta-endorphin.
It _____ _____ and stress.
W: Okay. Then let's go bike riding.

UNIT 10 Social Issues

Answers p. 8

1

M: How often does your family _____
_____ _____ together? Due to an
increase in double-income couples and
family members' _____ _____, it's
hard to have a family meal. However,
according to various studies, there are
_____ _____ to family meals. First, it's
good for developing children's brains.
Surprisingly, children learn _____
_____ _____ new words during family
meals than when reading books. Also,
children get to eat healthier food like fruits
and vegetables _____ _____ junk food.
Moreover, children who take part in regular
family meals are _____ _____ _____
smoke, drink alcohol, or take drugs.

2

W: Johnny, let's _____ _____ for milk and
fruit.
M: All right. Are you going to Joe's Groceries
near the house?
W: No. I'm going to the _____ _____
_____ which just opened.
M: Has another large discount store opened?
I heard that many small groceries are

_____ _____ _____ _____

because of big discount stores.
W: It's natural for people to go to big discount
stores. They have a _____ _____ and
bigger discounts.
M: But if everybody goes to them, small
grocery stores will shut down. It can affect
our _____ _____.
W: Oh, I've never thought about that.
M: In the long run, only large discount stores
owned by big companies will survive.
W: I _____ _____. Then let's go to Joe's
Groceries today.

113

3

W: Lately, the "_____ _____" have become a serious problem around the world. This term first appeared in the US _____ _____ _____ _____. It refers to people who work hard but still remain poor. These people have low income jobs which could be lost _____ _____ _____. If they lose their jobs or become sick, they can directly fall into the poorest class. The number of working poor around the world has been increasing since _____ _____ _____. The main reason is that the number of full-time jobs is decreasing, while _____ _____ _____ part-time jobs is increasing.

Listening ∗ **Practice**   Answers p. 8

A [1-2]

M: Jenny, how have you been doing?

W: Great, thanks. I'm _____ _____ in a coffee shop to save money.

M: For what? Are you going to travel abroad?

W: No. I'm not _____ _____ my small eyes. So I want to get plastic surgery this summer.

M: What? You look fine as you are. And _____ _____ there are side effects?

W: The technology has been upgraded, so there are fewer side effects nowadays.

M: Still, _____ _____ _____ plastic surgery. Women with self-confidence look more beautiful to me.

W: That's why I've decided to do it. I think I can _____ _____ by changing my eyes.

M: If you were my sister, I would persuade you not to do it. Please think about it again.

W: Anyway, _____ _____ _____ _____.

B [1-2]

W: A _____ _____ is a serious social problem in Singapore. To increase the birthrate, the Singapore government has been trying _____ _____ for a long time. The Singapore government founded a wedding consulting agency in 1984. This agency has _____ _____ _____ such as cooking classes and blind dating on a riverboat. Also, the government encouraged colleges to open "dating classes" to _____ _____ _____. After the average birthrate per woman dropped from 1.24 in 2003 to 1.04 in 2004, the government decided to _____ _____ _____. It gives some money to families with children and cuts taxes for them. With these efforts, Singapore's birthrate _____ _____ in 2008.

C [1-2]

M: Julie, how was your trip to California?

W: Well... there was a problem _____ _____ _____. I had to wait for four hours before the departure.

M: What happened? Was there _____ _____ _____ weather problem?

W: No. A man called the airline and said there was a bomb on the flight.

M: Oh, my god!

W: All the passengers _____ _____ had to get off. Then the police searched the plane.

M: So did they find it?

W: No. It _____ _____ to be a false bomb threat.

M: I can't believe it.

W: The worst part is he did it for no reason. That kind of behavior is _____ _____ _____ _____. Bomb threats are a serious issue around the world.

M: People who make false bomb threats should be _____ _____ so that they won't do it again.

W: Right. People should realize how much trouble their behavior can cause for others.

D [1-2]

M: Have you heard about "_____ _____"?

They are parents who are always around their children, and who care too much about everything _____ _____ _____. They frequently call the school, showing concern about things like homework or lunch menus. _____ _____ their children become adults, they insist on telling them what to do _____ _____ _____ _____ jobs, dating, and even marriage. This is to prevent their kids from making mistakes or failing at something. But helicopter parents are not _____ _____ _____ _____. These children don't learn problem solving abilities and have a hard time _____ _____ _____.
As a result, they can't be successful in society.

Listening ★ Challenge   Answers p. 8

A [1-2]

W: You've _____ _____ _____ than anyone this year. How do you feel?

M: I feel very good about myself.

W: Recently, _____ _____ have become a serious problem. When did you start donating blood?

M: In 1984. I've donated blood _____ _____ _____ since then.

W: How did you start? Did someone suggest you do it?

M: Well... I have a special story. When my wife _____ _____, it was hard to get extra blood. That's when I realized the importance of _____ _____.

W: I see. Could you tell our viewers about the benefits of blood donation?

M: Well, best of all, you can _____ _____ _____ with little effort.

W: Anything else?

M: Yes. I became healthier. Because it's not possible to donate blood _____ _____ _____, I pay more attention to my body by working out and eating a healthy diet.

W: I see. We hope many viewers will donate blood _____ _____ _____ _____.

B [1-2]

W: Hello, everyone. Today, we'll be talking about _____ _____ with Professor Jackson. Hello, professor.

M: Thank you for having me.

W: Shootings are increasing _____ _____. Yesterday, 12 students lost their lives because of campus shootings.

M: Yes. And _____ _____ _____ are killed by guns every year in America.

W: What could be the reason?

M: The main reason is that people can _____ _____ _____ _____. After the age of 21, people can buy guns with a simple identification check.

W: At first, people were allowed to keep guns _____ _____, right?

M: Right. But now it has caused many problems.

W: What's more, it seems there's been a _____ _____ in the number of shootings recently.

M: Shootings tend to increase when the economy is bad.

W: I see. Surprisingly, some of these shootings are _____ _____ by teenagers.

M: I think it's mainly because of the media. They copy shooting scenes from _____ _____ _____ _____.

Critical ★ Thinking   Answers p. 8

M1: I'm Nick. Lately, many elementary school students are _____ _____ alone to learn foreign languages. But how hard will it be for such small children to live _____ _____ _____? Because their parents aren't there to guide them, these kids can be led in the wrong direction.

W: I'm Anna. Children can _____ _____ _____ fast by studying abroad at an early age. It may be _____ _____

_____, but children usually get used to a new environment quickly. The language ability that they get through studying abroad will be useful when they _____ _____ _____ _____ in the future.

M2: I'm Jay. The problem is that elementary school is too early for children to _____ _____ _____. They will feel confused about their identity since they haven't fully learned their own culture and language yet. _____ _____ _____ _____ being good at foreign languages without first establishing your own identity?

UNIT 11 Sports

Listening * Start   Answers p. 9

1

M: Julie, what happened to your head? Did you _____ _____?

W: No. I went to a baseball stadium and _____ _____ in the head by a foul ball.

M: Oh, no! Are you okay?

W: Yes. I went to the hospital right away, and I'm fine now.

M: So that baseball team paid your _____ _____, right?

W: Surprisingly no. They said it was our responsibility to avoid foul balls.

M: What? _____ _____ _____.

W: But if a parked car outside of the stadium is damaged by a home run, the home team _____ _____ it.

M: Why?

W: Because a parked car can't avoid a ball.

2

W: This is Jamie Christine. _____ _____ _____ George Jackson.

M: Hello.

W: George, you led your team to victory with the goal _____ _____ _____ _____. How did you feel?

M: As you might guess, I was really happy.

W: After scoring the goal, you _____ _____ _____ _____ with your arms. Was it for your girlfriend?

M: Yes, it was. I kissed my ring last time I scored, and she liked it. So _____ _____ I prepared another celebration.

W: How sweet! Anyway, London United is only one game away from _____ _____ _____ _____.

M: That's right. I'll try to score a goal in the finals. Then I'll carry the coach on my back.

W: I'm _____ _____ _____ seeing that celebration.

3

M: Do you know who won the most gold medals _____ _____ _____? It is American swimming hero Michael Phelps. He won a total of 14 gold medals, _____ _____ _____ in the 2004 Olympics, and eight more in the 2008 Olympics. And he set _____ _____ _____ in the 2008 Olympics. This amazing record could be achieved mainly because Michael has a _____ _____ for swimming. He's 193 cm tall, which is similar to other swimmers. But the length of his open arms is _____ _____ other swimmers. Also, his big feet help him swim faster.

Listening * Practice   Answers p. 9

A [1-2]

W: Henry, I heard you _____ _____ onto the school soccer team.

M: Yes. I received my uniform today. _____ _____ _____ wear it to practice.

W: You look really happy.

M: Of course. And I can't believe I can wear number 9.

W: _____ _____ _____ about the number 9?

M: The number 9 usually represents the

team's No. 1 striker.

W: Really? I thought the players just chose
_____ _____ they like.

M: No. Each number has a symbolic meaning
in soccer. For example, the number 7 goes
to the team's _____ _____ _____.

W: Oh, I remember David Beckham wore the
number 7.

M: Right. And the number 1 is only _____
_____ _____. Field players can't wear
that number.

W: Interesting. Anyway, when is your first
practice?

M: This Friday. _____ _____ it would
come soon.

B [1-2]

W: Usain Bolt _____ _____ _____
Jamaica in 1986. When he was a high
school student, his cricket coach discovered
his talent and recommended that he
_____ _____ _____. He ran in the
2004 Olympics in Athens, but dropped out
in the first round because of _____
_____ _____. However, four years
later, in the 2008 Beijing Olympics, he
showed his great ability. He _____
_____ _____ _____ in the 100 meter
event. Surprisingly, he slowed down before
the finish line to celebrate, but he still
_____ _____ _____ _____. His left
shoelace was even untied! He also won the
200 meter race and the _____ _____
_____ _____, setting new world records.

C [1-2]

W: What did you do yesterday?

M: I stayed home and _____ _____
_____.

W: Me, too. I watched the women's fencing
semifinal. It was such an exciting match.

M: Oh, I _____ _____ _____. I was
watching women's weightlifting.

W: What were the results?

M: Sarah Wilkins only won a silver medal.
She _____ _____ lift 95 kg in her final

attempt. I was really disappointed.

W: Why were you disappointed? She _____
_____ _____ _____!

M: But athletes practice hard for four years to
win a gold medal. Winning a gold medal
is _____ _____ _____ _____.

W: Being second best in the world at
something is pretty great too, though.

M: _____ _____ I agree with that.

W: In my opinion, winning any medal in the
Olympics is a great achievement. _____
_____ _____, silver or bronze, it
should be celebrated.

D [1-2]

M: Did you hear David Adams is joining the
LA Galaxy?

W: Really? I thought he would _____
_____ Chelsea FC in the Premier League.

M: Me, too.

W: Maybe Chelsea didn't offer a big _____
_____ _____.

M: No, they offered a lot.

W: Then, why did he reject it? It's every
soccer player's dream to _____ _____
_____ _____ _____.

M: He said there was no guarantee of being a
main player in Chelsea because there are
_____ _____ _____. But on the LA
Galaxy, the left-wing position is open.

W: I see. But I think he should've taken the risk.

M: Well, he could go to the Premier League
_____ _____ _____ in America.

W: This kind of opportunity doesn't come
often. I'm disappointed with his decision.

M: David Adams is _____ _____ _____
_____, so a Premier League team will
take him eventually.

Listening * Challenge   Answers p. 9

A [1-2]

W: Hello, Mr. Black. First of all, _____
_____ tonight's victory.

M: Thank you very much.

117

W: Including today's match, the last three games were all _____ _____.

M: Yes, that's true.

W: But the semifinal against Russia is only two days away. The players _____ _____ _____ _____.

M: I'm worried about that. But we'll do our best to win the game with Russia and _____ _____ _____.

W: The record shows your team has won 10 times and lost 14 against Russia. Could you tell us what _____ _____ will be?

M: As you know, the Russia team has many tall players with good blocking techniques.

W: And they're also very _____ _____.

M: Yes. But we'll use our quickness to beat them. I believe in my players.

W: I see. Well, I hope I get to see your team play _____ _____ _____.

M: Thanks.

B [1-2]

M: Do you know that you can't see _____ _____ _____ _____ from the last Olympics in the next Olympics? That's because the official Olympic events are not set. The _____ _____ _____ meets every four years to set the events for the next Olympics. For example, mixed doubles ping pong _____ _____ _____ the 2008 Beijing Olympics. Instead, the women's 3000-meter hurdles and 10 km swimming marathon were added. Also, 2008 was the _____ _____ for baseball and softball. They are not official events of the 2012 London Olympics. Taekwondo was _____ _____ the 2012 Olympics, but there's a high chance of it not being included in 2016. On the other hand, karate, golf and rugby _____ _____ _____ in 2016.

Critical ★ Thinking   Answers p. 9

M: Did you _____ _____ _____ _____ between the US and Spain yesterday? It was really exciting.

W: Yes. But the US lost the game because of _____ _____ _____.

M: Are you talking about when Spain got a penalty kick because of the US's foul?

W: Yes. Obviously, _____ _____ _____ _____. The US players appealed, but the referee didn't change his decision.

M: Well, I understand why he didn't change his decision, _____ _____ it was wrong.

W: Why not? His wrong decision changed the game's result.

M: Think about it. If referees start to _____ _____ _____, all the coaches and players will always complain until they do.

W: I don't think that _____ _____ _____ _____. They'll protest only when the decision is clearly wrong.

M: Do you really think so?

W: Yes. And even if they often protest, _____ _____ _____ _____ is more important.

M: Well, it's hard to say what's right.

UNIT 12 Environment

Listening ★ Start   Answers p. 9

1

M: Hey, let's _____ _____ _____ here.

W: Wait! Are you going to throw all the garbage into one trash bin?

M: Yeah. _____ _____?

W: It should be separated!

M: I know that. But it's too annoying.

W: Peter! We should _____ _____ the future of the environment.

M: How does that affect the future of our

environment?

W: We can save natural resources _____ _____. And we can reduce waste, too.

M: I heard that there isn't enough space for waste nowadays.

W: You're right. And if you _____ _____, it can be turned into other things. Plastic bottles can be used to make toys, T-shirts, and even _____ _____.

M: I see. I promise I'll be more careful when I throw away the garbage _____ _____ _____.

2

W: The earth is getting warmer and warmer. Because of _____ _____, unusual things are happening around the world. In Spanish mountain areas, bears are awake _____ _____ _____ during winter. Higher temperatures made it possible for them to stay active longer. In the Alps of France, you can see the buds of _____ _____ already during winter. In the past, they were only seen in spring. In New York in the US, _____ _____ _____ during the winter of 2007. It was the first time since 1877.

3

M: Hello. _____ _____ reporter Chris Jones at Richmond Middle School near the International Airport. As you see, a plane is _____ _____ and it's making serious noise. Students at this school hear _____ _____ several times a day. Students complain that it's difficult to focus on studying _____ _____. Because of the noise, they can't open the windows even during the summer. The noise from airplanes can cause _____ _____ _____ _____ and hurt the students' hearing ability. Furthermore, it can have bad effects on their _____ _____. The government needs to do something immediately.

Answers p. 10

Listening ∗ **Practice**

A [1-2]

W: Did you watch that documentary about _____ _____ yesterday?

M: Yes. I didn't know that environmental pollution was that serious.

W: After watching it, I decided to _____ _____ _____ _____ at our school.

M: Good idea! What do people do in that club?

W: They make guidebooks about protecting the environment. They _____ _____ _____ to students for free.

M: What else do they do?

W: They sell recycled products. _____ _____ _____, they show people that waste can be made into useful items. Plus, they hold lots of events like _____ _____ based on the environment.

M: I think I'd like to join the environment club, too. _____ _____ going to the student office and applying?

W: Great. But can I drop by a bookstore first? _____ _____ _____ _____ a book about the environment first.

M: No problem. I'll go with you.

B [1-2]

M: Hello, everyone. Our school is going to hold a poster painting contest _____ _____, June 4th. The purpose of this event is to show you how to protect our environment. You can _____ _____ that shows ways to protect the environment. The best posters will be exhibited in the _____ _____ _____. It will give you the chance to think about saving the earth. The contest is going to be held from 9:00 a.m. _____ _____ _____ _____. If you want to join, you must visit the teacher's room by next Friday. Bring an application form and _____ _____ _____ to Mr. Jones. Everyone is welcome to join!

C [1-2]

W: Ted, are you _____ _____ a photo of

119

environmental pollution on the Internet?

M: Yes. Did you find a good one? The homework is _____ _____.

W: Not yet. I'm going to search for one now. Is the seat next to you taken?

M: No, _____ _____ and search.

W: Okay.

M: Susan, look at this photo of a bird floating on water! I'm going to use it.

W: Is it a photo of a _____ _____?

M: No, the bird is alive, but the water is polluted with _____ _____.

W: That's terrible. Anyway, it's a great photo.

M: I'm finished. Do you want me to help you?

W: No thanks. _____ _____ _____ too.

M: Which one is it?

W: A photo of three birds in the water.

M: Oh my god! Waste water is pouring _____ _____ _____ next to them.

W: That's right. I feel sorry for them.

D [1-2]

W: A hybrid car is a special car made to _____ _____ _____. The biggest difference between a hybrid car and a regular car is that a hybrid car uses _____ _____ _____. It gets its driving power from both a gasoline engine and an electric motor. When the car _____ _____ _____, it only uses the electric motor. When it speeds up, it uses both the electric motor and the gasoline engine. But, when it _____ _____, the engine turns off and only the electric motor works. _____ _____ both a gasoline engine and an electric motor effectively, hybrid cars _____ _____ _____ and reduce the amount of harmful pollution.

Listening ∗ Challenge   Answers p. 10

A [1-2]

W: Hello, everyone. Today, our guest is an _____ _____, Dr. J. He is going to tell us about the changing environment of the Arctic and the problems _____ _____. Good morning, Dr. J.

M: Thank you for inviting me.

W: First, let's talk about _____ _____ in the Arctic. What's happening there?

M: Average temperatures in the Arctic are rising very fast. The ice is melting and _____ _____.

W: How does that affect the Arctic area?

M: If this trend continues, all the ice will melt _____ _____. It means animals will lose their homes and die out.

W: Will melting Arctic ice influence _____ _____?

M: Sure. If the entire ice cover melts, the sea level will rise all over the world. Then, people _____ _____ _____ _____ and islands may lose their homes.

W: Sounds tragic.

M: Yes. The problem happening in the Arctic may _____ _____ _____ as well. That's why we need to work on it.

B [1-2]

W: Do you know that _____ _____ are harmful to our environment? They have dangerous chemicals inside them. So when they are buried, they _____ _____ _____. They can even affect the water we drink. And once they're buried, the chemicals last _____ _____ _____ _____. But recycling can turn them into useful resources, while protecting the environment. To make this happen, we _____ _____ _____ called "Save the Earth!" every year. It was planned to encourage cell phone recycling. The goal for this year is to _____ _____ _____ _____. From June 1 to July 31, bring your old cell phones to ABC Service Center. We'll sell the phones to a certain cell phone _____ _____. By donating your cell phones, you can save the environment. Call 3142-0357 to join us!

Critical★Thinking   Answers p. 10

W: These days, yellow dust is _____

_____ _____ I don't even want to go

out.

M: Right. It's getting worse _____ _____.

W: China is causing most of the yellow dust.

China should be held responsible for the

problem and _____ _____ for the

damages it causes.

M: But as long as the wind blows in desert

areas, they can't stop it.

W: The problem is that the _____ _____

doesn't pay much attention to the

environment.

M: That's true.

W: The government doesn't _____ _____

to stop people from cutting down trees.

It can increase the size of the desert and

_____ _____ _____.

M: You have a point. Still, it's hard for China

to solve the problem alone. We need to

_____ _____ _____ together.

W: Then, what do you think we should do?

M: We should help China bring water to dry

areas and _____ _____ _____ there.

We can prevent the desert from becoming

wider that way.

JUNIOR LISTENING EXPERT

A Theme-Based Listening Course for Young EFL Learners

Level 4

Answer Key

JUNIOR
LISTENING EXPERT

A Theme-Based Listening Course for Young EFL Learners

Answer Key

Level **4**

★ ★

UNIT 01 Outdoor Activities

Getting ★ Ready p. 8
A 1 ⓔ 2 ⓖ 3 ⓐ 4 ⓒ 5 ⓓ 6 ⓑ
B 1 ⓐ 2 ⓕ 3 ⓔ

Listening ★ Start p. 9
1 ④ 2 ①, ③ 3 ②

Listening ★ Practice p. 10
A 1 ② 2 ④ B 1 ③ 2 ④ C 1 ③ 2 ④
D 1 ③ 2 (1) F (2) T (3) T

Listening ★ Challenge p. 12
A 1 ① 2 ② B 1 ② 2 ③

Critical ★ Thinking p. 13
1 ③ 2 ②

Dictation

Listening ★ Start p. 90
1 going camping, changed my mind, best of
   all, set up a tent
2 enjoy horseback riding, 10 years, Soon after,
   burns more calories, feel more relaxed
3 start rafting, with shoelaces, Make sure,
   Standing up, you'll sink

Listening ★ Practice p. 90
A go trekking, enjoy beautiful scenery, three
   good trails, Which trail, the most beautiful,
   checking out
B is looking for, nearby beaches, per month,
   you're afraid of, scuba diving's basic skills
C dressed like, war game, shoot members,
   win a game, the other team's flag, that's
   why
D $150 each, hold 20 people, from the sky,
   I've ever seen, on board

Listening ★ Challenge p. 91
A going climbing, in winter, gets dark, very

cold, body temperature, feel cold, get lost,
   there's any way
B I'd like to ask, what activities, outdoor
   cooking, carried out, much higher, only for,
   register your older daughter

Critical ★ Thinking p. 92
as though, left behind, destroying trees,
enjoy nature, maintain parks, protecting
nature, putting up

UNIT 02 Entertainment

Getting ★ Ready p. 14
A 1 ⓓ 2 ⓑ 3 ⓐ 4 ⓒ 5 ⓕ 6 ⓔ
B 1 ⓐ 2 ⓔ 3 ⓒ

Listening ★ Start p. 15
1 ③ 2 (1) ⓑ (2) ⓐ (3) ⓕ 3 ①

Listening ★ Practice p. 16
A 1 ④ 2 ② B 1 ③ 2 ③
C 1 ② 2 ④ D 1 ④ 2 ④

Listening ★ Challenge p. 18
A 1 ① 2 ③ B 1 ② 2 (1) ⓓ (2) ⓐ (3) ⓒ

Critical ★ Thinking p. 19
1 ④ 2 ②

Dictation

Listening ★ Start p. 92
1 do you mind, her latest song, on another
   channel, Are you certain, It's supposed to
2 related to, really fantastic, a lot of
   information, serious TV programs, laugh
   hard
3 become a necessity, it's better, watching
   TV, fully developed, gaining weight

Listening ∗ Practice p. 93

A Wednesday evenings, math homework, tape every episode, blank tape, got married, watch it myself, from the Internet

B would-be singers, perfect chance, at the end, record a debut album, come true, It'll be an honor

C sick of, promote their movies, silly jokes, in a different language, get together, as a group

D At 7 p.m., one million dollars, their new songs, such as, make its debut

Listening ∗ Challenge p. 94

A my little niece, in the newspaper, kill each other, are to blame, need to monitor, bad for their children, growing children

B I'm pleased, many categories, have been nominated, amazing actors, the most popular show, look real, open the envelope

Critical ∗ Thinking p. 94

too many details, stars' lives, 24 hours a day, people's gossip, get more attention, private lives, entertainers themselves

UNIT 03 Daily Life

Getting ∗ Ready p. 20

A 1 ⓑ　2 ⓓ　3 ⓐ　4 ⓔ　5 ⓒ　6 ⓕ

B 1 ⓑ　2 ⓕ　3 ⓔ

Listening ∗ Start p. 21

1 ③　2 ③　3 ②, ④

Listening ∗ Practice p. 22

A 1 ④　2 ④　**B** 1 ①　2 ④

C 1 ②　2 (1) T　(2) F　(3) F　**D** 1 ④　2 ③

Listening ∗ Challenge p. 24

A 1 ②　2 ③　**B** 1 ③　2 ②

Critical ∗ Thinking p. 25

1 ③　2 ②

Dictation

Listening ∗ Start p. 95

1 had some food delivered, make an additional order, so salty that, it's no excuse

2 take care of, professional system, as follows, seven days a week

3 have your hair done, with curly hair, look good, really damaged, get a hair treatment

Listening ∗ Practice p. 95

A left my wallet, bus number, dark brown, any identification, yellow stripes, It's possible

B on this CD, Four by six, for customers, How much, extra $10, the same

C we're affected by, electronic goods, Bigger TVs, large leaves, come out of it, keep flowing

D subscribe to, 10% discount, regular price, start from, in October, a credit card

Listening ∗ Challenge p. 97

A billing address, signing up for, very often, few benefits, get a 20% discount, higher annual fee

B This is, washing clothes, lemon juice, put some toothpaste, through the washing machine, as well as

Critical ∗ Thinking p. 97

go to a bank, business hours, make bankers work, time to relax, on weekends, get paid for

3

★ ★

^{UNIT}04 Food

Getting ⋆ Ready p. 26
A 1 ⓓ 2 ⓑ 3 ⓐ 4 ⓔ 5 ⓒ 6 ⓕ
B 1 ⓒ 2 ⓕ 3 ⓐ

Listening ⋆ Start p. 27
1 (1) ④ (2) ① 2 ③ 3 (1) ⓔ (2) ⓐ (3) ⓒ

Listening ⋆ Practice p. 28
A 1 ④ 2 ① B 1 ③ 2 ①, ④
C 1 ④ 2 ④ D 1 ① 2 ③

Listening ⋆ Challenge p. 30
A 1 ② 2 ①, ④ B 1 ② 2 ①

Critical ⋆ Thinking p. 31
1 ④ 2 ①

Dictation

Listening ⋆ Start p. 97
1 Japanese dish, boiling water, traditional
Korean food, such as, not only, but also
2 a chicken salad, I've never tried, the most
popular, bigger than, one well-done, order
a steak
3 shouldn't be eaten, an example, destroys
the vitamin C, prevents you from taking,
take in

Listening ⋆ Practice p. 98
A come over here, so sure, not to mention,
burn off, In that case, dark place, in the
cabinet
B talk to the manager, had a reservation,
apologize for, too sweet, lost my appetite,
sounds fine
C How about, Is it tasty, What kind of food,
loves seafood, rice dish, You'd better, every
Friday
D Welcome back, so widely known that, as a
juice, as soon as possible, don't forget

Listening ⋆ Challenge p. 99
A Japanese restaurant, running this
restaurant, from the beginning, change
their minds, come up with, are interested
in
B got a table, Calm down, based on, tire
company, because of, such as, thank me

Critical ⋆ Thinking p. 100
canned corn, genetically modified food,
such food, healthier for our bodies, what will
happen, food shortage problem

^{UNIT}05 Fashion

Getting ⋆ Ready p. 32
A 1 ⓔ 2 ⓗ 3 ⓒ 4 ⓓ 5 ⑨ 6 ⓐ
B 1 ⓐ 2 ⓑ 3 ⓔ

Listening ⋆ Start p. 33
1 ① 2 (1) ⓒ (2) ⓐ (3) ⓔ 3 ①

Listening ⋆ Practice p. 34
A 1 ② 2 ④ B 1 ④ 2 ③
C 1 ② 2 ③ D 1 ② 2 ①

Listening ⋆ Challenge p. 36
A 1 (1) T (2) T (3) F 2 ② B 1 ③ 2 ②

Critical ⋆ Thinking p. 37
1 ④ 2 ②

Dictation

Listening ⋆ Start p. 100
1 this fall's trends, colorful accessories,
Stay away, one colorful accessory, look
especially fashionable
2 the worst dressers, how short she is,
attractive color, Asian-style white dress,
how many

4

3 write articles, hard work, That's not all, cover concept, are busy monitoring, newest fashion trends

Listening ★ Practice p. 101

A It's been a while, Time flies, simple yet practical, in the finale, means a lot, good cause

B look taller, at least, from head to toe, look slimmer, focus on

C latest fashion trends, According to, in their collections, any more, something to encourage

D more stylish, have a crush on, a lot of effort, wearing clothes, take them off, follow trends, I'll try

Listening ★ Challenge p. 102

A at low prices, based on, What's the problem, lots of new clothes, wear clothes, outdated quickly, From now on

B French fashion designer, during the 50 years, blue jeans, held a solo exhibition, changed the world, raised women's status

Critical ★ Thinking p. 102

wearing too many accessories, should have seen him, much bigger, That's different, I can't understand, such short miniskirts, wear skirts, The most embarrassing part

UNIT 06 Ads & Announcements

Getting ★ Ready p. 38

A 1 ⓔ 2 ⓒ 3 ⓕ 4 ⓐ 5 ⓓ 6 ⓑ
B 1 ⓕ 2 ⓐ 3 ⓑ

Listening ★ Start p. 39

1 ③ **2** (1) 3rd (2) 1st (3) 2nd **3** ③

Listening ★ Practice p. 40

A 1 ② 2 ③ **B** 1 ④ 2 ②
C 1 ① 2 ④ **D** 1 ① 2 ③

Listening ★ Challenge p. 42

A 1 ③ 2 ④ **B** 1 ③ 2 ③

Critical ★ Thinking p. 43

1 ③ **2** ②

Dictation

Listening ★ Start p. 103

1 look beautiful, all natural materials, feel the change, as smooth as, beauty secret

2 different theme, traditional costumes, royal family items, famous paintings, enjoy our collections

3 a men's bag, on the 5th floor, it's yours, closes at

Listening ★ Practice p. 103

A work out, exercise equipment, sit in the chair, for 30 minutes, original price, on our website

B Where have you been, Why not, some skin problems, telling the truth, read an article, give wrong information, customer reviews

C Attention, please, is being delayed, 11 o'clock, one more notice, Gate 16

D what it is advertising, have to do with, product information, in detail, very curious, getting attention

Listening ★ Challenge p. 104

A on board, During this time, on Wednesday, taste various foods, duty free shops, gather together

B junk food ads, due to, why this is, ban those ads, 5 to 8, junk food companies, come first, Thank you for coming

5

Critical ★ Thinking **p. 55**
1 (1) For (2) Against (3) Against
2 (1) ⓑ (2) ⓐ (3) ⓒ

Listening ★ Start **p. 108**
1 sensitive to smell, fall to the ground, blind people, waits for an order
2 a sixth sense, it seems, Indian Ocean, none of the animals, higher places, predict earthquakes
3 protect themselves, turn white, in danger, are well-known for

Listening ★ Practice **p. 108**
A talked on the phone, much cuter, giving her away, take care of, control the temperature
B go to the beach, while surfing, on the arm, off the coast, swim alone, see a shark
C getting a pet, raising a pig, common misunderstanding, by themselves, as smart as, the amount of food
D strange costume, raise money, supposed to walk, such a wonderful event, decreasing fast, Do you mind if

Listening ★ Challenge **p. 109**
A hot summer weather, preparing food, I'm sure, for about 10 minutes, come from, spray cold water
B seems to be abandoned, a female dog, broke her leg, after a month, put to sleep, hold 100 dogs, adoption fee

Critical ★ Thinking **p. 110**
Animal testing, we're not sure, saved millions of people, feel pain, stop cruel experiments, Even if, for nothing

UNIT **09** Psychology

Getting ★ Ready **p. 56**
A 1 ⓐ **2** ⓔ **3** ⓑ **4** ⓗ **5** ⓕ **6** ⓓ
B 1 ⓕ **2** ⓑ **3** ⓔ

Listening ★ Start **p. 57**
1 ③ **2** (1) ⓑ (2) ⓐ (3) ⓓ **3** ②

Listening ★ Practice **p. 58**
A 1 ② **2** ②　　**B 1** ④ **2** ④
C 1 ④ **2** ①, ③　**D 1** ③ **2** ①

Listening ★ Challenge **p. 60**
A 1 (1) T (2) F (3) T **2** ③ **B 1** ④ **2** ②, ③

Critical ★ Thinking **p. 61**
1 ① **2** ①, ②

Listening ★ Start **p. 110**
1 blind date, black pants, far from stylish, good first impression, I see, pay more attention
2 buy wallpaper, help people concentrate, reduce stress, in a kitchen, less violence
3 your parents, look so much alike, an article, good and bad, similar facial expressions, look like

Listening ★ Practice **p. 111**
A doing better, changed the way, something wrong, a lot of interest, seemed embarrassed
B on a street, decide to, around them, tend to feel, pick one specific person
C different strategies, with 99 cents, one cent difference, fake price tag, real price
D next Thursday night, take care of, switch presentation times, asking him a favor, help him with, he owes me

Listening ★ Challenge p. 112

A look tired, What was it about, a kind of, hurt themselves, pay more attention to, named after, main symptom

B visited a fortune teller, worried about, feel lonely, completely true, that makes sense, their own story, tend to trust

Critical ★ Thinking p. 113

lost my appetite, look so depressed, feel better, overcoming depression, change our mood, next 12 hours, relieves pain

UNIT 10 Social Issues

Getting ★ Ready p. 62
A 1 ⓓ 2 ⓕ 3 ⓑ 4 ⓒ 5 ⓔ 6 ⓐ
B 1 ⓑ 2 ⓔ 3 ⓐ

Listening ★ Start p. 63
1 ③ 2 ① 3 (1) F (2) T (3) F

Listening ★ Practice p. 64
A 1 ④ 2 ① B 1 ② 2 ①
C 1 ③ 2 ③ D 1 ② 2 ③

Listening ★ Challenge p. 66
A 1 ③ 2 ①, ② B 1 (1) T (2) F (3) T 2 ④

Critical ★ Thinking p. 67
1 (1) Against (2) For (3) Against
2 (1) ⓐ (2) ⓓ (3) ⓒ

Dictation
Listening ★ Start p. 113

1 have a meal, busy schedules, many advantages, ten times more, rather than, less likely to

2 go shopping, large discount store, going out of business, wide selection, local

economy, get it

3 working poor, in the mid 90's, at any time, the year 2000, the number of

Listening ★ Practice p. 114

A working part-time, satisfied with, what if, I'm not for, get self-confidence, thanks for your concern

B low birthrate, various policies, held many events, teach dating techniques, provide financial support, reached 1.08

C at the airport, some kind of, on board, turned out, no longer a joke, punished heavily

D helicopter parents, their children do, Even after, when it comes to, helpful for their children, dealing with failures

Listening ★ Challenge p. 115

A donated more blood, blood shortages, every three months, had surgery, blood donation, save people's lives, if I'm sick, after watching this program

B gun control, these days, about 30,000 people, get guns too easily, for self-defense, sudden increase, carried out, movies and TV shows

Critical ★ Thinking p. 115

going abroad, without their parents, learn foreign languages, difficult at first, look for a job, face different cultures, What's the point of

UNIT 11 Sports

Getting ★ Ready p. 68
A 1 ⓓ 2 ⓔ 3 ⓗ 4 ⓐ 5 ⓑ 6 ⓕ
B 1 ⓒ 2 ⓐ 3 ⓑ

Listening ★ Start p. 69
1 ④　**2** ③　**3** ③

Listening ★ Practice p. 70
A 1 ②　**2** ①　**B 1** (1) T　(2) F　(3) T　**2** ④
C 1 ④　**2** ①　**D 1** ④　**2** ②

Listening ★ Challenge p. 72
A 1 ④　**2** ①　**B 1** ③　**2** ③

Critical ★ Thinking p. 73
1 ③　**2** ①

Dictation
Listening ★ Start p. 116
1 fall down, got hit, hospital bills, That's not fair, pays for
2 I'm here with, in the second half, made a heart shape, this time, winning the Champions League, looking forward to
3 at the Olympics, six of them, seven world records, suitable body, longer than

Listening ★ Practice p. 116
A got accepted, I'm anxious to, What's so special, whatever number, most famous player, for the goalkeeper, I wish
B was born in, become a runner, a leg injury, won a gold medal, broke the world record, 400 meter team relay
C watched the Olympics, missed that one, failed to, won a silver medal, the most important thing, I guess, Whether it's gold
D transfer to, enough transfer fee, play in the Premier League, so many stars, after gaining experience, a great soccer player

Listening ★ Challenge p. 117
A congratulations on, very tight, must be very tired, make the finals, your strategy, powerful spikers, in the finals
B some of the events, International Olympic Committee, was removed from, last Olympics, selected for, might be included

Critical ★ Thinking p. 118
watch the soccer game, a referee's mistake, it wasn't a foul, even though, change their decisions, is likely to happen, making the correct decision

UNIT **12** Environment

Getting ★ Ready p. 74
A 1 ⓕ　**2** ⓒ　**3** ⓐ　**4** ⓑ　**5** ⓓ　**6** ⓔ
B 1 ⓑ　**2** ⓐ　**3** ⓓ

Listening ★ Start p. 75
1 ③　**2** (1) ⓐ　(2) ⓒ　(3) ⓑ　**3** (1) F　(2) T　(3) F

Listening ★ Practice p. 76
A 1 ③　**2** ①　**B 1** ①　**2** ④
C 1 ③　**2** ②　**D 1** ③　**2** ②

Listening ★ Challenge p. 78
A 1 ④　**2** ③　**B 1** ④　**2** ③

Critical ★ Thinking p. 79
1 ④　**2** (1) T　(2) F　(3) T

Dictation
Listening ★ Start p. 118
1 throw the garbage, What's wrong, think about, by recycling, separate garbage, park benches, from now on
2 global warming, instead of sleeping, chestnut trees, it didn't snow
3 This is, flying overhead, such noise, during class, a lot of stress, academic achievements

★ ★

Listening ★ Practice **p. 119**

A environmental pollution, join the environment club, hand them out, By doing so, painting contests, How about, I'd like to buy

B next Saturday, paint anything, local art gallery, at the school gym, hand it in

C looking for, due tomorrow, sit here, dead bird, black waste, I've found one, out of pipes

D protect the environment, two power sources, starts to move, slows down, By using, use less gasoline

Listening ★ Challenge **p. 120**

A environmental expert, it's causing, environmental change, getting thinner, by 2040, other areas, living in coastal areas, affect our lives

B cell phones, pollute the land, for a long time, conduct a campaign, collect 4,000 cell phones, recycling company

10

Critical ★ Thinking **p. 121**

so serious that, every year, pay money, Chinese government, try hard, worsen yellow dust, work on it, plant strong vegetables

★ ★

UNIT 01 Outdoor Activities

Getting ★ Ready p. 8

A 1 ⓔ 2 ⓖ 3 ⓐ 4 ⓒ 5 ⓓ 6 ⓑ
B 1 ⓐ 2 ⓕ 3 ⓔ

B 1 여: 숲에서 길을 잃으면 어떻게 해야 하지?
남: 있던 곳에 머물면서 구조를 기다려.
2 여: 여름 캠프 프로그램에 포함된 활동은 무엇이니?
남: 아이들은 하이킹과 야외 취사 같은 활동에 참가할 거야.
3 여: 페인트볼 경기 어떻게 하는지 알아?
남: 선수들이 2개 팀으로 나뉘어서 페인트볼 총으로 서로 싸우는 거야.

Listening ★ Start p. 9

1 ④ 2 ①, ③ 3 ②

1

M: When my dad first suggested going camping, I didn't want to go because I thought a camping trip would be uncomfortable. But the camping experience totally changed my mind. It's fun to play in the water, catch fish, and have a campfire in the evening. And of course, I can enjoy beautiful nature. But best of all, it's a great way to become closer with family members. When camping, we have to work together to set up a tent or cook a meal. While doing those jobs, we can talk and laugh a lot.

남: 아빠가 처음 캠핑을 가자고 제안했을 때 전 캠핑 여행은 불편할 거라고 생각해서 가고 싶지 않았어요. 그런데 캠핑 체험은 제 생각을 완전히 바꿨어요. 물놀이를 하고, 물고기를 잡고, 저녁엔 캠프파이어를 하는 게 재미있어요. 그리고 물론 아름다운 자연을 즐길 수 있죠. 하지만 무엇보다도 캠핑은 가족들끼리 더 가까워지는 좋은 방법이에요. 캠핑을 하는 동안 텐트를 세우거나 음식을 요리하기 위해 함께 일해야 하니까요. 그런 일들을 하는 가운데 우리는 많은 대화를 나누고 웃을 수 있답니다.

어휘
camping [kǽmpiŋ] [명] 야영, 캠핑 experience [ikspí(:)əriəns] [명] 경험 totally [tóutəli] [부] 완전히 campfire [kǽmpfàiər] [명] 캠프파이어, 모닥불 nature [néitʃər] [명] 자연 set up 세우다 meal [mi:l] [명] 식사 [문제] relationship [riléiʃənʃìp] [명] 관계

문제 해설
Q: 남자는 주로 무엇에 대해 이야기하고 있는가?
① 가족 캠핑 여행으로 좋은 장소
② 가족 캠핑 여행을 계획하는 데 필요한 조언
③ 가족 관계를 더 좋게 하기 위한 비결
④ 가족 구성원끼리 캠핑을 가면 좋은 점
가족 캠핑을 가면 재미있는 활동들을 하고 자연을 즐길 수 있으며, 가족끼리 더 친해진다며 가족 캠핑의 장점을 이야기하고 있다.

2

M: This is Alex Kim reporting for NTV. These days, many people enjoy horseback riding. Let's hear from riders why they do it. Hello.
W: Hello.
M: How long have you been riding horses?
W: It's been 10 years.
M: Was there any special reason you started horseback riding?
W: I just wanted to do something with animals. Soon after I started horseback riding, I started to love it.
M: What's so good about it?
W: It's a good way to stay in shape. It burns more calories than swimming.
M: That's surprising. I didn't know that.
W: Also, as I spend time with the horses, I feel more relaxed.
M: I see. Thanks for the interview.

남: 전 NTV의 기자 Alex Kim입니다. 요즘 많은 사람들이 승마를 즐깁니다. 승마를 하는 사람들에게 왜 승마를 하는지 들어보겠습니다. 안녕하세요.
여: 안녕하세요.
남: 승마를 하신지 얼마나 되셨어요?
여: 10년이요.
남: 승마를 시작한 특별한 이유가 있으셨나요?
여: 그저 뭔가 동물과 함께 하는 것을 하고 싶었어요. 승마를 시작하고는 바로 좋아하게 됐지요.
남: 무엇이 그렇게 좋나요?
여: 건강을 유지하는 데 좋은 방법이에요. 수영보다 열량을 더 많이 소모하거든요.
남: 놀랍네요. 그건 몰랐어요.
여: 또, 말들과 시간을 보내면 더 편안해져요.
남: 알겠습니다. 인터뷰해 주셔서 감사합니다.

어휘
report [ripɔ́:rt] [동] 보도하다 horseback riding 승마 rider [ráidər] [명] 말을 타는 사람, 기수 stay in shape 건강을 유지하다 burn [bə:rn] [동] 태우다, 소모하다 calorie [kǽləri] [명] 칼로리, 열량 relaxed [rilǽkst] [형] 긴장을 푼,

편안한 [문제] relieve[rilíːv] ⑧ 해소하다, 줄이다
confident[kánfədənt] ⑱ 자신감이 있는

Q: 여자에 따르면 승마의 두 가지 좋은 점은?
　여자는 승마가 열량 소비가 많아 건강을 유지하는 데 좋은
　운동이며 마음을 편안하게 해 준다고 했다.

3

W: Hello. Before we start rafting, I'll tell you the safety guidelines you should follow. First, wear shoes with shoelaces and tighten them. It is easy to lose your shoes if they aren't tied. The second guideline is about helmets and life jackets. Make sure they fit tightly. Never take them off. Next, once we start rafting, don't stand. Standing up inside the boat is dangerous. Lastly, if you fall into the water, just relax. That will help you float. If you struggle, you'll sink.

여: 안녕하세요. 래프팅을 시작하기 전에 따르셔야 할 안전 수칙을 말씀드릴게요. 우선, 신발끈이 있는 신발을 신고 끈을 꽉 조이세요. 단단히 묶지 않으면 신발을 잃어버리기 쉽습니다. 두 번째 수칙은 헬멧과 구명조끼에 관한 것인데요. 반드시 꽉 맞게 착용하세요. 절대 벗지 마세요. 다음으로 일단 래프팅이 시작되면 일어나면 안 됩니다. 배 안에서 일어나는 것은 위험합니다. 마지막으로 물 속으로 떨어지면 그냥 긴장을 푸세요. 그렇게 하면 물에 뜰 거예요. 몸부림을 치면 가라앉게 됩니다.

어휘
rafting[rǽftiŋ] ⑱ 래프팅, 뗏목 타기　safety guideline 안전 수칙　shoelace[ʃúːlèis] ⑱ 신발끈　tighten[táitən] ⑧ 꽉 죄다　tie[tai] ⑧ ~을 묶다　life jacket 구명조끼　fit[fit] ⑧ 꼭 맞다　tightly[táitli] ⑨ 단단히　take off 벗다　relax[rilǽks] ⑧ 긴장을 풀다　float[flout] ⑧ 뜨다　struggle[strʌ́gl] ⑧ 몸부림치다　sink[siŋk] ⑧ 가라앉다 (sink-sank-sunk)　[문제] remain seated 앉아 있다

Q: 래프팅 수칙을 따르지 않은 사람은?
　신발끈이 있는 신발을 신고 끈을 단단히 조이라고 했다.

Listening ★ Practice　p. 10

A 1 ② 　2 ④ 　B 1 ③ 　2 ④ 　C 1 ③ 　2 ④
D 1 ③ 　2 (1) F　(2) T　(3) T

A [1-2]

M: Maria, let's go trekking tomorrow.
W: Trekking? I've never done it before.
M: Then you should try it! You can enjoy

beautiful scenery while walking in nature.
W: Okay. Where should we go?
M: I'm thinking of Yellowwood National Park. There are three good trails there: the riverside trail, the wildflower trail, and the deep forest trail.
W: Both the riverside trail and the wildflower trail sound wonderful. Which trail do you have in mind?
M: I looked up photos of each trail on the homepage, and I thought the wildflower trail was the most beautiful.
W: Did you? Then let's take that one.
M: Or, if you want, you can decide after checking out those photos.
W: Well, it will be too difficult to decide even if I do see the photos. Just tell me what I should prepare for tomorrow.
M: Okay.

남: Maria, 내일 트레킹 가자.
여: 트레킹? 한 번도 해 본 적이 없는데.
남: 그럼 한번 해 봐! 자연 속을 걸으면서 아름다운 풍경을 즐길 수 있어.
여: 좋아. 어디로 갈 거야?
남: Yellowwood 국립공원을 생각 중이야. 그곳에는 좋은 길이 세 개 있는데, 강가 길과 야생화 길, 깊은 숲 속 길이야.
여: 강가 길과 야생화 길 둘 다 멋질 것 같다. 어떤 길을 고려 중인데?
남: 홈페이지에서 각 길의 사진을 찾아봤는데 야생화 길이 가장 아름다운 것 같았어.
여: 그랬니? 그럼 그 길로 가자.
남: 아니면, 원한다면 네가 그 사진들을 확인해 본 다음 결정해도 돼.
여: 음, 사진을 본다고 하더라도 결정하기 너무 힘들 거야. 그냥 내일 뭘 준비해야 될지 알려 줘.
남: 좋아.

어휘
trekking[trékiŋ] ⑱ 트레킹, 도보 여행　scenery[síːnəri] ⑱ 풍경　trail[treil] ⑱ 오솔길, 산길　riverside[rívərsàid] ⑱ 강가　wildflower[wáildflàuər] ⑱ 야생화　forest [fɔ́(ː)rist] ⑱ 숲　have ~ in mind ~에 관해 생각하고 있다　look up ~을 찾아보다　even if 비록 ~할지라도

Q1: 그들이 선택할 트레킹 길은?
　남자의 의견에 따라 강가 길과 야생화 길 중에 더 아름다워 보이는 야생화 길을 가기로 결정했다.

Q2: 그들이 다음에 할 일은?
　여자가 남자에게 내일 트레킹에 필요한 게 뭔지 알려달라고 했으므로 그 얘기를 나눌 것이다.

12

B [1-2]

W: Dream Scuba Diving Club is looking for new members. We practice every Saturday in indoor swimming pools or in the sea at nearby beaches. Also, there are two scuba diving tours to foreign countries every year. Our membership fee is $50 per month, not including overseas tour fees. We welcome both experienced scuba divers and beginners. If you're afraid of trying scuba diving, please come to the California University school pool this Saturday. You can learn some of scuba diving's basic skills for free. Experience it for yourself and decide if you want to join us.

여: Dream Scuba Diving Club이 새 회원을 찾고 있습니다. 우리는 매주 토요일에 실내 수영장이나 가까운 해변의 바다에서 연습합니다. 또한, 매년 두 차례 외국으로 스쿠버 다이빙 여행을 갑니다. 회원비는 한 달에 50달러이고 해외 여행비는 포함되어 있지 않습니다. 경험이 많은 스쿠버 다이버와 초보자 모두 환영합니다. 스쿠버 다이빙을 시도하기가 두려우시면 이번 토요일에 California University 학교 수영장에 와 보세요. 무료로 몇몇 스쿠버 다이빙 기초 기술을 배울 수 있습니다. 스스로 체험해 보시고 가입할 것인지 결정하세요.

어휘

scuba diving 스쿠버 다이빙 indoor[índɔːr] 🕲 실내의 nearby[nìərbái] 🕲 가까운 foreign[fɔ́ːrən] 🕲 외국의 membership fee 회원비 overseas[óuvərsíːz] 🕲 해외로 가는 experienced[ikspí(ː)əriənst] 🕲 경험 있는, 노련한 beginner[bigínər] 🕲 초보자 be afraid of ~이 두렵다 basic[béisik] 🕲 기초의 [문제] newcomer[njúːkʌ̀mər] 🕲 신참

문제 해설

Q1: 틀린 정보를 고르시오.
　매년 두 번의 해외 여행 일정이 있다고 했다.

Q2: 이번 주 토요일에 Dream Scuba Diving Club에서 열리는 행사는?
　이번 토요일에는 초보자들을 위한 기초 강습을 한다고 했다.

C [1-2]

M: Wow, look at you in this picture. You're dressed like a soldier and covered in paint!
W: Oh, yes. That picture was taken after a paintball game.
M: A paintball game?
W: It's a kind of war game. Players are divided into two teams and fight each other with paintball guns.
M: They try to shoot members of the other team, right?
W: Yes. A person who gets hit by a paintball is out of the game.
M: Does one team need to shoot all the other team's members to win a game?
W: No, the game ends when one team comes back to the starting point after catching the other team's flag.
M: It sounds so exciting. I guess it's important to think of a good plan to catch the flag quickly.
W: Exactly. That's the most interesting part and that's why I love paintball.

남: 와, 이 사진 속의 너 좀 봐. 군인처럼 옷을 입었는데 페인트가 묻었네!
여: 아, 그래. 그 사진은 페인트볼 게임 후에 찍은 거야.
남: 페인트볼 게임?
여: 전쟁 게임의 일종이야. 선수들이 두 팀으로 나뉘어서 페인트볼 총을 가지고 서로 싸우는 거야.
남: 상대팀 멤버를 쏘려고 하는 거지, 그렇지?
여: 응. 페인트볼에 맞은 사람은 게임에서 빠져야 해.
남: 한 팀이 상대팀의 멤버를 모두 쏴야 게임을 이기는 거야?
여: 아니, 게임은 한 팀이 상대팀의 깃발을 잡아서 출발점으로 돌아오면 끝나.
남: 아주 흥미진진할 것 같다. 깃발을 빨리 잡기 위해 좋은 계획을 생각해내는 게 중요할 것 같아.
여: 바로 그거야. 그게 가장 흥미로운 부분이고 내가 페인트볼을 좋아하는 이유지.

어휘

soldier[sóuldʒər] 🕲 군인 divide[diváid] 🕲 나누다 gun[gʌn] 🕲 총 shoot[ʃuːt] 🕲 쏘다 get hit 맞다 starting point 출발점 flag[flæg] 🕲 깃발 [문제] thrill[θril] 🕲 스릴, 전율 workout[wɔ́ːrkàut] 🕲 운동 strategy[strǽtədʒi] 🕲 전략

문제 해설

Q1: 페인트볼 게임을 이기기 위해 팀이 해야 하는 일은?
　① 상대팀의 깃발을 먼저 찾는다.
　② 상대팀의 팀원을 모두 쏜다.
　③ 상대팀의 깃발을 가지고 돌아온다.
　④ 상대팀으로부터 페인트볼 총을 뺏는다.
　상대팀의 깃발을 가지고 출발점으로 다시 돌아오면 게임에 이긴다.

Q2: 여자가 페인트볼을 좋아하는 이유는?
　여자는 깃발을 빨리 가져오기 위한 전략을 잘 세우는 것이 매우 흥미로우며, 이것이 자신이 게임을 좋아하는 이유라고 했다.

D [1-2]

M: This morning, I went on a hot-air balloon ride with my friend. We paid $150 each for a 30-minute ride. The basket under the balloon was large enough to hold 20 people, and it was almost full. At first, I thought it would be boring to look at the city from the sky. But watching the city and nearby forests was more amazing than I expected. I also watched the sun rise, and it was the most beautiful thing I've ever seen. Thirty minutes in the air felt really short. After landing on the ground, we packed up the air balloon with the other people on board.

남: 오늘 아침, 저는 친구와 열기구를 타러 갔습니다. 30분의 탑승을 위해 각자 150달러를 지불했어요. 기구 아래의 바구니는 20명을 수용할 수 있을 만큼 컸는데, 거의 가득 찼습니다. 처음에는 하늘에서 도시를 내려다 보는 것이 지루할 거라 생각했어요. 하지만 도시와 근처의 숲을 바라보는 것은 기대했던 것보다 더 훌륭했어요. 또 해가 뜨는 것도 봤는데 제가 여태껏 본 것 중에서 가장 아름다웠어요. 공중에서의 30분은 정말 짧게 느껴졌어요. 땅에 내려온 후에 탑승했던 다른 사람들과 풍선을 접었어요.

어휘

hot-air balloon 열기구 basket[bǽskit] 명 바구니 expect[ikspékt] 동 기대하다 rise[raiz] 동 (해·달이) 뜨다 (rise-rose-risen) land[lænd] 동 착륙하다 ground [graund] 명 땅, 육지 pack up 싸다, 접다 on board 탑승한 [문제] scary[skɛ́(:)əri] 형 무서운 take off 이륙하다 sunrise[sʌ́nràiz] 명 일출

문제 해설

Q1: 남자가 열기구 비행에 대해 했을 말은?
 ① 예상했던 것보다 더 지루했어.
 ② 나빠진 않았지만 너무 비쌌어.
 ③ 아주 재미있어서 시간이 너무 빨리 갔어.
 ④ 아름다운 풍경을 보는 것은 좋은데 무서웠어.
 예상보다 아름다웠고 시간이 짧게 느껴졌다고 했다.

Q2: 사실이면 T, 사실이 아니면 F에 ✓표 하시오.
 비행은 한 사람당 150달러가 들었고, 하늘에서 일출을 봤다고 했으므로 그 전에 이륙했을 것이며, 바구니는 20명을 수용할 만큼 크다고 했다.

Listening ★ Challenge   p. 12

A 1 ① 2 ② B 1 ② 2 ③

A [1-2]

W: Dad, I'm going climbing in the mountains with my friends this Saturday.

M: Only with your friends? Don't you know how dangerous the mountains are in winter?

W: Well, they're not high mountains, so we'll be okay.

M: Even so, be sure to come down before it gets dark. The sun sets early these days.

W: Okay. Dad, what clothes should I wear? The weather forecast says it'll be very cold.

M: Put on many thin items of clothing under a warm winter coat. That'll help you control your body temperature.

W: I see.

M: And eat some chocolate or candy while you're climbing. You'll feel cold if you get hungry.

W: Okay. I'll buy some tomorrow.

M: One more thing! If you get lost in the woods, don't move around. Stay where you are and wait for rescue.

W: I don't think there's any way we will get lost.

M: Oh, I can't relax. Maybe I should go with you.

W: Dad!

여: 아빠, 이번 주 토요일에 친구들이랑 등산하러 갈 거예요.

남: 친구들하고만? 겨울에 산이 얼마나 위험한지 모르니?

여: 음, 높은 산들이 아니라 괜찮을 거예요.

남: 그렇다고 해도, 어두워지기 전에 꼭 내려오도록 해라. 요즘 해가 일찍 지거든.

여: 알았어요. 아빠, 무슨 옷을 입어야 해요? 일기예보에서는 아주 추울 거래요.

남: 따뜻한 겨울 코트 안에 얇은 옷을 여러 개 입어. 그러면 체온을 조절하는 데 도움이 될 거야.

여: 알았어요.

남: 그리고 등산하는 동안 초콜릿이나 사탕을 좀 먹어. 배가 고파지면 추위를 느끼게 되니까.

여: 알았어요. 내일 좀 살게요.

남: 하나 더! 숲에서 길을 잃으면 돌아다니지 마. 현재 있는 곳에 머물면서 구조를 기다려.

여: 길을 잃을 일은 있을 거 같지 않아요.

남: 아, 안심이 안 된다. 내가 같이 가야 될 것 같구나.

여: 아빠!

어휘

be sure to-v 반드시 ~하라 set[set] 동 (해·달이) 지다 (set-set-set) weather forecast 일기예보 body temperature 체온 get lost 길을 잃다 wood[wud] 명 ((~s)) 숲, 삼림 rescue[réskju:] 명 구조

14

문제 해설

Q1: 그들은 주로 무엇에 관해 이야기하고 있는가?

① 겨울에 등산하는 데 필요한 정보

② 겨울에 등산하는 것의 위험

③ 겨울에 등산하는 것의 좋은 점

④ 산에서 길을 잃었을 때를 위한 조언

겨울 등산을 가는 딸에게 아버지가 겨울 등산에 필요한 정보들을 알려주고 있다.

Q2: 남자의 현재 심정은?

친구들과 겨울 등산을 가는 딸에 대해 걱정하고 있다.

B [1-2]

(*Telephone rings.*)

M: Pine Camp office, how may I help you?

W: Hello. I'd like to ask about the summer camp program at Bear Lake that starts on July 7th.

M: Sure.

W: I'm wondering what activities are included in the program.

M: For 5 days, children will participate in basic camp activities like hiking and outdoor cooking. Plus, there'll be special programs including swimming and canoeing.

W: My younger daughter is afraid of deep water. Will she be okay?

M: Water activities will be carried out in shallow water, so don't worry about it.

W: Great. How much is it?

M: It is $400 per child. It's more expensive than other camps, but the quality is much higher.

W: Okay. I want to send my two daughters. They're 10 and 6 years old.

M: Ma'am, I'm sorry but this camp is only for ages 8 to 12.

W: Really? I didn't even think about the age limit.

M: Would you like to register your older daughter only?

W: Well... yes, please.

(전화벨이 울린다.)

남: Pine Camp 사무실입니다. 무엇을 도와드릴까요?

여: 안녕하세요. 7월 7일에 시작하는 Bear Lake에서의 여름 캠프 프로그램에 대해서 여쭤보고 싶어서요.

남: 말씀하세요.

여: 프로그램에 어떤 활동들이 포함되는지 궁금해요.

남: 5일 동안 아이들은 하이킹이나 야외 취사 같은 기본적인 캠프 활동에 참여하게 됩니다. 덧붙여서 특별 프로그램에는 수영과 카누가 있습니다.

여: 제 작은 딸이 깊은 물을 무서워하는데요. 괜찮을까요?

남: 수상 활동은 얕은 물에서 진행되니까 걱정하지 마세요.

여: 좋아요. 얼마죠?

남: 한 아이당 400달러예요. 다른 캠프보다 더 비싸지만 질은 훨씬 높습니다.

여: 알겠어요. 두 딸을 보내고 싶어요. 10세와 6세예요.

남: 고객님, 죄송하지만 이 캠프는 8세에서 12세까지만 가능해요.

여: 정말이요? 나이 제한을 생각하지 못했네요.

남: 큰 딸만 등록하시겠어요?

여: 음… 그렇게 해 주세요.

어휘

wonder[wʌ́ndər] [동] 궁금해하다 activity[æktívəti] [명] 활동 participate in ~에 참여하다 outdoor[áutdɔ̀ːr] [형] 야외의 canoe[kənúː] [동] 카누를 타다 carry out 실행하다 shallow[ʃǽlou] [형] 얕은 quality[kwɑ́ləti] [명] 품질 limit[límit] [명] 제한 register[rédʒistər] [동] 등록하다

문제 해설

Q1: 틀린 정보를 고르시오.

7월 7일에 시작하는 5일짜리 캠프라고 했다.

Q2: 여자가 큰 딸만 캠프에 등록시킨 이유는?

작은 딸도 보내려 했으나 나이 제한에 걸려 보내지 못한다.

Critical ★ Thinking p. 13

1 ③ 2 ②

M: Sally, I'm glad I came here to hike. I feel as though I can breathe better in this fresh air.

W: Me, too. Anyway, shall we set up a tent over there?

M: Okay. Oh, no! Look at all that trash left behind by hikers!

W: That's awful!

M: You know what? Besides throwing garbage on the ground, I heard many hikers are destroying trees by cutting them down for fires. I don't know why they don't care more about nature.

W: You're right. If they want to enjoy nature, they should try to protect it.

M: It might be better if national parks weren't open to hikers.

W: But it would be hard to maintain parks without visitors' entrance fees. Instead, I think hikers should realize the importance of protecting nature.

M: I agree. Then, why don't we make a little

effort first? Let's clean up the trash before putting up our tent.
W: Good idea.

남: Sally, 하이킹 오길 잘 한 것 같아. 상쾌한 공기 속에 있으니까 숨이 더 잘 쉬어지는 것 같아.
여: 나도 그래. 어쨌든, 저기에 텐트를 세울까?
남: 좋아. 아, 이런! 등산객들이 버리고 간 쓰레기들 봐!
여: 끔찍하다!
남: 그거 알아? 쓰레기를 땅에 버리는 거 외에도 많은 등산객들이 불을 피우려고 나무를 꺾어서 그것들을 훼손하고 있다고 들었어. 왜 자연에 대해서 좀 더 신경을 쓰지 않는지 모르겠어.
여: 맞아. 자연을 즐기기 원한다면 보존하려고 노력해야지.
남: 국립공원을 등산객들에게 개방하지 않았다면 더 나았을지도 몰라.
여: 하지만 방문객들의 입장료 없이 공원을 유지하기는 어려울 거야. 대신, 등산객들이 자연 보호의 중요성을 깨달아야 한다고 생각해.
남: 동의해. 그럼, 우리가 먼저 작은 노력부터 해보는 게 어때? 텐트를 세우기 전에 쓰레기를 치우자.
여: 좋은 생각이야.

어휘

as though 마치 ~인 것처럼 breathe[briːð] [동] 숨을 쉬다 trash[træʃ] [명] 쓰레기 leave behind 두고 가다 hiker [háikər] [명] 도보여행객, 등산객 awful[ɔ́ːfəl] [형] 끔찍한 besides[bisáidz] [전] ~이외에도 throw[θrou] [동] 버리다 garbage[gáːrbidʒ] [명] 쓰레기 destroy[distrɔ́i] [동] 훼손하다 protect[prətékt] [동] 보호하다 entrance fee 입장료 realize[ríː(ː)əlàiz] [동] 깨닫다 make an effort 노력하다 put up 세우다 [문제] environmental[invàiərənméntəl] [형] 환경의

문제 해설

Q1: 여자의 의견은?
① 공원 관리인은 공원을 더 잘 관리해야 한다.
② 국립공원은 입장료를 올려야 한다.
③ 등산객들은 자연 보호에 대한 생각을 바꿔야 한다.
④ 등산객들이 국립공원에 들어가는 것을 금지해야 한다.
등산객들이 자연 보호에 대해 더 많은 관심을 가져야 한다는 생각이다.

Q2: 그들이 다음에 할 일은?
텐트를 세우기 전에 자연 보호 노력의 일환으로 남들이 남겨두고 간 쓰레기를 치우자고 했다.

UNIT 02 Entertainment

Getting ★ Ready p. 14

A 1 ⓓ 2 ⓑ 3 ⓐ 4 ⓒ 5 ⓕ 6 ⓔ
B 1 ⓐ 2 ⓔ 3 ⓒ

B 1 남: 'Doctors'가 언제 하는지 알아?
여: 오후 8시에 방영될 예정이야.
2 남: 이 리얼리티 쇼의 경쟁은 어떻게 이루어져?
여: 각 에피소드마다 투표로 한 명씩 떨어질 거야.
3 남: 어제 'Henry V' 봤니? 난 못 봤어.
여: 너 어제 에피소드는 꼭 봤어야 했는데.

Listening ★ Start p. 15

1 ③ 2 (1) ⓑ (2) ⓐ (3) ⓕ 3 ①

1

M: Jane, do you mind turning to Channel 11?
W: No, I don't mind. Is there a special program on?
M: Yes. *ABC Music* is on now. My favorite singer, Christina, will be performing her latest song for the first time.
W: Wow, let's watch it together... well, that's weird. The evening news is on Channel 11 now.
M: Really? Maybe it's on another channel. Check some other channels.
W: I don't see any music programs on the other channels, either. Are you certain about the time?
M: Let me check the TV schedule... uh-oh. It looks like I got mixed up.
W: What does the schedule say?
M: It's supposed to be broadcast tomorrow.

남: Jane, 채널 11번으로 돌려도 괜찮겠니?
여: 응, 상관없어. 특별한 프로그램을 하니?
남: 응. 지금 'ABC Music'이 방송 중이야. 내가 제일 좋아하는 가수인 Christina가 신곡을 처음으로 공연할 거야.
여: 와, 같이 보자… 음, 이상하다. 지금 채널 11에서는 저녁 뉴스를 하는걸.
남: 정말? 아마 다른 채널에서 하나 봐. 다른 채널을 확인해봐.
여: 다른 채널에서도 음악 프로그램은 안 하는데. 이 시간에 하는 거 맞니?

★ ★

남: TV 편성표를 확인해 볼게… 이런. 내가 혼동했던 거 같아.

여: 편성표엔 뭐라고 써 있니?

남: 내일 방송될 예정이래.

어휘

mind[maind] 통 싫어하다, 꺼림칙하게 생각하다 channel
[tʃǽnəl] 명 (방송의) 채널 perform[pərfɔ́:rm] 통 공연하다
latest[léitist] 형 최신의 for the first time 처음으로
weird[wiərd] 형 이상한 schedule[skédʒuːl] *명 예정표,
일정표; 통 ~을 예정하다 get mixed up 혼동하다 be
supposed to-v ~할 예정이다 broadcast[brɔ́ːdkæ̀st]
통 방송하다; 명 방송 [문제] replace[ripléis] 통 대체하다.
대신하다

문제 해설

Q: 그들이 음악 프로그램을 볼 수 없었던 이유는?
  내일 방송될 프로그램을 오늘 하는 것으로 착각했다.

2

M1: I'm Adam. I like watching programs related to animals, especially the lives of animals in Africa. Last week, I watched one about the wildlife of southern Africa. It was really fantastic.

W: I'm Betty. I'm curious about what is happening around the world. So I like programs that provide a lot of information. TV shows about events around the world give me a lot of food for thought.

M2: I'm Chris. I hate serious TV programs. So I watch shows full of silly jokes. The day's stress disappears when I laugh hard.

남1: 난 Adam이야. 난 동물, 특히 아프리카에 사는 동물들의 삶과 관련된 프로그램을 보는 걸 좋아해. 지난주에는 남아프리카의 야생 생물에 대한 걸 봤어. 정말 멋지더라.

여: 난 Betty야. 난 세계에서 일어나고 있는 일들에 대해 호기심이 많아. 그래서 많은 정보를 제공해주는 프로그램을 좋아해. 세계에서 일어나는 사건에 대한 TV 프로그램들로 인해 생각할 거리가 많이 생기거든.

남2: 난 Chris야. 난 심각한 TV 프로그램을 싫어해. 그래서 실없는 농담이 많이 나오는 쇼를 봐. 실컷 웃으면 그날의 스트레스가 사라지지.

어휘

related[riléitid] 형 관계가 있는 wildlife[wáildlàif] 명
야생 생물 provide[prəváid] 통 제공하다 food for
thought 생각할 거리 silly[síli] 형 바보 같은, 시시한
joke[dʒouk] 명 농담 disappear[dìsəpíər] 통 사라지다
[문제] soap opera 드라마

문제 해설

Q: 각 인물이 좋아하는 프로그램의 종류는?

Adam은 야생 동물의 생활을 다루는 다큐멘터리를, Betty는 세계의 정보를 제공해주는 뉴스를, Chris는 웃을 수 있는 가벼운 프로그램인 코미디 쇼를 좋아한다.

3

W: TV has become a necessity we can't live without. Some people say that TV can help us in many ways. But I believe it's better not to watch too much TV. Why? As you know, our brains don't do any work while we're watching TV, because we're only receiving TV images. It's especially bad for children whose brains are not fully developed. Also, people don't burn calories while sitting watching TV. A study showed that people who watch a lot of TV have a higher chance of gaining weight.

여: TV는 우리 생활에 없어서는 안 될 필수품이 되었습니다. 어떤 사람들은 TV가 많은 면에서 도움이 될 수 있다고 말합니다. 하지만, 전 TV를 너무 많이 보지 않는 것이 좋다고 믿습니다. 왜냐고요? 아시다시피, TV를 보는 동안 우리의 뇌는 TV 이미지만 받아들이고 있기 때문에 전혀 활동을 하지 않습니다. 이것은 특히 뇌가 완전히 발달하지 않은 아이들에게 나쁩니다. 또한 앉아서 TV를 보는 동안에는 열량을 소모하지 않습니다. 한 연구에서는 TV를 많이 보는 사람이 살이 찔 확률이 더 높다는 것이 밝혀졌습니다.

어휘

necessity[nəsésəti] 명 필수품 brain[brein] 명 뇌
develop[divéləp] 통 발달하다 calorie[kǽləri] 명 칼로리
chance[tʃæns] 명 가능성 gain weight 살이 찌다 [문제]
negative[négətiv] 형 부정적인 effect[ifékt] 명 영향, 효과
relationship[riléiʃənʃip] 명 관계

문제 해설

Q: 여자는 주로 무엇에 대해 이야기하고 있는가?
  ① TV 시청의 부정적인 영향
  ② 아이들을 위한 유용한 TV 프로그램
  ③ TV가 없으면 생길 수 있는 일들
  ④ TV와 몸무게 사이의 관계
  뇌의 활동 중지 및 체중 증가와 같은 TV를 많이 시청하는 것의 나쁜 영향에 대해 설명하고 있다.

Listening ★ Practice p. 16

A 1 ④ 2 ② B 1 ③ 2 ③
C 1 ② 2 ④ D 1 ④ 2 ④

17

A [1-2]

M: Did you watch *Love Triangle* yesterday?

W: Of course. You know I always watch it on Wednesday evenings.

M: I missed yesterday's episode.

W: Why did you miss it? Did you go to bed early?

M: No, I had a lot of math homework, so I had to work on it all night.

W: What a pity! You shouldn't have missed yesterday's episode.

M: You tape every episode, right? Can you lend it to me?

W: Sorry, but I couldn't tape the last episode because I didn't have a blank tape.

M: Oh, that's too bad.

W: I can tell you what happened, though. Sophie and James finally got married and...

M: Stop it! I don't want to know the ending in advance. I'm going to watch it myself.

W: Are you going to watch the rerun?

M: I'm not patient enough to wait that long. I'll just download it from the Internet.

W: (laughs) All right.

남: 어제 'Love Triangle' 봤니?

여: 물론이지. 나 수요일 저녁이면 항상 보는 거 알잖아.

남: 난 어제 에피소드 놓쳤어.

여: 왜 놓쳤니? 일찍 잤어?

남: 아니, 수학 숙제가 많아서 밤새 그걸 해야 했어.

여: 안됐구나! 어제 에피소드는 놓치지 말았어야 했는데.

남: 너 모든 에피소드를 녹화하지? 나에게 빌려줄 수 있어?

여: 미안하지만 공테이프가 없어서 지난 에피소드는 녹화하지 못했어.

남: 아, 그거 유감이다.

여: 하지만 무슨 일이 있었는지 말해 줄 수는 있어. Sophie와 James는 결국 결혼하게 되었는데…

남: 그만 해! 미리 결말을 알고 싶지 않아. 내가 직접 볼 거야.

여: 재방송 보려고?

남: 그렇게 오래 기다릴 만큼 참을성이 있진 않아. 그냥 인터넷에서 다운로드할 거야.

여: [웃으며] 알았어.

어휘

triangle[tráiæŋɡl] 몡 삼각형; *삼각 관계   miss[mis] 통 그리워하다; *놓치다   episode[épisòud] 몡 에피소드, 시리즈의 1회분   What a pity! 안됐구나!   tape[teip] 통 (테이프에) 녹화하다   blank tape 공테이프   get married 결혼하다   ending[éndiŋ] 몡 결말   in advance 미리   rerun[ríːrÀn] 몡 재방송   patient[péiʃənt] 혱 참을성이 있는   [문제] rent[rent] 통 빌리다

Q1: 소년이 어제 저녁에 한 일은?

　　밤새 숙제를 하느라 TV를 볼 수 없었다고 했다.

Q2: 소년이 'Love Triangle'을 볼 방법은?

　　재방송을 기다릴 수가 없어 인터넷에서 다운로드해서 보겠다고 했다.

B [1-2]

M: Did you hear that KBC is looking for would-be singers for its new reality show?

W: Is it like *American Idol*?

M: Yes. The program is called *Star*. It's a perfect chance for you.

W: How does the competition work?

M: There are 12 competitors and two of them compete each week. The person who remains at the end is the winner.

W: But what if I fail?

M: How do you know what will happen without trying? The winner gets the chance to record a debut album and win $10,000.

W: I don't know...

M: Being a singer is your dream, right? If you don't try, it'll never come true.

W: Do you know who the judges are?

M: Famous singers like Madonna and Sting.

W: Wow. It'll be an honor just to sing in front of them.

M: So try it. Don't be afraid of failure.

남: KBC의 새로운 리얼리티 쇼에서 예비 가수를 찾고 있다는 거 들었어?

여: 'American Idol' 같은 거야?

남: 응. 'Star'라는 프로그램이야. 너를 위한 완벽한 기회야.

여: 어떻게 경쟁이 이루어지는데?

남: 12명의 경쟁자들이 있고 그들 중 2명이 매주 경쟁해. 마지막에 남는 사람이 우승자야.

여: 하지만 떨어지면 어떻게 해?

남: 해 보지도 않고 무슨 일이 생길지 어떻게 알아? 우승자는 데뷔 앨범을 녹음할 기회를 얻고 10,000달러를 타게 돼.

여: 모르겠어…

남: 가수가 되는 게 네 꿈이잖아, 그렇지? 시도하지 않으면 절대 이루어지지 않을 거야.

여: 심사위원이 누군지 알아?

남: Madonna와 Sting 같은 유명한 가수들이야.

여: 와. 그들 앞에서 노래하는 것만으로도 영광이겠다.

남: 그러니 시도해 봐. 실패를 두려워하지 마.

어휘

would-be[wúdbìː] 혱 ~이 되려고 하는, 지망의   reality

show 리얼리티 쇼　idol[áidəl] 몡 우상　competition
[kὰmpətíʃən] 몡 경쟁　competitor[kəmpétitər] 몡 경쟁자
compete[kəmpíːt] 통 경쟁하다　remain[riméin] 통 남다
debut[déibjuː] 몡 데뷔, 첫 출연　come true 이루어지다
judge[dʒʌdʒ] 몡 심사위원　honor[ánər] 몡 영광　failure
[féiljər] 몡 실패　[문제] participate in ～에 참가하다

문제 해설

Q1: 남자가 여자에게 제안한 것은?
　가수가 될 수 있는 리얼리티 쇼에 도전해 보라고 제안했다.

Q2: 'Star'에 관해 사실이 아닌 것은?
　우승자는 데뷔 앨범을 녹음할 수 있고, 우승 상금으로
　10,000달러를 받는다.

C [1-2]

M: I'm so sick of variety shows these days.

W: What's wrong with them?

M: The same entertainers are on every channel. They're only there to promote their movies or songs.

W: That's true.

M: And it's not just that. The programs all follow the same concept, which is all about silly jokes.

W: I think the bigger problem is copying other countries' entertainment shows. It's like watching the same program in a different language.

M: I agree. There's a lot to be changed.

W: How about making our opinions heard? We could call the broadcasting companies to protest or get together with others who have the same opinion.

M: Why don't we create an online community? It will be more effective if we raise our voices as a group.

W: Good idea. Let's start one right now.

남: 난 요즘 버라이어티 쇼에 아주 질려버렸어.

여: 뭐가 문제인데?

남: 똑같은 연예인들이 모든 채널에 나오잖아. 그들은 오직 자신
　의 영화나 노래를 홍보하기 위해 거기에 나오는 거야.

여: 그건 사실이지.

남: 그리고 그뿐만이 아니야. 그 프로그램들은 모두 시시한 농담
　이 전부인 똑같은 컨셉을 따르고 있지.

여: 더 큰 문제는 다른 나라의 연예 프로그램을 모방하는 거라고
　생각해. 마치 다른 언어로 된 같은 프로그램을 보는 것 같아.

남: 동감이야. 바뀌어야 할 것이 많아.

여: 우리 의견을 피력하는 게 어때? 방송사에 전화해서 항의하거
　나 우리와 같은 의견을 가진 사람들이 모일 수 있을 거야.

남: 온라인 커뮤니티를 만들어 보는 게 어때? 단체로 목소리를
　높이는 것이 더욱 효과적일 거야.

여: 좋은 생각이야. 당장 하나 시작해 보자.

어휘

be sick of ～이 지겹다, ～에 넌더리 나다　variety show
버라이어티 쇼　entertainer[èntərtéinər] 몡 연예인
promote[prəmóut] 통 선전하다, 판매를 촉진하다
concept[kánsept] 몡 개념, 발상　copy[kápi] 통 모방하다
broadcasting company 방송사　protest[prətést] 통
항의하다　create[kriéit] 통 창조하다　effective[iféktiv]
몡 효과적인　raise one's voice 소리를 높이다, 의견을 주
장하다　[문제] viewer[vjúːər] 몡 시청자

문제 해설

Q1: 그들은 주로 무엇에 대해 이야기하고 있는가?
　① 자신들이 싫어하는 연예인
　② 버라이어티 쇼의 나쁜 점
　③ 시청자의 중요한 역할
　④ 외국 프로그램을 모방한 프로그램
　버라이어티 쇼는 동일한 연예인들이 여러 프로그램에 출연
　하고, 시시한 농담이 주를 이루며, 외국 것을 모방하는 등의
　문제점을 안고 있다고 했다.

Q2: 그들이 다음에 할 일은?
　자신들과 같은 의견을 가진 사람들을 모으기 위해 커뮤니티
　를 인터넷에 만들기로 했다.

D [1-2]

M: Here's tonight's Fun TV schedule. At 7 p.m., *Focus* will be broadcast. Competitors answer ten questions, and the winner of the final round takes home one million dollars! *Jimmy's Show* is going to air at 8:30 p.m. Usher and Britney, who released new albums recently, will sing their new songs. *With Anne* is scheduled at 10 p.m. We'll inform you of what's been going on in Hollywood this week, such as who's dating and what's new at the box office. At 11 p.m., famous drama writer Jason Smith's *Specialists, Season 1,* will make its debut. Come check out what's happening at the hospital.

남: 오늘 밤의 Fun TV 편성표입니다. 오후 7시에는 'Focus'가 방
　송될 것입니다. 경쟁자들은 10개의 질문에 답하고 결승전
　의 승자는 백만 달러를 가지고 돌아가게 됩니다. 'Jimmy's
　Show'가 오후 8시 30분에 방영됩니다. 최근에 새 앨범을 발
　표한 Usher와 Britney가 자신들의 신곡을 부를 것입니다.
　'With Anne'은 오후 10시에 예정되어 있습니다. 누가 데이트
　를 하고 새로 나온 영화는 무엇인지 등 금주에 할리우드에서
　있었던 일들을 전해 드릴 것입니다. 오후 11시에는 유명한 드

19

라마 작가인 Jason Smith의 'Specialists, 시즌 1'이 첫 방송 됩니다. 병원에서 어떤 일이 일어나는지 와서 확인해 보세요.

어휘

million[míljən] [형] 백만의 **air**[ɛər] [동] 방송되다 **release** [rilíːs] [동] 발표하다, 공개하다 **recently**[ríːsəntli] [부] 최근에 **inform A of B** A에게 B를 알려주다 **box office** *박스 오피스; 영화 매표소 **specialist**[spéʃəlist] [명] 전문가 **make one's debut** 데뷔하다

문제 해설

Q1: 오늘 밤의 Fun TV 편성표에 관해 틀린 정보를 고르시오.

'Specialists, 시즌 1'은 오후 11시에 방영된다고 했다.

Q2: 'With Anne'은 어떤 종류의 프로그램인가?

할리우드 스타들의 데이트나 박스 오피스 소식 등 할리우드와 관련된 정보를 전해주는 연예 뉴스 프로그램이다.

Listening ★ Challenge p. 18

A 1 ① 2 ③ B 1 ② 2 (1) ⓓ (2) ⓐ (3) ⓒ

A [1-2]

W: Have you watched cartoons on TV recently?

M: No. But my little niece and nephews watch them every day.

W: If I were you, I would be worried about them. I saw an article in the newspaper saying that violence in cartoons is a serious problem.

M: Are there many violent scenes?

W: Yes. Characters fight or kill each other in many scenes.

M: I can't believe it. That could be a bad influence on little kids.

W: I know. I think the TV stations are to blame. They show these kinds of cartoons in the early evening when kids watch TV the most.

M: I think parents also need to monitor what their children are watching and not allow them to watch violent shows. Usually, parents don't think cartoons could be bad for their children.

W: But I think TV stations should do something first. They should select educational cartoons that are good for growing children.

여: 최근에 TV에서 하는 만화를 본 적 있니?

남: 아니. 하지만 내 어린 조카들은 매일 봐.

여: 내가 너라면 그 애들이 걱정될 거야. 만화의 폭력성이 심각한 문제라는 신문 기사를 봤거든.

남: 폭력적인 장면이 많이 있어?

여: 응. 등장인물들이 서로 싸우거나 죽이는 장면이 많아.

남: 믿을 수가 없어. 어린 아이들에게 나쁜 영향을 미칠 텐데.

여: 그러니까. 난 TV 방송국의 잘못이라고 생각해. 방송국에서 아이들이 TV를 가장 많이 보는 때인 이른 저녁에 이런 종류의 만화를 보여주잖아.

남: 부모들 역시 아이들이 무엇을 보는지 체크하고 폭력적인 프로그램은 보지 못하게 할 필요가 있다고 생각해. 일반적으로 부모들은 만화가 아이들에게 나쁠 수 있다고 생각하지 않잖아.

여: 하지만 난 TV 방송국들이 뭔가 우선적으로 해야 한다고 생각해. 자라나는 아이들에게 좋은 교육적인 만화를 선별해야 해.

어휘

cartoon[kɑːrtúːn] [명] 만화 **niece**[niːs] [명] 여자 조카 **nephew**[néfjuː] [명] 남자 조카 **article**[ɑ́ːrtikl] [명] 기사 **violence**[váiələns] [명] 폭력 **violent**[váiələnt] [형] 폭력적인 **scene**[siːn] [명] 장면 **character**[kǽriktər] [명] 등장인물, (만화) 캐릭터 **influence**[ínfluəns] [명] 영향 **station**[stéiʃən] [명] 방송국 **be to blame** 책임이 있다, ~이 나쁘다 **monitor**[mánitər] [동] 감시하다, 관리하다 **educational** [èdʒukéiʃənəl] [형] 교육적인

문제 해설

Q1: 그들은 주로 무엇에 대해 이야기하고 있는가?

① TV 만화의 폭력성

② 좋은 TV 만화를 만드는 방법

③ 아이들에게 비교육적인 TV 프로그램

④ 만화 시청의 나쁜 영향

아이들이 보는 만화의 심각한 폭력성에 대한 대화이다.

Q2: 여자와 같은 의견을 가진 사람은?

① Jack: 부모는 아이들이 어떤 프로그램을 보는지 신경을 써야 해.

② Nora: TV 방송국은 만화를 더 적게 방영해야 해.

③ Paul: TV 방송국은 교육적인 만화의 방영을 고려할 필요가 있어.

여자는 방송국이 아이들을 위한 교육적인 만화를 골라 방영해야 한다고 주장하고 있다.

B [1-2]

W: Good evening. I'm Amy Jones. I'm pleased to be part of the Best TV Drama Awards.

M: Good evening. I'm Justin Watson. Awards in many categories have been announced so far. Now, I'm curious about the Best Drama of the Year.

W: Me, too. Three dramas have been nominated for this award.

M: Yes. Let's check them out one by one.

W: Okay. First, we have *Witches*. Wonderful performances by amazing actors made this drama unforgettable.

M: And here's another strong one, *The Boys*.

The exciting plot made this series the most popular show of the year.

W: And lastly, there's *Dream*. This show takes place 100 years in the future. Amazing special effects made the future look real.

M: What a difficult choice to make!

W: All right, Justin. We can't wait any longer. Could you please open the envelope?

M: Okay. I think it's time to find out.

여: 안녕하세요. Amy Jones입니다. Best TV Drama Awards에 참가하게 되어 기쁩니다.

남: 안녕하세요. Justin Watson이에요. 지금까지 많은 부문의 상이 발표되었는데요. 이제 올해의 최고 드라마상이 궁금해지네요.

여: 저도 그렇습니다. 세 개의 드라마가 이 상의 후보로 올랐는데요.

남: 네. 하나씩 살펴보도록 하죠.

여: 좋습니다. 우선, 'Witches'가 있습니다. 훌륭한 배우들의 멋진 연기가 이 드라마를 인상 깊게 했죠.

남: 그리고 다른 막강한 후보, 'The Boys'가 있습니다. 흥미진진한 줄거리로 인해 이 시리즈가 올해의 가장 인기 있는 쇼가 되었죠.

여: 그리고 마지막으로 'Dream'이 있습니다. 이 쇼는 100년 후 미래에서 벌어지는데요. 놀라운 특수 효과가 미래를 실제처럼 보이게 만들었습니다.

남: 아주 어려운 선택인데요!

여: 그렇습니다, Justin. 더 이상 기다릴 수 없겠는데요. 봉투를 열어 주시겠어요?

남: 좋아요. 밝힐 시간이 왔군요.

어휘

pleased[pli:zd] 혱 기쁜　award[əwɔ́:rd] 몡 상, 상패　category[kǽtəgɔ̀:ri] 몡 부문, 카테고리　announce [ənáuns] 통 발표하다　so far 지금까지　nominate [námənèit] 통 후보로 지명하다　witch[witʃ] 몡 마녀　performance[pərfɔ́:rməns] 몡 연기　unforgettable [ʌ̀nfərgétəbl] 혱 잊을 수 없는　plot[plɑt] 몡 줄거리　take place 일어나다　special effect 특수 효과　real[ríːəl] 혱 실제의, 현실의　envelope[énvəlòup] 몡 봉투　[문제] host [houst] 몡 진행자, 사회자　camerawork[kǽmərəwɜ̀:rk] 몡 촬영기술　sound effect 음향 효과

문제 해설

Q1: 그들이 다음에 할 일은?

최고 드라마상의 후보를 발표하고 나서 봉투를 연다고 했으므로 수상작을 발표할 것이다.

Q2: 각 드라마의 특별한 점을 고르시오.

'Witches'는 배우들의 연기가 훌륭했고, 'The Boys'는 줄거리가 흥미진진했고, 'Dream'은 특수 효과가 멋졌다고 평했다.

Critical ★ Thinking　p. 19

1 ④　2 ②

M: I'm Ted. Entertainment news on TV gives too many details about stars' private lives. But stars also need their privacy. Although the general public wants to know every single detail of the stars' lives, the privacy of these people should be respected. How would you feel if the paparazzi were around you 24 hours a day and your mistakes were all over the news?

W: I'm Nell. Entertainers already knew their lives would be other people's gossip when they joined the entertainment business. Also, some entertainers make their lives open to the media to get more attention. It's natural for the general public to be interested in entertainers. News about their private lives satisfies people's curiosity. It's good for not only the entertainment business and the public, but also the entertainers themselves.

남: 난 Ted야. TV에서 하는 연예 뉴스는 스타들의 개인 생활에 대해 너무 세세하게 알려줘. 그런데 스타들도 사생활이 필요한 거잖아. 비록 일반 대중들이 스타들의 삶에 대해 시시콜콜 다 알고 싶다고 하더라도 그들의 사생활은 존중되어야 해. 파파라치가 하루 24시간 네 주변에 있고 네가 저지른 실수들이 뉴스에 다 나온다면 어떨 것 같아?

여: 난 Nell이야. 연예인은 그들이 연예계에 들어갈 때 자신들의 생활이 다른 사람들의 가십이 될 거라는 걸 이미 알고 있었어. 또한 몇몇 연예인들은 대중 매체에 자신의 생활을 공개해서 더 많은 관심을 끌기도 하지. 대중들이 연예인들에게 관심이 있는 것은 자연스러운 거야. 그들의 사생활에 대한 뉴스가 사람들의 호기심을 만족시키지. 그것은 연예계와 대중뿐만 아니라 연예인 자신들에게도 좋은 일이야.

어휘

detail[ditéil] 몡 사소한 일, 세부　private[práivit] 혱 사적인　privacy[práivəsi] 몡 사생활, 프라이버시　general public 일반 대중　respect[rispékt] 통 존중하다　paparazzo [pàːpəráːtsou] 몡 파파라치 (복수형 paparazzi)　gossip [gásəp] 몡 가십, 남의 뒷말　the media 미디어, 대중 매체　satisfy[sǽtisfài] 통 만족시키다　curiosity[kjùəriásəti] 몡 호기심　[문제] be responsible for ~에 대해 책임이 있다

문제 해설

Q1: 그들은 주로 무엇에 대해 이야기하고 있는가?

① 파파라치를 법으로 금지해야 하는가?

② 연예인의 사생활을 어떻게 보호할 수 있을까?

21

③ 연예계 가십에 대해 누가 책임이 있는가?

④ 연예인의 사생활이 미디어에 나와야 하나?

연예인들의 사생활에 대한 뉴스가 미디어에 보도되어야 하는지에 대한 토론이다.

Q2: 남자의 의견은?

① 연예인은 자신의 개인 생활을 포기해야 한다.

② 미디어는 유명인들의 개인 생활을 보호해야 한다.

③ 몇몇 연예인들은 관심을 얻기 위해 미디어를 이용한다.

④ 연예인 자신들이 가십에 대해 책임이 있다.

남자는 연예 뉴스에서 유명인들의 사생활을 다루는 것이 좋지 않다고 생각한다.

UNIT 03 Daily Life

Getting ★ Ready　p. 20

A 1 ⓑ　2 ⓓ　3 ⓐ　4 ⓔ　5 ⓒ　6 ⓕ

B 1 ⓑ　2 ⓕ　3 ⓔ

B 1 여: 오늘 머리를 어떻게 하고 싶으세요?

　　남: 짧게 자를지 파마를 할지 결정을 못하겠어요.

　2 여: 이 카드의 연회비는 얼마죠?

　　남: 연회비를 부과하지 않습니다.

　3 여: 배달이 뭐 때문에 이렇게 늦은 거죠?

　　남: 주문이 많이 밀려서요.

Listening ★ Start　p. 21

1 ③　2 ③　3 ②, ④

1

(*Telephone rings.*)

W: Hello, Grand Chinese Restaurant.

M: Yes. My address is 603 Main Street and I had some food delivered about an hour ago.

W: I remember. You're one of my regular customers. Do you want to make an additional order?

M: That's not the reason I called. My food was cold when it arrived.

W: I'm sorry. We had a rush of orders, so your delivery may have been delayed.

M: That's not all. It was so salty that I couldn't have more than one bite.

W: Was it? We are really short of hands, so

maybe our chef made a mistake.

M: I understand that you're busy, but it's no excuse for bad food.

W: I'm so sorry.

(전화벨이 울린다.)

여: 여보세요. Grand 중식당입니다.

남: 네. 제 주소는 메인가 603번지이고 한 시간 전쯤에 음식을 배달시켰어요.

여: 기억해요. 저희 단골 중 한 분이시잖아요. 추가 주문을 원하세요?

남: 그것 때문에 전화를 한 건 아니고요. 음식이 도착했을 때 식어 있었어요.

여: 죄송합니다. 주문이 밀려들어서 배달이 지연되었나 봐요.

남: 그게 다가 아니에요. 음식이 너무 짜서 한 입 먹고선 더 이상 먹을 수가 없었어요.

여: 그랬나요? 일손이 정말 모자라서 아마 주방장이 실수를 했나 봅니다.

남: 바쁘신 건 이해하지만 형편없는 음식에 대한 변명은 안 되죠.

여: 정말 죄송합니다.

어휘

deliver[dilívər] 통 배달하다　regular customer 단골 고객　additional[ədíʃənəl] 형 추가의　order[ɔ́ːrdər] 명 주문　rush[rʌʃ] 명 분주; *(주문) 쇄도　delivery[dilívəri] 명 배달　delay[diléi] 통 늦추다, 지체시키다　bite[bait] 명 한 입　be short of hands 일손이 부족하다　chef[ʃef] 명 요리사　excuse[ikskjúːs] 명 변명　[문제] complain[kəmpléin] 통 불평하다

문제 해설

Q: 남자가 전화한 이유는?

　남자는 배달된 음식이 다 식어 있었고, 너무 짜서 먹을 수 없었던 것에 대해 불평하기 위해 전화했다.

2

M: Are you planning to move soon? If so, one call to Speed Movers will take care of all your moving needs. With 20 years of experience, we have maintained a great reputation. Using our professional system and packaging techniques, we provide moving services to any place, even overseas. Our main services are as follows: packing, moving, new house cleaning, unpacking, and arranging unpacked items. We are here for you seven days a week from 9 a.m. to 7 p.m. Please call 143–9012 to schedule an appointment.

남: 곧 이사할 계획이세요? 그렇다면, Speed Movers에 전화 한 통만 거시면 이사할 때 필요한 모든 사항을 책임져 드릴

것입니다. 저희는 20년 간의 경험으로 좋은 명성을 유지해 왔습니다. 전문적인 시스템과 포장 기술을 사용해서 어느 곳이든, 해외로까지도 이사 서비스를 제공해 드립니다. 저희의 주된 서비스는 다음과 같습니다: 짐 싸기와 이사, 새집 청소, 짐 풀기, 푼 물건 정리하기입니다. 일주일 내내 오전 9시부터 오후 7시까지 대기하고 있습니다. 143-9012로 전화 주셔서 예약을 하세요.

어휘

take care of ~을 책임지다 reputation [rèpju(ː)téiʃən] 명 명성, 평판 professional [prəféʃənəl] 형 전문적인 packaging [pǽkidʒiŋ] 명 포장, 짐 싸기 technique [tekníːk] 명 기술 provide [prəváid] 동 제공하다 overseas [òuvərsíːz] 부 해외로 pack [pæk] 동 꾸리다, 싸다 unpack [ʌnpǽk] 동 (짐을) 풀다 arrange [əréindʒ] 동 배치하다, 정리하다 schedule an appointment 약속 시간을 잡다

문제 해설

Q: 틀린 정보를 고르시오.

일주일 내내 근무한다고 했다.

3

M: How would you like to have your hair done today?

W: I can't decide between cutting it short and getting a perm.

M: In my opinion, you'll look prettier with curly hair. How about some curls just on the edge?

W: Well... I've never thought about that kind of style.

M: Try it. I'm sure it'll look good on you.

W: If you say so, I'll give it a try. Plus, I want to dye my hair light brown.

M: Well, your hair is really damaged now. I don't think it's a good idea to do both at the same time.

W: Oh, I see. I didn't know the condition of my hair was that bad.

M: Why don't you get a hair treatment instead?

W: Okay.

남: 오늘은 머리를 어떻게 하고 싶으세요?

여: 짧게 자르는 거랑 파마를 하는 거 사이에서 결정을 못하겠어요.

남: 제 생각에는 곱슬머리가 더 귀여워 보일 것 같아요. 끝에만 컬을 넣는 건 어떨까요?

여: 음… 그런 스타일은 생각해 보지 않았어요.

남: 해 보세요. 분명히 잘 어울릴 거예요.

여: 그렇게 말씀하시니까 한 번 해 볼게요. 그리고 머리를 밝은 갈색으로 염색하고 싶어요.

남: 음, 머리가 지금 많이 상해 있어요. 두 가지를 한꺼번에 하는

건 좋은 생각이 아닌 것 같아요.

여: 아, 알겠어요. 제 머리 상태가 그렇게 나쁜지 몰랐어요.

남: 대신 헤어 트리트먼트를 받는 것이 어때요?

여: 좋아요.

어휘

have one's hair done 머리 손질을 하다 get a perm 파마를 하다 curly [kə́ːrli] 형 곱슬곱슬한 curl [kəːrl] 명 컬 edge [edʒ] 명 끝 give it a try 한 번 해 보다 dye [dai] 동 염색하다 damaged [dǽmidʒd] 형 손상된 at the same time 동시에 condition [kəndíʃən] 명 상태 hair treatment 헤어 트리트먼트(상한 머리에 영양분을 주는 미용법)

문제 해설

Q: 여자가 시술 받으려고 하는 서비스를 두 개 고르시오.

여자는 파마를 하고 상한 머리를 위해 헤어 트리트먼트를 하기로 했다.

Listening ★ Practice　**p. 22**

A 1 ④　2 ④　B 1 ①　2 ④
C 1 ②　2 (1) T　(2) F　(3) F　D 1 ④　2 ③

A [1-2]

(*Telephone rings.*)

M: BG transportation company.

W: Hello. I rode one of your buses this morning and left my wallet on it. Do you happen to have it?

M: Let me check. Do you remember the bus number?

W: It was 14.

M: Okay. Could you describe the wallet? I'm looking up the lost and found list on the computer.

W: It's a dark brown wallet. Please check carefully. I have to find it.

M: Hmm... we have several brown wallets. Is there any identification inside?

W: Unfortunately, no. But my wallet has light yellow stripes on it.

M: I'm sorry but we don't have a wallet with yellow stripes. Are you sure you left it on the bus?

W: Yes. As soon as I got off the bus, I realized I lost it.

M: It's possible that one of the other passengers took it.

W: Oh, no! I hoped I would find it.

(전화벨이 울린다.)

남: BG 운수 회사입니다.

여: 안녕하세요. 오늘 아침에 거기 버스 중 하나를 탔었는데 제 지갑을 두고 내렸어요. 혹시 가지고 있으세요?

남: 한번 확인해 볼게요. 버스 번호 기억하세요?

여: 14번이었어요.

남: 알았어요. 지갑을 설명해 주시겠어요? 컴퓨터로 분실물 리스트를 찾아보고 있어요.

여: 짙은 갈색 지갑이에요. 신중하게 확인해 주세요. 꼭 찾아야 해요.

남: 음… 갈색 지갑이 몇 개 있네요. 안에 신분증이 있어요?

여: 불행히도 없어요. 하지만 제 지갑은 밝은 노란색 줄무늬가 있어요.

남: 유감이지만 노란 줄무늬가 있는 지갑은 없어요. 버스에 두고 간 거 확실해요?

여: 네. 버스에서 내리자마자 잃어버린 걸 알았거든요.

남: 다른 승객 중 한 명이 가지고 갔을 가능성이 있어요.

여: 아, 안돼요! 찾을 걸로 기대했는데.

어휘

transportation[trænspərtéiʃən] 몡 운송, 수송 wallet
[wɔ́lit] 몡 지갑 describe[diskráib] 통 설명하다, 묘사하다
lost and found 분실물 보관소 identification
[aidèntəfikéiʃən] 몡 신분증 unfortunately[ʌnfɔ́ːrtʃənətli]
흰 불행히도 stripe[straip] 몡 줄무늬 as soon as ~하
자마자 possible[pásəbl] 혱 가능성이 있는 passenger
[pǽsəndʒər] 몡 승객

문제 해설

Q1: 여자의 지갑을 고르시오.

　 여자의 지갑은 갈색에 밝은 노란색 줄무늬가 있는 지갑이다.

Q2: 여자의 심정은 어떻게 변했나?

　 지갑을 잃어버려서 걱정스러워하는 마음이었다가 지갑을 찾기 어려울 것 같다는 것을 알고 실망한 상태이다.

B [1-2]

M: What can I do for you?

W: I'd like to get the photos on this CD developed.

M: What size would you like, three by five or four by six?

W: Four by six, please.

M: Would you write down your name and phone number here?

W: Okay... oh, what a nice photo album. Do you make these for customers?

M: Yes. It's a hot trend among young couples these days.

W: I was thinking of making one for my boyfriend. How much does it cost?

M: The album you saw is $60. It has 30 pages with two photos per page. Putting

comments costs an extra $10.

W: I want to order one with comments. But can I just put one big picture per page?

M: Sure. The price is the same.

남: 무엇을 도와드릴까요?

여: 이 CD에 있는 사진을 현상하고 싶어요.

남: 어떤 사이즈를 원하세요, 3x5요, 아니면 4x6이요?

여: 4x6으로 해주세요.

남: 이름과 전화번호를 여기 써 주시겠어요?

여: 좋아요… 오, 멋진 포토앨범이네요. 판매용으로 이걸 만드시나요?

남: 네. 요즘 젊은 연인들 사이에 대유행이지요.

여: 제 남자 친구를 위해 하나 만들까 생각 중이었거든요. 얼마예요?

남: 보신 앨범은 60달러예요. 한 페이지당 두 장의 사진이 들어가고, 30페이지짜리입니다. 문구를 써 넣는 것은 추가 10달러가 됩니다.

여: 문구가 있는 것으로 주문하고 싶어요. 하지만 한 페이지에 한 장의 큰 사진을 넣을 수 있을까요?

남: 물론이지요. 가격은 같습니다.

어휘

develop[divéləp] 통 현상하다 customer[kʌ́stəmər] 몡
고객 trend[trend] 몡 유행 comment[káment] 몡 문구,
짧은 말 extra[ékstrə] 혱 추가의

문제 해설

Q1: 여자가 사진관에 간 이유는?

　 여자는 찍은 사진을 현상하기 위해 사진관에 간 것이다.

Q2: 여자가 원하는 포토앨범을 고르시오.

　 여자는 한 페이지당 하나의 큰 사진이 들어가 있고 문구를 적을 수 있는 앨범을 골랐다.

C [1-2]

M: In our daily lives, we're affected by lots of electromagnetic waves but aren't aware of them. They flow in the air when we use electronic goods such as TVs and cell phones. Therefore, keep at least two meters away from the TV when watching it. Bigger TVs produce more electromagnetic waves, so always watch them from far away. Plants with large leaves or high water content absorb the waves, so put some near your TV. When using your cell phone, don't touch the antenna. Lots of electromagnetic waves come out of it. And even if you turn electronic devices off, make sure to unplug them. Otherwise, the electromagnetic waves keep flowing.

남: 일상생활에서 우리는 많은 양의 전자파의 영향을 받지만 그것을 알지 못합니다. 전자파는 우리가 TV나 휴대전화와 같은 전자 제품을 사용할 때 공중에서 흐릅니다. 그러므로 TV를 볼 때 적어도 2미터 떨어지세요. 더 큰 TV일수록 더 많은 전자파를 만들어 내기 때문에 항상 멀리서 봐야 합니다. 큰 잎사귀를 가졌거나 높은 수분 함량을 가진 식물은 전자파를 흡수하므로 몇 개를 TV 가까이에 두세요. 휴대전화를 사용할 때 는 안테나를 만지지 마세요. 많은 양의 전자파가 거기에서 나옵니다. 그리고 전자 기기를 비록 껐다고 하더라도 반드시 플러그를 뽑으세요. 그렇지 않으면 전자파는 계속 흐르고 있습니다.

어휘

be affected by ~에 영향을 받다 electromagnetic wave 전자파 be aware of ~을 알다 flow[flou] [동] 흐르다 electronic[ilektránik] [형] 전자의 goods[gudz] [명] 물품, 상품 at least 최소한 water content 수분 함량 absorb[æbsɔ́ːrb] [동] 흡수하다 antenna[ænténə] [명] 안테나 device[diváis] [명] 도구, 기기 turn off ~을 끄다 make sure to-v 반드시 ~하도록 하다 unplug[ʌnplʌ́g] [동] 플러그를 빼다

문제 해설

Q1: 남자는 주로 무엇에 관해 이야기하고 있나?
① 전자파가 어떻게 작용하는지
② 어떻게 전자파를 피할 수 있는지
③ 전자파가 얼마나 위험한지
④ 전자파가 어떻게 우리 삶에 영향을 주는지
TV나 휴대전화 사용 시 발생하는 전자파를 피하기 위한 방법을 소개하고 있다.

Q2: 전자파에 관해 사실이면 T, 사실이 아니면 F를 쓰시오.
(1) 작은 TV는 큰 TV보다 전자파를 더 적게 만들어 낸다.
(2) 전자파는 휴대전화 사용 시 대부분 화면에서 나온다.
(3) 전자 제품을 끄면 흐르지 않는다.
TV가 클수록 전자파가 많이 나온다고 했고 휴대전화 사용 시 전자파는 안테나에서 가장 많이 나온다고 했으며 전자 제품을 끈 상태에서도 플러그를 뽑지 않으면 전자파가 계속 흘러나오는 것이라고 설명했다.

D [1-2]

(*Telephone rings.*)
W: Top Magazine.
M: Hello. I want to subscribe to your magazine for six months. How much will that be?
W: That's $27. One issue is $5, so it's a 10% discount.
M: Well, the discount isn't as big as I expected.
W: If you subscribe for a year, there's a 20% discount.
M: Really? Since the regular price is $60, that means I can save $12. I'll go with an annual subscription.
W: Great. Do you want to start from this month?
M: I already bought this month's issue. So I'd like my subscription to start in October.
W: All right. What's your name and address?
M: It's James Pitt and my address is 160 Clinton Street.
W: All right. Will you pay with a credit card?
M: No, I'd prefer to pay by bank transfer.
W: All right.

(전화벨이 울린다.)
여: Top Magazine입니다.
남: 여보세요. 잡지를 여섯 달 동안 구독하고 싶어요. 얼마죠?
여: 27달러예요. 한 호가 5달러이니까 10% 할인입니다.
남: 음, 할인액이 예상했던 것만큼 크진 않군요.
여: 일 년 구독하시면 20% 할인해 드립니다.
남: 그래요? 정가가 60달러이니까 12달러가 절약된다는 뜻이군요. 일 년 구독으로 할게요.
여: 좋습니다. 이번 달부터 받으시겠습니까?
남: 이번 달 호는 이미 샀어요. 그래서 10월에 구독을 시작하고 싶어요.
여: 알겠습니다. 이름과 주소가 어떻게 되시죠?
남: 전 James Pitt이고 주소는 Clinton가 160번지예요.
여: 알겠습니다. 신용카드로 지불하실 건가요?
남: 아니요, 계좌 이체로 할게요.
여: 알겠습니다.

어휘

subscribe[səbskráib] [동] 구독하다 issue[íʃuː] [명] 발행물 discount[dískaunt] [명] 할인, 할인액 since[sins] [접] ~이기 때문에 annual[ǽnjuəl] [형] 일년의 subscription[səbskrípʃən] [명] 구독 credit card 신용카드 prefer[prifə́ːr] [동] 선호하다 bank transfer 계좌 이체

문제 해설

Q1: 틀린 정보를 고르시오.
남자는 신용카드보다 계좌 이체를 선호한다고 했다.

Q2: 남자가 지불할 금액은?
일 년 정기구독을 신청했으므로 정가 60달러의 20% 할인가인 48달러이다.

Listening ★ Challenge p. 24

A 1 ② 2 ③ B 1 ③ 2 ②

A [1-2]

(*Telephone rings.*)
W: BT Credit Card. How may I help you?
M: I called to change my billing address.
W: Could you tell me your name and social

security number?

M: I'm Tom Wilson, and my number is 555–21–0707.

W: Have you considered signing up for e-billing service? You wouldn't need to change your address with e-billing.

M: No, thanks. I don't use email very often.

W: Okay. What's your new address?

M: 97 Victoria Street.

W: It's done. But your card is old and has few benefits. Why don't you change it to a new card?

M: Well, I don't know.

W: We have a new card called the "Green Card." You can get a 20% discount on hotels and a 15% discount in most family restaurants.

M: Is there a discount for gasoline?

W: I'm sorry but there isn't.

M: Wouldn't it have a higher annual fee?

W: We don't charge an annual fee.

M: Great. Then I'll get the new card.

(전화벨이 울린다.)

여: BT 신용카드입니다. 무엇을 도와드릴까요?

남: 청구지 주소를 변경하려고 전화했어요.

여: 성함과 사회보장번호를 알려주시겠어요?

남: Tom Wilson이고 번호는 555–21–0707입니다.

여: 이메일 청구서 신청을 생각해 본 적 있으세요? 이메일 청구서는 주소를 바꿀 필요가 없거든요.

남: 감사합니다만 괜찮아요. 전 이메일을 그렇게 자주 사용하지 않아요.

여: 알겠습니다. 새 주소가 어떻게 되시죠?

남: 빅토리아가 97번지예요.

여: 되셨습니다. 하지만 카드가 오래 되었고 혜택도 얼마 안 되네요. 새 카드로 바꾸시는 게 어떨까요?

남: 음, 모르겠어요.

여: '그린 카드'라는 새 카드가 있어요. 호텔에서 20% 할인이 되고 대부분의 패밀리 레스토랑에서 15% 할인을 받을 수 있어요.

남: 주유 할인은 있나요?

여: 죄송하지만 그건 없습니다.

남: 연회비가 더 높지는 않나요?

여: 연회비는 없어요.

남: 좋네요. 그럼 새 카드를 받을게요.

어휘

billing address 청구지 주소 social security number 사회 보장 번호 consider[kənsídər] [동] 고려하다, 생각하다 sign up for ~을 신청하다 e-billing service 이메일 청구서 서비스 benefit[bénəfit] [명] 혜택 gasoline[gǽsəlì:n] [명] 가솔린, 휘발유 annual fee 연회비

문제 해설

Q1: 남자가 전화한 이유는?

남자는 청구지 주소를 바꾸기 위해 신용카드 회사에 전화했다.

Q2: 그린 카드의 혜택이 아닌 것은?

연회비가 없고 호텔 할인과 패밀리 레스토랑 할인이 되지만, 주유 할인은 없다고 했다.

B [1-2]

W: Hello. This is Janet from *Guess What*. Today, I'll give you clear answers about the questions you asked about washing clothes. First, white socks are easy to get dirty and hard to get clean. But if you wash them after soaking them in water with lemon juice and salt for a while, they'll be as good as new. If your sneakers are still dirty after washing them, put some toothpaste on the dirty parts and dry it. When a dress shirt collar is dirty, rub shampoo on it before running it through the washing machine. Then the dirt will go away. Next week, I'll tell you about cleaning techniques for kitchens and bathrooms, as well as how to remove bad smells from your house. Please join us next week.

여: 안녕하세요. 'Guess What'의 Janet입니다. 오늘은 옷 세탁과 관련해 여러분이 질문한 문제들에 대해 분명한 답을 드리겠습니다. 우선, 흰색 양말은 더러워지기 쉽고 깨끗해지기가 어렵습니다. 하지만 레몬즙과 소금을 넣은 물 속에 잠시 동안 담근 후에 세탁하면 새것처럼 될 것입니다. 운동화가 세탁 후에도 여전히 더럽다면 더러운 부분에 치약을 바른 다음 말리세요. 와이셔츠의 깃이 더러우면 세탁기에 돌리기 전에 그 위에 샴푸를 바르고 문지르세요. 그러고 나면 때가 사라질 것입니다. 다음 주에는 집 안의 나쁜 냄새를 없애는 방법뿐만 아니라 부엌과 목욕탕을 청소하는 방법에 대해서도 알려 드리겠습니다. 다음 주에도 함께 해 주세요.

어휘

soak[souk] [동] 적시다, 담그다 salt[sɔ:lt] [명] 소금 sneakers[sní:kərz] [명] 운동화 toothpaste[tú:θpèist] [명] 치약 dress shirt 와이셔츠 collar[kálər] [명] 깃 rub[rʌb] [동] 문지르다 washing machine 세탁기 dirt[də:rt] [명] 때 remove[rimú:v] [동] 없애다

문제 해설

Q1: 여자의 충고를 올바르게 따르고 있는 사람은?

① Ian: 흰색 양말을 세탁할 때는 소금과 치약을 물에 넣어.

② Kate: 운동화를 세탁하기 전에 레몬즙이 든 물에 넣어.

③ Lily: 세탁하기 전에 셔츠 깃에 샴푸를 문질러.

와이셔츠 깃 부분의 때는 세탁 전에 샴푸를 문지르면 없어진다고 했다.

Q2: 다음 주에 언급되지 않을 것 같은 것은?
다음 주에는 집안의 나쁜 냄새를 없애는 방법, 부엌과 욕실의 청소 방법에 대한 내용이 나올 것이다.

Critical ★ Thinking p. 25

1 ③ 2 ②

W1: I'm Eve. It's difficult to find time to go to a bank, because they are closed when I finish work. I think if they can't extend their weekday business hours, banks should open on the weekends.
M: I'm Tom. I have a different opinion. Wouldn't it be unfair to make bankers work on weekends? We can't force them to work more days just for our convenience. They also need time to relax and rest.
W2: I'm Janet. It's true that many workers have a hard time using banks. But I don't think all banks need to open on weekends. Opening a few branches in each region will be enough. Bank clerks could rotate their schedules and get paid for weekend overtime work.

여1: 난 Eve야. 내가 일을 마치면 은행은 문을 닫기 때문에 은행에 가기가 힘들어. 은행이 주중 업무 시간을 연장할 수 없다면 주말에 열어야 한다고 생각해.
남: 난 Tom이야. 난 다른 의견이야. 은행 직원을 주말에 일하도록 하는 것은 불공평하지 않을까? 우리의 편의를 위해 그들에게 더 많은 날을 일하라고 강요할 수는 없지. 그들도 편하게 쉴 시간이 필요해.
여2: 난 Janet이야. 많은 직장인들이 은행을 이용하기가 힘든 건 사실이야. 그러나 모든 은행이 주말에 열어야 할 필요가 있다고 생각하지는 않아. 각 지역마다 몇 개 지점만을 여는 것으로 충분해. 은행 직원은 순환 근무를 하고 주말 추가 근무에 대한 수당을 받을 수 있잖아.

어휘
extend [iksténd] [동] 연장하다 weekday [wí:kdèi] [명] 주중 business hours 업무 시간 unfair [ʌnfέər] [형] 불공평한 force A to-v A를 ~하도록 강요하다 convenience [kənví:njəns] [명] 편의, 편리 have a hard time v-ing ~하는 데 힘들어하다 branch [bræntʃ] [명] 지점 region [rí:dʒən] [명] 지역 clerk [klə:rk] [명] 직원 rotate [róuteit] [동] 교대하다, 순환하다 overtime work 시간외 근무, 초과 근무

문제 해설
Q1: 그들은 주로 무엇에 대해 이야기하고 있나?
① 왜 초과 근무 수당이 지불되어야 하나?
② 은행은 언제 문을 닫아야 하나?
③ 은행은 주말 동안 문을 열어야 하나?
④ 은행에서 일하는 것의 힘든 점은 무엇인가?
은행이 주말에 문을 열어야 할지에 대한 의견을 교환하고 있다.

Q2: Janet과 같은 의견을 가진 사람은?
① Jack: 은행은 주중에 근무 시간을 늘려야 한다.
② Matt: 은행 지점 몇 개를 주말에 열어야 한다.
③ Laura: 사람들의 편의를 위해 모든 은행은 주말에 열어야 한다.
Janet은 지역당 몇 개의 지점만 주말에 열어야 한다는 의견을 가지고 있으므로 Matt와 같은 의견이다.

UNIT 04 Food

Getting ★ Ready p. 26

A 1 ⓓ 2 ⓑ 3 ⓐ 4 ⓔ 5 ⓒ 6 ⓕ
B 1 ⓒ 2 ⓕ 3 ⓐ

B 1 남: 올리브 오일의 건강상의 혜택은 뭐죠?
여: 콜레스테롤 수치를 낮추는 데 도움이 됩니다.
2 남: 주문하시겠어요?
여: 네. 에피타이저로 감자 샐러드를 먹을게요.
3 남: 어제 갔던 음식점 어땠어?
여: 끔찍했어. 예약을 했는데도 자리에 앉기까지 1시간을 기다렸어.

Listening ★ Start p. 27

1 (1) ④ (2) ① 2 ③ 3 (1) ⓔ (2) ⓐ (3) ⓒ

1

M: (1) This is a Japanese dish which includes various vegetables and sliced beef. I lightly cook them by putting them in boiling water for a while. Then I dip them in a delicious sauce and eat them.
W: (2) This is a traditional Korean food. It is served in a large bowl. It contains rice, vegetables such as carrot, cucumber, mushroom and spinach, and an egg. I mix them together with red pepper paste. This food is not only delicious but also healthy.

남: 이것은 다양한 채소와 얇게 썬 쇠고기가 들어가는 일본 음식입니다. 그것들을 끓는 물에 잠시 넣어서 가볍게 익힙니다. 그리고 나서 맛있는 소스에 찍어서 먹습니다.

여: 이것은 전통적인 한국 음식입니다. 이것은 큰 그릇에 담겨 나옵니다. 밥과 당근, 오이, 버섯, 시금치와 같은 채소와 달걀이 들어 있습니다. 이것들을 고추장과 함께 섞습니다. 이 음식은 맛있을 뿐만 아니라 건강에 좋습니다.

어휘

dish[diʃ] 몡 요리 　vegetable[védʒitəbl] 몡 채소 　sliced [slaist] 휑 얇게 썬 　beef[bi:f] 몡 쇠고기 　boiling[bɔ́iliŋ] 휑 끓는 　dip[dip] 동 (살짝) 담그다 　sauce[sɔ:s] 몡 소스 traditional[trədíʃənəl] 휑 전통적인 　bowl[boul] 몡 그릇 contain[kəntéin] 동 포함하다 　carrot[kǽrət] 몡 당근 cucumber[kjú:kʌmbər] 몡 오이 　mushroom [mʌ́ʃru(:)m] 몡 버섯 　spinach[spínitʃ] 몡 시금치 　red pepper paste 고추장

문제 해설

Q: 각 인물이 설명하는 음식을 고르시오.

다양한 채소와 얇은 쇠고기를 끓는 물에 데쳐 소스에 찍어 먹는 음식은 샤브샤브이고, 밥과 채소를 섞어 고추장에 비벼 먹는 음식은 비빔밥이다.

2

M: Can I take your order?

W: Yes. I'd like to have a chicken salad as an appetizer.

M: All right. We have Thousand Island, honey mustard, and French dressing.

W: I've never tried French dressing, so I want to try it this time. Can you recommend a steak?

M: Our rib-eye steak and New York steak are the most popular.

W: Why is there such a price difference between them?

M: The New York steak is bigger than the rib-eye steak.

W: I see. Then we'll have two rib-eye steaks, one well-done and the other rare.

M: Okay. Would you like to have some wine? It's offered at a 20% discount when you order a steak.

W: Yes. One glass of red wine, please.

M: Okay.

남: 주문하시겠어요?

여: 네. 에피타이저로 치킨 샐러드를 먹을게요.

남: 좋습니다. 사우전드 아일랜드와 허니 머스터드, 프렌치 드레싱이 있습니다.

여: 프렌치 드레싱은 먹어본 적이 없어서 이번엔 그걸 먹어보고 싶어요. 스테이크를 추천해 주실래요?

남: 립아이 스테이크와 뉴욕 스테이크가 가장 인기가 많습니다.

여: 둘의 가격은 왜 차이가 많이 나죠?

남: 뉴욕 스테이크가 립아이 스테이크보다 더 큽니다.

여: 알겠어요. 그럼 립아이 스테이크 2개를 하나는 웰던, 다른 하나는 레어로 먹을게요.

남: 좋습니다. 와인을 드시겠어요? 스테이크를 주문하시면 20% 할인 가격에 제공됩니다.

여: 네. 레드 와인 한 잔 주세요.

남: 알겠습니다.

어휘

Can I take your order? 주문하시겠어요? 　appetizer [ǽpətàizər] 몡 전채요리 　honey[hʌ́ni] 몡 꿀 　mustard [mʌ́stərd] 몡 겨자 　dressing[drésiŋ] 몡 드레싱, 소스 recommend[rèkəménd] 동 추천하다 　well-done [wéldʌ́n] 휑 (고기가) 완전히 익은 　rare[rɛər] 휑 덜 익은 offer[ɔ́(:)fər] 동 제공하다

문제 해설

Q: 틀린 정보를 고르시오.

스테이크를 하나는 웰던, 또 하나는 레어로 주문했다.

3

W: Recent research has shown that certain foods shouldn't be eaten together. It's because some foods destroy the nutrients in other food. Let me give you an example. When you make a salad, you should avoid using cucumbers and carrots together. An element in carrots destroys the vitamin C in cucumbers. Here's another example. Some people eat tomatoes with sugar on them. But that's not a good idea because sugar prevents you from taking in vitamin B from the tomatoes. Also, putting honey in black tea makes it hard for our bodies to take in iron.

여: 최근 연구에서 어떤 음식들은 함께 먹으면 안 된다는 것이 밝혀졌습니다. 그것은 어떤 음식이 다른 음식에 들어 있는 영양소를 파괴하기 때문입니다. 예를 들어 볼게요. 샐러드를 만들 때 오이와 당근을 함께 사용하는 것을 피하세요. 당근에 있는 한 성분이 오이에 있는 비타민 C를 파괴합니다. 또 다른 예가 있습니다. 어떤 사람들은 토마토에 설탕을 얹어서 먹습니다. 하지만 설탕이 토마토로부터 비타민 B를 섭취하는 것을 막기 때문에 좋은 생각이 아닙니다. 또한 홍차에 꿀을 넣으면 우리 몸이 철분을 섭취하는 것이 어려워집니다.

어휘

recent[rí:snt] 휑 최근의 　research[risə́:rtʃ] 몡 연구 destroy[distrɔ́i] 동 파괴하다 　nutrient[njú:triənt] 몡 영

양소 avoid[əvɔ́id] 통 피하다 element[éləmənt] 명 요소, 성분 prevent A from v-ing A가 ~하는 것을 막다 take in ~을 섭취하다 iron[áiərn] 명 철분

어휘
besides[bisáidz] 부 게다가 reduce[ridʒúːs] 통 줄이다 cholesterol level 콜레스테롤 수치 not to mention ~은 말할 것도 없이 corn[kɔːrn] 명 옥수수 calorie [kǽləri] 명 칼로리, 열량 burn off 소모하다, 연소시키다 in the first place 진작에, 처음부터 store[stɔːr] 통 보관하다, 저장하다 fridge[friʤ] 명 냉장고 (= refrigerator) cloudy[kláudi] 형 탁한 cabinet[kǽbənit] 명 진열장, 캐비닛

문제 해설
Q: 같이 먹으면 안 되는 음식을 고르시오.
　　오이를 당근과 먹으면 오이의 비타민 C가 파괴되고, 토마토를 설탕과 먹으면 비타민 B를 섭취하기 어려우며 홍차에 꿀을 넣어 먹으면 철분의 섭취를 막는다고 했다.

문제 해설
Q1: 남자가 올리브 오일을 사기로 결정한 이유는?
　　올리브 오일의 열량이 쉽게 연소되어 다이어트 프로그램에 널리 사용된다는 여자의 말을 듣고 결정했다.

Q2: 올리브 오일을 보관하는 최고의 방법은?
　　서늘하고 어두운 찬장에 넣어두는 것이 좋다고 했다.

Listening ★ Practice　p. 28

A 1 ④　2 ①　B 1 ③　2 ①, ④
C 1 ④　2 ④　D 1 ①　2 ③

A [1-2]

M: Julie, come over here. Help me choose a cooking oil.
W: There's no need to think it over. Pick the olive oil.
M: What makes you so sure?
W: I think food tastes better with olive oil. Besides, it's helpful in reducing cholesterol levels, not to mention good for your heart.
M: Well... it's more expensive than corn oil.
W: But the calories in olive oil are easier to burn off than those in other oils. That's why olive oil is widely used in diet programs.
M: In that case, I should buy it! Why didn't you say that in the first place?
W: (laughs) Don't forget to store it in a cool, dark place.
M: Okay, I'll put it in the fridge.
W: No, that'll make the oil turn cloudy and thick. Just put it in the cabinet.

남: Julie, 여기로 와 봐. 식용유 고르는 걸 도와줘.
여: 고심할 필요 없어. 올리브 오일을 골라.
남: 어떻게 그렇게 확신하는 거야?
여: 음식에 올리브 오일을 넣으면 훨씬 맛이 좋아지는 것 같아. 게다가 심장에 좋은 것은 말할 필요도 없고 콜레스테롤 수치를 줄여주는 데도 도움이 돼.
남: 음… 옥수수 오일보다 더 비싸네.
여: 하지만 올리브 오일의 열량은 다른 오일에 있는 것보다 더 쉽게 연소돼. 올리브 오일이 다이어트 프로그램에 널리 사용되는 이유가 그거지.
남: 그렇다면 그걸 사야겠구나! 처음부터 왜 그걸 말하지 않았니?
여: [웃으며] 서늘하고 어두운 장소에 보관하는 거 잊지 마.
남: 알았어. 냉장고에 넣을게.
여: 아니, 그러면 오일이 탁해지고 뭉치게 돼. 그냥 찬장에 넣어둬.

B [1-2]

M: Would you like something else to drink?
W: No, thanks. I'd like to talk to the manager.
M: Oh. Is there some kind of problem?
W: Yes. Today, I waited for an hour to be seated even though I had a reservation. But I put up with the inconvenience in order to enjoy your delicious food.
M: I apologize for that. We have too many customers tonight.
W: Well, what's worse is that my chicken salad is too sweet and these ribs are tough.
M: I'm sorry to hear that. I'll serve you the food again after talking about it with the chef.
W: No, thanks. I've already lost my appetite.
M: Let me bring you today's special steak. I'm sure you'll like it. And there'll be no charge.
W: Hmm... okay, that sounds fine.

남: 다른 마실 것을 드릴까요?
여: 아니, 괜찮아요. 매니저와 얘기하고 싶어요.
남: 아. 무슨 문제가 있으세요?
여: 네. 오늘 제가 예약을 했음에도 불구하고 자리에 앉기까지 1시간이나 기다렸어요. 하지만 이곳의 맛있는 음식을 먹기 위해 불편을 참았어요.
남: 사과 드립니다. 오늘 밤 손님들이 너무 많네요.
여: 음, 더 문제는 치킨 샐러드가 너무 달고 립은 질기다는 것이에요.
남: 정말 유감이네요. 주방장과 얘기해보고 음식을 다시 올리도록 하겠습니다.
여: 아니, 괜찮아요. 이미 식욕을 잃었어요.
남: 오늘의 특별 스테이크를 가져오겠습니다. 분명히 좋아하실 거예요. 그리고 돈을 받지 않겠습니다.
여: 음… 알겠어요, 그건 좋네요.

어휘

even though ~임에도 불구하고   reservation
[rèzərvéiʃən] 몡 예약   put up with ~을 참다
inconvenience[ìnkənví:njəns] 몡 불편   apologize for
~에 대해 사과하다   rib[rib] 몡 갈비, 립   tough[tʌf] 몡
질긴   chef[ʃef] 몡 주방장   appetite[æpətàit] 몡 식욕
charge[tʃɑːrdʒ] 몡 청구 금액, 지불 요금   [문제] tasty[téisti]
몡 맛이 있는

문제 해설

Q1: 화자 간의 관계는?

여자가 먹은 음식에 대해 불평하고 음식을 서빙하는 사람이
해명하는 내용이므로 웨이터와 손님의 대화임을 알 수 있다.

Q2: 여자가 마음에 들지 않았던 두 가지 점은?

여자는 예약을 했음에도 1시간이나 기다렸고 음식이 너무 달
고 질겼다고 불평했다.

C [1-2]

W: This Friday is Dan's birthday. Can you
   suggest a good restaurant?

M: How about El Cruce? The chef is from
   Spain, so the food is really great.

W: I haven't tried Spanish food. Is it tasty?

M: Sure. Garlic and red pepper are usually
   used in Spanish food, so you will like the
   taste.

W: What kind of food do the Spanish enjoy
   eating?

M: Since Spain is surrounded by the sea,
   seafood is pretty popular.

W: Great. Dan loves seafood.

M: Also, many Spanish dishes use rice. One of
   the nicest dishes is paella, which is a rice
   dish that contains an Indian spice called
   saffron.

W: Sounds good. I'll make a reservation.

M: You'd better hurry. That restaurant has been
   popular since it opened twelve years ago.

W: When does it close?

M: At 11 p.m. Oh, and you can watch a
   flamenco performance there every Friday.

여: 이번 금요일이 Dan의 생일이야. 좋은 음식점을 추천해 줄래?

남: El Cruce는 어때? 주방장이 스페인 출신이라서 음식이 아
   주 훌륭해.

여: 스페인 음식을 먹어본 적이 없는데. 맛이 있니?

남: 물론이지. 스페인 음식에는 마늘과 고추가 주로 쓰여서, 네
   가 그 맛을 좋아할 거야.

여: 스페인 사람들은 어떤 종류의 음식을 즐겨 먹어?

남: 스페인이 바다로 둘러싸여 있어서 해산물이 꽤 인기 있어.

여: 잘됐다. Dan은 해산물을 좋아해.

남: 또, 많은 스페인 요리에 밥이 들어가. 가장 맛있는 음식 중의
   하나가 파엘랴인데 사프란이라고 불리는 인도산 향신료가
   들어가는 밥 요리야.

여: 좋을 것 같다. 예약을 할래.

남: 서두르는 게 좋아. 그 음식점은 12년 전에 문을 연 이후로 줄
   곧 인기가 많거든.

여: 언제 문을 닫아?

남: 오후 11시야. 아, 그리고 금요일마다 플라멩코 공연을 볼 수
   있어.

어휘

Spanish[spǽniʃ] 몡 스페인의; 몡 스페인 사람   be
surrounded by ~로 둘러싸이다   seafood[síːfùːd] 몡 해
산물   paella[pɑːéiljə] 몡 파엘랴(쌀, 고기, 해물, 야채 등을 찐
스페인식 밥 요리)   spice[spais] 몡 향신료, 양념   saffron
[sǽfrən] 몡 사프란   flamenco[fləménkou] 몡 플라멩코(스
페인 전통 춤)   performance[pərfɔ́rməns] 몡 공연   [문제]
midnight[mídnàit] 몡 자정

문제 해설

Q1: 스페인 음식에 관해 사실이 아닌 것은?

인도산 향신료인 사프란을 특정 요리에 사용한다는 내용은
있지만 인도 요리와 비슷하다는 언급은 없었다.

Q2: El Cruce 음식점에 관해 사실인 것은?

예약을 서둘러야 한다고 했으므로 예약 시스템이 있고, 11시
에 문을 닫으며, 12년 전부터 계속 인기가 있다.

D [1-2]

M: Welcome back! It's time for *All about Super
   Foods*! Today's super food is cabbage. Its
   medical benefits are so widely known that
   it's called "the doctor of the poor." In
   particular, cabbage is good for the stomach. Its effect
   increases when you drink it as a juice. If you
   can't stand the bitter taste of cabbage, mix
   it with lemon or orange. Make sure you drink
   cabbage juice as soon as possible because
   its nutrients are quickly destroyed. If you
   want to eat cabbage by boiling it, don't forget
   to drink the boiled water too, because many
   of the nutrients go into the water.

남: 다시 오신 걸 환영합니다! 지금은 'All about Super Foods'
   시간입니다! 오늘의 슈퍼 푸드는 양배추입니다. 양배추의 의
   학적인 이점은 널리 알려져 있어서 '가난한 자들의 의사'라고
   불립니다. 특히 양배추는 위에 좋습니다. 주스로 마실 때 효
   능이 더 증가합니다. 양배추의 쓴맛을 참을 수가 없다면 레몬
   이나 오렌지를 섞으세요. 양배추 주스는 영양소가 빠르게 파
   괴되니까 가능한 한 빨리 마시도록 하세요. 양배추를 삶아서
   먹으려면, 많은 영양분이 물로 들어가니 끓인 물도 마시는 걸
   잊지 마세요.

★ ★

p. 31

어휘

cabbage[kǽbidʒ] 명 양배추 medical[médikəl] 형 의학적인 benefit[bénəfit] 명 혜택, 이점 in particular 특히 stomach[stʌ́mək] 명 위 effect[ifékt] 명 효능 stand[stænd] 동 참다 bitter[bítər] 형 쓴 as soon as possible 가능한 한 곧 boil[bɔil] 동 끓이다

문제 해설

Q1: 남자는 주로 무엇에 대해 이야기하고 있나?

① 양배추를 건강에 좋게 먹는 방법

② 양배추를 가열하면 어떤 일이 생기나

③ 의사들이 어떤 채소를 먹으라고 제안하는지

④ 양배추가 어떤 영양분을 포함하고 있는지

양배추 속의 영양소를 최대한 섭취하려면 어떻게 양배추를 먹어야 하는지를 소개했다.

Q2: 남자의 조언을 따르고 있지 않은 사람은?

① Cindy: 난 종종 양배추 주스에 레몬즙을 넣어.

② Ben: 난 양배추 주스를 만든 다음 빨리 마셔.

③ Joshua: 양배추를 끓인 후에 그 물을 버리고 양배추만 먹어.

남자는 양배추를 끓인 물에 영양분이 들어가 있으므로 꼭 마시라고 조언했다.

Listening ★ Challenge p. 30

A 1 ② 2 ①, ④ B 1 ② 2 ①

A [1-2]

W: Good morning, viewers. Today I'm visiting a famous Japanese restaurant. The owner of this restaurant, Michael Taka, is here. Hello, Mr. Taka.

M: Hello. Welcome to Taka Sushi Bar.

W: How long have you been running this restaurant?

M: It's been 20 years.

W: I heard that more than 200 customers visit here each day. Was this place popular from the beginning?

M: Not at all. At first, Americans thought eating raw fish was nonsense.

W: How did you change their minds?

M: I created a new kind of sushi to appeal to American tastes. You can't imagine how hard I worked to come up with these delicious sushi rolls.

W: What do you think was the key to your success, apart from that?

M: I recognized that many Americans are

interested in Eastern culture. So I decorated my restaurant with Japanese items so that customers would feel as though they were in Japan.

여: 안녕하세요, 시청자 여러분. 오늘은 유명한 일본 음식점을 가보겠습니다. 이 음식점의 주인이신 Michael Taka 씨가 나와 계십니다. 안녕하세요, Taka 씨!

남: 안녕하세요. Taka Sushi Bar에 오신 걸 환영합니다.

여: 이 음식점을 운영하신지 얼마나 되셨나요?

남: 20년이에요.

여: 매일 200명 이상의 손님들이 온다고 들었어요. 이 곳이 처음부터 인기가 있었나요?

남: 전혀요. 처음에 미국인들은 날생선을 먹는 건 말도 안 된다고 생각했죠.

여: 그들의 생각을 어떻게 바꾸셨나요?

남: 미국인 입맛을 끄는 새로운 종류의 스시를 만들어냈죠. 이 맛있는 스시롤을 생각해내기 위해 얼마나 힘들게 일했는지 상상 못하실 거예요.

여: 그 외에 성공의 비결은 뭐였다고 생각하세요?

남: 많은 미국인들이 동양 문화에 관심이 있다는 것을 깨달았어요. 그래서 손님들이 일본에 와 있는 것처럼 느끼도록 음식점을 일본 물건들로 장식했죠.

어휘

owner[óunər] 명 소유자, 주인 run[rʌn] 동 운영하다 raw[rɔː] 형 날것의, 익히지 않은 nonsense[nánsèns] 명 터무니 없는 일, 말이 되지 않는 일 create[kriéit] 동 고안하다, 창작하다 appeal[əpíːl] 동 ~의 마음에 들다, 마음을 끌다 come up with ~을 생각해내다 apart from ~은 제외하고 recognize[rékəgnàiz] 동 깨닫다 Eastern[íːstərn] 형 동양의 decorate[dékərèit] 동 꾸미다, 장식하다 [문제] negative[négətiv] 형 부정적인 favorable[féivərəbl] 형 우호적인 indifferent[indífərənt] 형 무관심한 ingredient[ingríːdiənt] 명 재료 food tasting event 시식 행사

문제 해설

Q1: 미국인들의 스시에 대한 첫 느낌은 어땠나?

처음에는 날생선을 먹는 것은 말도 안 되는 일이라고 생각할 정도로 거부감이 있었다.

Q2: Taka 씨의 두 가지 성공 전략은?

미국인들의 입맛에 맞는 새로운 스시롤을 만들어냈고, 음식점 장식을 일본풍으로 한 것이 성공을 가져왔다.

B [1-2]

M: We finally got a table.

W: I can't believe this! We've waited almost for an hour. I feel like we've wasted our time.

M: Calm down. This restaurant got two stars in the Red Guide.

W: What's the Red Guide?

M: It's a restaurant guidebook. It evaluates restaurants based on food, service and interior design. André Michelin from France first published it.

W: Oh, he was the owner of a tire company, right? Isn't that book called the Michelin Guide?

M: Yes. But it's also known as the Red Guide because of the color of its cover.

W: I thought it was a guidebook only for restaurants in France.

M: At first, but then versions for countries such as the US, the UK, and Japan were also published.

W: Oh, now I feel honored to be served in a two-star restaurant from the Michelin Guide.

M: (laughs) You should thank me for bringing you here.

W: Thanks. I'm sorry for complaining earlier.

남: 마침내 자리를 잡았군.

여: 어떻게 이럴 수가! 거의 한 시간이나 기다렸어. 시간만 낭비한 것 같아.

남: 진정해. 이 음식점은 Red Guide에서 별 2개를 받았어.

여: Red Guide가 뭔데?

남: 음식점 안내서야. 음식과 서비스, 실내 디자인을 기준으로 음식점을 평가해. 프랑스 출신의 André Michelin이 처음 출판했지.

여: 아, 그 사람 타이어 회사의 소유주였잖아, 맞지? 그 책은 Michelin Guide라고 불리지 않니?

남: 맞아. 하지만 책 표지색 때문에 Red Guide로도 알려져 있어.

여: 난 그게 프랑스에 있는 음식점만을 대상으로 한 안내서인 줄 알았어.

남: 처음엔 그랬지만 이후 미국, 영국, 일본과 같은 나라들의 버전 역시 출판되었어.

여: 아, 이제 Michelin Guide의 별 2개짜리 음식점에서 식사를 하게 된 게 영광스럽군.

남: [웃으며] 널 여기로 데려온 나에게 감사해라.

여: 고마워. 좀 전에 불평한 거 미안해.

어휘

calm down 진정하다   evaluate[ivǽljuèit] 동 평가하다
based on ~에 기반하여   publish[pʌ́bliʃ] 동 출판하다
tire[taiər] 명 타이어   version[və́ːrʒən] 명 ~판, 버전
honored[ɑ́nərd] 형 영광스러운   complain[kəmpléin]
동 불평하다   [문제] annoyed[ənɔ́id] 형 화가 난
depressed[diprést] 형 우울한   embarrassed[imbǽrəst]
형 난처한

문제 해설

Q1: Michelin Guide에 관해 사실인 것은?

① 음식만을 기준으로 음식점을 평가한다.

② 타이어 회사의 주인이 처음으로 출판했다.

③ Red Guide로 이름을 바꾸었다.

④ 세계의 프랑스 음식점에 대한 안내서이다.

음식과 서비스, 실내 디자인을 모두 평가하며, Red Guide는 책의 또 다른 이름이고, 프랑스뿐만 아니라 미국판, 영국판, 일본판도 출판된다.

Q2: 여자의 심정은 어떻게 변했나?

처음에는 너무 오래 기다려 기분이 상했다가 인정받는 음식점임을 알게 되고 나서 만족스러운 마음이 되었다.

Critical ★ Thinking   p. 31

1 ④ 2 ①

W: What are we going to buy next?

M: We need some canned corn. Oh, there it is.

W: Hmm... how about choosing some other brand? This one says it's a genetically modified food.

M: Can't you see the price tag? It's much cheaper.

W: But this corn was genetically changed by humans. I don't want to eat such food.

M: Look! It says it contains more vitamins. GM technology made that possible. It's healthier for our bodies.

W: No way! I would eat GM food if it guaranteed our health in the long run. But nobody can be sure about what will happen in the future if we keep eating it.

M: I've only heard about the benefits of GM food.

W: And I bet you've heard that GM food can solve the world food shortage problem.

M: That's right. We can produce more food with GM technology.

W: Yes, but I think it's useless if it can harm our health.

여: 다음엔 뭘 살까?

남: 옥수수 통조림이 필요해. 아, 저기 있다.

여: 음… 다른 브랜드를 고르는 게 어때? 이건 유전자 변형 식품이라고 되어 있네.

남: 가격표 안 보여? 훨씬 싸잖아.

여: 하지만 이 옥수수는 인간에 의해 유전자가 변형된 거야. 그런 식품은 먹고 싶지 않아.

남: 봐! 비타민이 더 많이 들어 있대. GM 기술이 그걸 가능하게 한 거지. 우리 건강에 더 좋은 거야.

여: 아니야! 장기적으로 우리 건강을 보장해주기만 한다면 GM 식품을 먹겠어. 하지만 그걸 계속 먹었을 때 미래에 어떤 일이 일어날지는 아무도 확실히 알지 못해.

남: 나는 GM 식품의 장점만 들어봤는데.

여: GM 식품이 세계 식량 부족 문제를 해결할 수 있다고도 들었겠구나.

남: 맞아. GM 기술로 더 많은 식량을 생산해 낼 수 있어.

여: 그래. 하지만 우리의 건강을 해친다면 아무 소용이 없다고 생각해.

어휘

canned[kænd] 형 통조림의 genetically[dʒənétikəli] 부 유전적으로 modified[mɑ́dəfàid] 형 변형된 price tag 가격표 GM(genetically modified) 유전자 변형의 guarantee[gæ̀rəntíː] 동 보장하다 in the long run 장기적으로 shortage[ʃɔ́ːrtidʒ] 명 부족 [문제] beneficial [bènəfíʃəl] 형 유익한

문제 해설

Q1: 그들은 주로 무엇에 대해 이야기하고 있나?
GM 식품이 건강에 어떤 해를 주게 될지 확신할 수 없으므로 먹지 말아야 한다는 의견과 영양 성분을 강화해서 건강에 좋게 만들었으니 괜찮다는 의견이 대립하고 있다.

Q2: 여자와 같은 의견인 사람은?
① Anne: 안전하다고 증명될 때까지 GM 식품을 먹지 않을 거야.
② Ted: 장점이 많은 GM 식품을 선호해.
③ Mark: GM 식품은 세계의 사람들이 굶주리게 되는 것을 막을 수 있어.
안전하다고 확신할 수 없는 상태이므로 GM 식품을 먹지 않겠다는 것이 여자의 의견이다.

UNIT 05 Fashion

Getting ★ Ready p. 32

A 1 ⓔ 2 ⓗ 3 ⓒ 4 ⓓ 5 ⓖ 6 ⓐ
B 1 ⓐ 2 ⓑ 3 ⓔ

B 1 여: 나 이 핑크 드레스 입으니까 어때?
    남: 네 피부 톤과 잘 어울리지 않아.

  2 여: 왜 이 상점에서 쇼핑하기를 좋아하니?
    남: 최신 디자인들을 취급하거든.

  3 여: 어떤 외투를 사야 할까? 결정을 못 하겠어.
    남: 어두운 색깔의 것이 날씬해 보이지.

1 ① 2 (1) ⓒ (2) ⓐ (3) ⓔ 3 ①

1

W: Hello, all. Welcome to *Fashion World*. Today, let's learn about this fall's trends. There are two key points you should keep in mind, "back to basics" and "colorful accessories." This season is about simple designs which show the lines of your body. Stay away from bright colors like yellow and pink or large prints. Choose black, white, and beige clothes. And don't forget to wear one colorful accessory. A brightly colored hat, scarf, tie, or large necklace will make you look especially fashionable.

여: 안녕하세요, 여러분. 'Fashion World'에 오신 걸 환영합니다. 오늘은 이번 가을 유행에 대해 알아봅시다. 명심해야 할 두 가지 핵심이 있는데, '기본으로 돌아가라'와 '화려한 액세서리'입니다. 이번 계절의 핵심은 신체 라인을 드러내는 단순한 디자인입니다. 노랑과 핑크 같은 밝은 색이나 큰 프린트는 피하세요. 검정과 흰색, 베이지 색의 옷을 고르세요. 그리고 화려한 액세서리를 한 가지 하는 것을 잊지 마세요. 밝은 색의 모자나 스카프, 넥타이, 큰 목걸이가 당신을 특히 패셔너블해 보이게 만들어 줄 것입니다.

어휘

trend[trend] 명 경향, 유행 keep in mind 명심하다 basic[béisik] 명 기본 colorful[kʌ́lərfəl] 형 색채가 풍부한, 화려한 accessory[əksésəri] 명 액세서리, 장신구 stay away from ~을 멀리하다, 피하다 beige[beiʒ] 형 베이지 색 necklace[néklis] 명 목걸이 fashionable[fǽʃənəbl] 형 패셔너블한, 유행에 맞는

문제 해설

Q: 'Fashion World'에 따르면 가을 시즌의 유행은?
몸의 라인이 잘 드러나는 검정, 흰색, 베이지 색의 옷에, 스카프 같은 화려한 액세서리를 하는 패션이 유행한다고 했다.

2

W: Let's look at the monitor and talk about the worst dressers at the Cannes Film Festival. Let's discuss Jane Stewart first.

M: Oh, my goodness. Her dress is too long for how short she is.

W: It looks like she's sweeping the red carpet with it.

M: Next is Susan Morris, wearing a yellow dress.

W: That is an attractive color, but unfortunately, it doesn't go well with her skin tone.

M: You're right. I like the slim line, though.
W: Finally, it's Kate Smith. She's wearing an Asian-style white dress.
M: I think it looks great.
W: The problem is not the dress, but the accessories. I can't count how many she's wearing.
M: Wearing just one necklace would've been better.

여: 모니터를 보며 칸 영화제의 워스트 드레서에 대해 얘기해 봅시다. 우선 Jane Stewart에 대해 얘기를 나눠보죠.
남: 아, 이런. 드레스가 아주 작은 그녀에 비해 너무 길군요.
여: 드레스로 레드 카펫을 쓸고 다니는 것처럼 보이네요.
남: 다음은 노란 드레스를 입은 Susan Morris입니다.
여: 매력적인 색이긴 한데, 불행히도 그녀의 피부 톤과는 어울리지 않는군요.
남: 맞습니다. 그래도 슬림한 라인은 좋네요.
여: 마지막은 Kate Smith입니다. 그녀는 동양풍의 흰색 드레스를 입고 있네요.
남: 멋진 것 같은데요.
여: 문제는 옷이 아니고 액세서리예요. 몇 개를 했는지 셀 수가 없네요.
남: 목걸이를 하나만 하는 게 더 나았을 거예요.

어휘
monitor[mánitər] 몡 모니터, 화면 worst dresser 최악의 드레서 festival[féstəvəl] 몡 축제 sweep[swiːp] 통 쓸다, 청소하다 attractive[ətrǽktiv] 혱 매력적인 unfortunately[ʌnfɔ́ːrtʃənətli] 囝 불행히도 go well with ~와 잘 어울리다 tone[toun] 몡 색조 slim[slim] 혱 슬림한, 날씬한 count[kaunt] 통 세다

문제 해설
Q: 각 인물에게 맞는 조언을 고르시오.
Jane Stewart는 작은 키에 맞지 않는 너무 긴 드레스를 입었으므로 더 짧은 드레스를 입으라는 조언을, Susan Morris는 노란색이 피부 톤과 맞지 않는다고 했으므로 피부 톤을 고려하라는 조언을, Kate Smith에게는 액세서리를 몇 개 빼라는 조언을 하는 것이 적절하다.

3

M: Fashion editors are people who write articles about fashion in magazines. It may seem like a fancy job, but they do a lot of hard work. They visit fashion shows, watch fashion trends, and interview fashion people. That's not all. They manage all the things related to photo shoots. They think of the cover concept and get clothing sponsors. On the day of a photo shoot, they are busy monitoring models' hair, makeup, and clothes. And fashion editors sometimes take trips to other countries to keep up-to-date with the newest fashion trends.

남: 패션 에디터는 잡지에 패션에 관한 기사를 쓰는 사람입니다. 화려한 직업처럼 보일지 모르지만, 힘든 일을 많이 합니다. 패션쇼에 가서 패션 경향을 살피고 패션계의 인물들을 인터뷰합니다. 그것이 다가 아닙니다. 사진 촬영과 관련된 모든 일을 감독합니다. 표지 컨셉을 생각해내고 의상 협찬사를 구합니다. 사진 촬영 날에는 모델의 머리와 화장, 의상을 체크하느라 바쁩니다. 그리고 패션 에디터는 때때로 최신 패션 유행을 따라잡기 위해 다른 나라로 여행을 가기도 합니다.

어휘
editor[éditər] 몡 편집자 article[áːrtikl] 몡 기사 fancy[fǽnsi] 혱 멋진, 화려한 manage[mǽnidʒ] 통 관리하다. 감독하다 related to ~에 관련된 shoot[ʃuːt] 몡 사진 촬영 cover[kávər] 몡 표지 concept[kánsept] 몡 구상, 컨셉 sponsor[spánsər] 몡 협찬사, 후원자 monitor[mánitər] 통 감시하다, 관리하다 makeup[méikʌp] 몡 화장 up-to-date[ʌ́ptədéit] 혱 최신의 [문제] career[kəríər] 몡 경력

문제 해설
Q: 남자는 주로 무엇에 대해 이야기하고 있나?
① 패션 에디터가 하는 일
② 패션 에디터가 되면 좋은 이유
③ 패션 에디터가 되기 위해 필요한 것
④ 패션 에디터가 경력을 개발하는 방법
패션 에디터의 다양한 업무에 대한 내용이다.

Listening ★ Practice p. 34

A 1 ② 2 ④ B 1 ④ 2 ③
C 1 ② 2 ③ D 1 ② 2 ①

A [1-2]

M: Sarah, welcome. It's been a while.
W: Yes. It's been two years since I last worked with you.
M: Wow! Time flies. So did you see the clothes you'll be wearing? How do they look?
W: The silhouettes are pretty. They're simple yet practical. You really are talented.
M: You're so kind. The hairstyle and makeup will be natural.
W: Okay. Then, walking should be casual, right?
M: Yes. You are in the finale, so you have a big responsibility.
W: I'll do my best.

M: Thank you again for doing my show for free. It means a lot to me.

W: Well, all the profits go to a facility for the disabled. How could I refuse to do something for a good cause?

M: You really have a good heart. Okay. Let's do the fitting.

남: Sarah, 환영해요. 오랜만이네요.

여: 네. 선생님과 마지막으로 일한 이후 2년만이네요.

남: 와! 시간이 빨리 가네요. 그래서 입을 옷은 봤어요? 어떤 것 같아요?

여: 실루엣이 예뻐요. 단순하지만 실용적이고요. 선생님은 정말 재능이 있으시다니까요.

남: 참 친절하시네요. 헤어스타일과 화장은 자연스러울 거예요.

여: 알겠어요. 그러면 워킹도 가벼워야겠죠?

남: 네, 마지막 무대에 서니까 책임이 커요.

여: 최선을 다할게요.

남: 무료로 제 쇼에 나와주어서 다시 한번 감사해요. 저에겐 의미가 참 큽니다.

여: 음, 모든 수익이 장애인을 위한 시설로 가잖아요. 좋은 취지로 하는 일을 어떻게 거절할 수 있겠어요?

남: 마음이 참 따뜻하시네요. 좋습니다. 옷을 입어 봅시다.

어휘

Time flies. 시간이 빠르다. silhouette[sìlu(:)ét] 명 실루엣, 윤곽 practical[prǽktikəl] 형 실용적인 talented [tǽləntid] 형 재능이 있는 casual[kǽʒuəl] 형 격식을 차리지 않은, 가벼운 finale[finǽli] 명 마지막 장면, 피날레 responsibility[rispànsəbíləti] 명 책임 profit[práfit] 명 수익 facility[fəsíləti] 명 시설 the disabled 장애인 refuse[rifjúːz] 동 거절하다 cause[kɔːz] 명 이유; *목적, 대의 fitting[fítiŋ] 명 피팅, 입어보기 [문제] raise money 모금하다

문제 해설

Q1: 화자 간의 관계는?

패션쇼의 의상과 워킹, 화장과 헤어스타일 등에 관해 상의하는 것으로 보아 디자이너와 쇼에 출연하는 모델이 나누는 대화임을 알 수 있다.

Q2: 여자가 쇼에 출연하기로 한 이유는?

여자는 수익금을 좋은 일에 쓰는 쇼에 돈을 받지 않고 출연한 것이므로 모금을 돕기 위한 것이다.

B [1-2]

W: Hello. I'm your fashion advisor, Christina. Many viewers asked about how to look taller and thinner. There are several ways. Follow these rules and you'll look tall and thin, at least while wearing clothes! First, match the top and bottom in similar tones. But don't dress in the same color from head to toe. Also, dark colored clothes will make you look slim. If you want to wear stripes, choose vertical ones, which make the body look slimmer. Lastly, wear your accessories above the chest. That way, other people will focus on your upper body and you'll look taller.

여: 안녕하세요. 여러분의 패션 조언자인 Christina입니다. 많은 시청자분들께서 더 키가 커 보이고 날씬해 보이는 방법에 대해서 물어보셨는데요. 몇 가지 방법이 있습니다. 이 규칙들을 따르면 최소한 옷을 입고 있는 동안은 키가 크고 날씬해 보일 것입니다! 우선, 상하의를 비슷한 색조로 맞추세요. 하지만 머리부터 발끝까지 똑같은 색깔로 입지는 마세요. 또한 진한 색의 옷은 날씬해 보이게 해 줍니다. 줄무늬 옷을 입고 싶으면 몸을 더 날씬하게 보이게 하는 세로 줄무늬를 입으세요. 마지막으로 가슴 위로 액세서리를 하세요. 그렇게 하면 다른 사람들이 당신의 상체에 집중하게 되어 더 키가 커 보일 거예요.

어휘

advisor[ədváizər] 명 조언자 match[mætʃ] 동 맞추다 top[tɑp] 명 상의 bottom[bátəm] 명 하의 stripe[straip] 명 줄무늬 vertical[vɔ́ːrtikəl] 형 세로의 chest[tʃest] 명 가슴 upper body 상체

문제 해설

Q1: 여자는 주로 무엇에 대해 이야기하고 있나?

상의와 하의를 비슷한 색으로 맞춘다거나, 세로 줄무늬를 입는 등 키가 커 보이고 날씬해 보이게 옷을 입는 방법을 소개하고 있다.

Q2: 여자의 조언을 가장 잘 따르고 있는 사람은?

비슷한 색깔의 옷으로 맞춰 입고 세로 줄무늬 셔츠를 입은 남자가 여자의 조언을 가장 충실하게 따랐다고 할 수 있다.

C [1-2]

M: Hello. I'm Tommy, helping you with the latest fashion trends. I'm on Tokyo's fashion street, Harajuku. Here, you can easily find men wearing skirts. According to one Japanese survey, 40% of men answered positively about wearing skirts. Recently, world famous designers like Mark Jacobs showed men's skirts in their collections. It might be shocking to many viewers, but some of the men think skirts aren't just for ladies any more. They especially love skirts during hot weather because they are cooler than pants. I think this kind of new fashion is something to encourage. I really want to praise their courage.

35

남: 안녕하세요. 최신 패션 경향에 대해 안내해 드리는 Tommy입니다. 전 도쿄의 패션 거리인 하라주쿠에 나와 있습니다. 여기에서는 치마를 입은 남자를 쉽게 볼 수 있는데요. 한 일본 설문 조사에 따르면 남자의 40%가 치마를 입는 것에 대해 긍정적으로 대답했습니다. 최근에 Mark Jacobs와 같은 세계적으로 유명한 디자이너들이 그들의 컬렉션에서 남성용 치마를 선보였습니다. 많은 시청자들께는 충격적일지도 모르지만 일부 남성들은 치마가 더 이상 여성만을 위한 것은 아니라고 생각합니다. 그들은 치마가 바지보다 더 시원해서 특히 더운 날씨에 치마를 입는 걸 좋아합니다. 저는 이런 새로운 패션이 권장되어야 할 것이라고 생각합니다. 그들의 용기를 아주 높이 사고 싶습니다.

어휘

latest[léitist] 형 최신의 survey[sə́ːrvei] 명 설문 조사
positively[pázitivli] 부 긍정적으로 recently[ríːsəntli]
부 최근에 collection[kəlékʃən] 명 컬렉션, 신작품 (발표회)
shocking[ʃákiŋ] 형 충격적인 encourage[inkə́ːridʒ] 동
장려하다, 촉진하다 praise[preiz] 동 칭찬하다 courage
[kə́ːridʒ] 명 용기 [문제] popularity[pàpjulǽrəti] 명 인기
designer brand 유명 디자이너 제품

문제 해설

Q1: 이 보도는 무엇에 관한 것인가?
  치마를 입는 남성들이 늘어나고 있는 것에 대한 내용이다.

Q2: 남자와 같은 의견인 사람은?
  ① Toby: 남자는 남자처럼 옷을 입어야 한다.
  ② Jen: 유명 디자이너 제품을 입으면 패션 리더가 될 것이다.
  ③ Mike: 새로운 옷을 입어보는 시도는 좋은 것이다.
  남자는 남성의 치마 착용을 권장되어야 하는, 긍정적인 것으로 보고 있다.

D [1-2]

M: Amy, I want to be more stylish, but don't know where to start.
W: Why do you suddenly feel this way?
M: There's a girl I have a crush on. But she told me that she didn't like how I dress. I was so disappointed.
W: You can't be fashionable overnight. It requires a lot of effort.
M: What am I doing wrong?
W: In my opinion, you never consider your shape when wearing clothes.
M: What do you mean?
W: Well, you always wear skinny jeans with dark T-shirts. But they make you look even thinner.
M: I should take them off right now! What else should I do?
W: Reading fashion magazines can help you follow trends.
M: What else?
W: Smart dressers always match accessories, shoes or bags nicely with their clothes.
M: I'll try. Will you help me?
W: You bet.

남: Amy, 난 더 세련되어 보이고 싶은데 어디서부터 시작해야 할지 모르겠어.
여: 왜 갑자기 그렇게 생각하는 거니?
남: 내가 반한 여자애가 있거든. 그런데 그 애가 내가 옷 입는 방식이 싫다고 했어. 정말 실망스러웠어.
여: 하룻밤 사이에 패셔너블해질 수는 없어. 많은 노력이 필요해.
남: 내가 무엇을 잘못 하고 있는 거지?
여: 내 생각엔 넌 옷을 입을 때 네 체형을 전혀 고려하지 않아.
남: 무슨 말이야?
여: 음, 넌 항상 어두운 색의 티셔츠와 스키니 진을 입잖아. 그런데 그런 옷들은 너를 훨씬 말라 보이게 해.
남: 당장 벗어버려야겠다! 또 뭘 해야 할까?
여: 패션 잡지를 읽는 것이 유행을 따르는 데 도움이 될 거야.
남: 또 다른 건?
여: 멋쟁이는 항상 옷에 잘 어울리는 액세서리, 구두나 가방을 맞춰 하지.
남: 노력해볼게. 네가 좀 도와줄래?
여: 물론이지.

어휘

stylish[stáiliʃ] 형 멋진, 맵시 있는 suddenly[sʌ́dnli] 부
갑자기 have a crush on ~에게 반하다 overnight
[óuvərnàit] 부 하룻밤 사이에, 갑자기 consider[kənsídər]
동 고려하다 shape[ʃeip] 명 체형 skinny jean 스키니 진
smart[smɑːrt] 형 영리한; *멋진, 세련된

문제 해설

Q1: 여자에 따르면 남자의 문제점은?
  여자는 남자가 스키니 진과 어두운 색 티셔츠를 입어 너무 말라 보인다는 점을 지적했다.

Q2: 여자의 조언이 아닌 것은?
  TV 스타의 옷차림을 따라해 보라는 조언은 하지 않았다.

Listening ★ Challenge p. 36

A 1 (1) T (2) T (3) F 2 ② B 1 ③ 2 ②

A [1-2]

W: Let's go to the Pineapple Store. They have various clothes at low prices.
M: Do you go there often?
W: Yes. They carry up-to-date designs.
M: Well, I don't think you should go there. That store is based on fast fashion.

W: Fast fashion?

M: It means clothing collections which reflect the latest fashion trends. The designs change almost every two weeks. It doesn't focus on materials, so it's very cheap.

W: What's the problem with it?

M: The problem is that it's not an environmentally-friendly store.

W: How come?

M: They produce lots of new clothes to reflect the latest fashions. Their unsold clothes become trash.

W: That isn't a good thing.

M: Also, do you wear clothes from the Pineapple Store for a long time?

W: No. I don't wear them for long because they become outdated quickly.

M: Exactly. That means more garbage. We need to protect our environment.

W: Good point. From now on, I'll consider the environment more before purchasing new clothes.

여: Pineapple Store에 가자. 거기 싼 옷들이 많아.

남: 거기 자주 가니?

여: 응. 거긴 최신 디자인을 취급하거든.

남: 음, 난 네가 거기 가지 않는 게 좋을 것 같아. 그 가게는 패스트 패션에 기반을 둔 곳이야.

여: 패스트 패션?

남: 그건 최신 패션 유행을 반영하는 옷 컬렉션이라는 뜻이야. 디자인이 거의 2주마다 바뀌지. 재질은 중요시하지 않으니까 아주 싸.

여: 그게 뭐가 문제인데?

남: 문제는 그 곳이 환경친화적인 가게가 아니라는 거지.

여: 왜?

남: 최신 유행을 반영하기 위해 새 옷들을 많이 생산하잖아. 팔리지 않은 옷들은 쓰레기가 되는 거야.

여: 그건 좋은 일이 아닌데.

남: 또, Pineapple Store의 옷을 오래 입니?

여: 아니. 금방 유행에 뒤떨어져서 오래 입지 않아.

남: 거봐. 그게 쓰레기가 더 많아진다는 의미야. 우린 환경을 보호해야 하잖아.

여: 좋은 지적이다. 앞으로는 새 옷을 사기 전에 환경을 더 생각할게.

어휘

be based on ~에 기반을 두다 reflect [riflékt] ⑧ 반영하다 material [mətí(:)əriəl] ⑨ 재료; *원단, 옷감 environmentally-friendly [invài ə rənméntlifréndli] ⑨ 환경 친화적인 How come? 어째서?, 왜? unsold [ʌ̀nsóuld]

⑨ 팔리지 않은 trash [træʃ] ⑨ 쓰레기 outdated [àutdéitid] ⑨ 시대에 뒤진 garbage [gɑ́ːrbidʒ] ⑨ 쓰레기 purchase [pə́ːrtʃəs] ⑧ 구입하다 [문제] negative [négətiv] ⑨ 부정적인 indifferent [indífərənt] ⑨ 무관심한

문제 해설

Q1: 패스트 패션에 관해 사실이면 T, 사실이 아니면 F에 √표 하시오.

값이 싸고 최신 스타일을 바로 반영하며, 디자인에만 중점을 두어 옷감은 중요시하지 않는다고 했다.

Q2: 남자의 패스트 패션에 대한 생각은?

남자는 패스트 패션이 옷 쓰레기를 많이 만들어내기 때문에 환경에 나쁜 영향을 미친다고 반대하는 입장이므로 부정적인 태도를 가지고 있다.

B [1-2]

W: Yves Saint Laurent was a French fashion designer who was born in 1936. Since childhood, he had great fashion sense, and created various looks during the 50 years of his designing career. He was the one who introduced "the safari look" and designer labeled blue jeans to the world. He was also the first person to hire black models for his shows. He even held a solo exhibition in the Metropolitan Museum of Art. But there's another reason why he is known as a fashion icon. He is considered to have changed the world through fashion by introducing pants suits for women. Pants suits gave freedom to women and raised women's status in society. This great designer retired in 2002 and died in June 2008.

여: Yves Saint Laurent은 1936년 태어난 프랑스의 패션 디자이너였습니다. 유년기부터 그는 훌륭한 패션 감각을 가졌고, 그의 디자이너 50년 경력 동안 다양한 디자인을 창작했습니다. 그는 사파리 룩과 디자이너 상표의 청바지를 세상에 소개한 사람입니다. 그리고 그는 처음으로 흑인 모델을 자신의 패션 쇼에 세운 사람이었습니다. 그는 Metropolitan Museum of Art에서 개인 전시회를 열기까지 했습니다. 그러나 그가 패션 아이콘으로 알려진 또 다른 이유가 있습니다. 그는 여성을 위한 바지 정장을 도입함으로써 패션을 통해 세상을 바꾸었다고 평가됩니다. 바지 정장은 여성들에게 자유를 주었고 사회에서의 여성의 지위를 높여주었습니다. 이 위대한 디자이너는 2002년에 은퇴했고 2008년 6월에 사망했습니다.

어휘

childhood [tʃáildhùd] ⑨ 어린 시절 look [luk] ⑨ 룩, 디자인 labeled [léibəld] ⑨ 라벨이 붙은 hire [haiər] ⑧ 고용

하다 solo exhibition 개인 전시회 icon[áikɑn] 몡 상징,
아이콘 pants suit 바지 정장 freedom[frí:dəm] 몡 자유
status[stéitəs] 몡 지위 retire[ritáiər] 통 은퇴하다 [문제]
work of art 예술품 protest[prətést] 통 항의하다
right[rait] 몡 권리

문제 해설

Q1: Yves Saint Laurent에 관해 사실이 **아닌** 것은?

그가 사파리 룩을 선보인 것은 맞으나 그의 첫 컬렉션에서
선보였다고는 하지 않았다.

Q2: Yves Saint Laurent이 세상을 바꾸었다고 평가되는 이유는?

① 그는 청바지를 대중화시켰다.

② 그는 여성을 위한 바지 정장을 디자인했다.

③ 그는 옷을 예술품으로 바꾸었다.

④ 그는 여성 권리를 위해 시위했다.

그는 여성용 바지 정장을 최초로 만들어서 여성의 사회적 지
위 향상에 기여했고 이로 인해 패션을 통해 세계를 바꾼 것
으로 평가받고 있다고 했다.

Critical ★ Thinking p. 37

1 ④ 2 ②

W: Today, I saw a guy wearing too many
accessories on the street.

M: What's wrong with that? It's just an expression
of personal preference.

W: You should have seen him. He was wearing
several gold bracelets and necklaces, along
with two big earrings. They were much
bigger than the kinds of earrings women
usually wear.

M: What about rock stars? They wear many
accessories.

W: That's different, because they look great
whatever they do.

M: That's a double standard. Actually, there's
something I can't understand about women.

W: Yes? Go on.

M: Why in the world do they wear such short
miniskirts?

W: I think miniskirts look cute. Don't men love
women wearing miniskirts?

M: Maybe. But some women wear skirts that
are too short. I don't know where to look
when I meet them on the street! The most
embarrassing part is that I sometimes see
their underwear when they walk up the
stairs.

여: 오늘 거리에서 액세서리를 너무 많이 한 남자를 봤어.

남: 그게 뭐가 어때서? 그건 개인적인 취향의 표현일 뿐이잖아.

여: 네가 그를 봤어야 했는데. 그는 여러 개의 금색 팔찌와 목걸
이를 하고 큰 귀걸이 두 개까지 하고 있었어. 여자들이 보통
하는 종류의 것보다 훨씬 더 큰 귀걸이였어.

남: 록 스타들은? 그들도 액세서리를 많이 하잖아.

여: 그건 다른 문제야. 왜냐하면 그들은 뭘 하든 멋지게 보이잖아.

남: 그건 이중 잣대야. 사실 여자들에 대해서 내가 이해할 수 없
는 것들이 있어.

여: 그래? 말해 봐.

남: 도대체 왜 그렇게 짧은 미니스커트를 입는 건데?

여: 미니스커트가 귀여워 보이잖아. 남자들은 미니스커트를 입
은 여자를 좋아하잖아?

남: 그럴지도. 하지만 어떤 여자들은 너무 짧은 치마를 입어. 거
리에서 만나면 어디를 봐야 할지 모르겠어! 가장 당황스러운
건 그들이 계단을 올라갈 때 가끔 속옷이 보인다는 거야.

어휘

expression[ikspréʃən] 몡 표현 personal[pə́rsənəl] 몡
개인적인 preference[préfərəns] 몡 취향, 선호도
bracelet[bréislit] 몡 팔찌 double standard 이중 잣대
in the world 도대체 embarrassing[imbǽrəsiŋ] 몡
당황스러운 underwear[ʌ́ndərwɛ̀ər] 몡 속옷 [문제]
current[kə́:rənt] 몡 현재의, 현재 유행하는

문제 해설

Q1: 그들은 주로 무엇에 대해 이야기하고 있나?

여자는 액세서리를 많이 한 남자의 차림새를 싫어하고, 남자
는 미니스커트를 너무 짧게 입은 여자의 차림새가 싫다고 말
하고 있다.

Q2: 미니스커트에 대해 남자와 같은 의견을 가진 사람은?

① Tara: 누구에게나 잘 어울린다.

② Bob: 어떤 미니스커트는 너무 짧다.

③ Judy: 날씬한 여자들에게만 잘 어울린다.

남자는 미니스커트를 너무 짧게 입은 경우는 보기 좋지 않다
는 생각을 드러내고 있다.

UNIT 06 Ads & Announcements

Getting ★ Ready p. 38

A 1 ⓔ 2 ⓒ 3 ⓕ 4 ⓐ 5 ⓓ 6 ⓑ
B 1 ⓕ 2 ⓐ 3 ⓑ

B 1 남: 왜 그 로션을 샀니?

여: 광고에서 피부 알레르기 테스트를 통과했다고 했어.

2 남: 무엇이 좋은 광고를 만드는 거라고 생각해?

여: 상품에 대해 자세하게 설명해 줘야 해.

3 남: 왜 TV에서 정크푸드 광고를 금지하기로 결정했나요?
여: 아이들에게 해롭다고 생각하거든요.

1 ③ 2 (1) 3rd (2) 1st (3) 2nd 3 ③

1

W: All my friends say I look beautiful these days. What's my secret? I've started using Shining Velvet.
M1: Shining Velvet is made with all natural materials. It contains vitamins B and E. It heals your dry, damaged hair. With Shining Velvet, you can feel the change in just three weeks.
W: Have a look! My hair is really shiny and feels as smooth as velvet. Also, it has the sweet smell of blueberries! You don't need to use any perfume when you use Shining Velvet.
M2: Hey, Vivian. You look great today.
W: See? Shining Velvet, it's my beauty secret.

여: 친구들 모두가 내가 요즘 예뻐 보인다고 그래요. 비밀이 뭐냐고요? 전 Shining Velvet을 쓰기 시작했답니다.
남1: Shining Velvet은 천연 물질로만 만들어졌습니다. 비타민 B와 E가 포함되어 있습니다. 여러분의 건조하고 상한 머리카락을 치료합니다. Shining Velvet을 쓰면 3주 만에 변화를 느낄 수가 있습니다.
여: 보세요! 제 머리카락이 아주 빛나고 벨벳처럼 부드러워요. 또, 블루베리의 달콤한 향이 나죠. Shining Velvet을 쓰면 향수를 쓸 필요가 없어요.
남2: 이봐, Vivian. 너 오늘 멋져 보여.
여: 보셨죠? Shining Velvet은 제 아름다움의 비밀이에요.

어휘
velvet[vélvit] 명 벨벳 material[mətí(ː)əriəl] 명 물질, 원료 contain[kəntéin] 동 포함하다 heal[hiːl] 동 치료하다 damaged[dǽmidʒd] 형 상한 shiny[ʃáini] 형 빛나는 smooth[smuːð] 형 매끈한, 윤기 있는 blueberry[blúːbèri] 명 블루베리 perfume[pə́ːrfjuːm] 명 향수 [문제] vitamin pill 비타민 정제(알약)

문제 해설
Q: 광고는 무엇에 관한 것인가?
상한 머리카락을 치료해 빛나고 부드럽게 한다고 했으므로 샴푸 광고임을 알 수 있다.

2

M: Thank you for visiting the Museum of Art and History. We have a different theme on each floor. On the first floor, we present a large collection of traditional costumes. It's a good place to learn about clothes in the old days. On the second floor, we have an exhibition of royal family items, such as jewelry, furniture, and books. In the gallery on the third floor, you can see famous paintings of the 18th century. The collection includes more than 300 paintings. We hope you enjoy our collections.

남: Museum of Art and History에 방문해 주셔서 감사합니다. 이곳은 각 층마다 다른 주제를 가지고 있습니다. 1층에서는 다수의 전통 의상 소장품을 보여드립니다. 옛날 의복에 관해 배울 수 있는 좋은 장소입니다. 2층에는 보석과 가구, 책과 같은 왕실 물품들이 전시되어 있습니다. 3층 전시실에서는 18세기의 유명한 그림들을 볼 수 있습니다. 전시품은 300개 이상의 그림을 포함하고 있습니다. 저희 전시품을 즐겁게 관람하시길 바랍니다.

어휘
theme[θiːm] 명 주제 present[prizént] 동 선보이다, 보여주다 collection[kəlékʃən] 명 전시품, 수집품 traditional[trədíʃənəl] 형 전통적인 costume[kάstjuːm] 명 의상 exhibition[èksəbíʃən] 명 전시 royal[rɔ́iəl] 형 왕실의 jewelry[dʒúːəlri] 명 보석 furniture[fə́ːrnitʃər] 명 가구 gallery[gǽləri] 명 전시실, 화랑

문제 해설
Q: 각 인물이 갈 층을 쓰시오.
(1) Tim: 난 유명한 그림을 보고 싶어.
(2) Katie: 옛날 스타일의 옷을 보고 싶어.
(3) Andrew: 왕들이 어떤 종류의 가구를 사용했는지 알고 싶어.
안내에 따르면 18세기의 유명한 그림은 3층 전시실에 전시되고, 고전 의복은 1층, 왕실의 물품은 2층 전시실에서 관람할 수 있다.

3

W: Attention, please. This is the Lost and Found Center. We just received a men's bag, which is made of black leather. It has a front pocket and a short handle. It was found at ABC Sports Store on the 5th floor at around 4:15. There are two books about marketing and a red handkerchief in the bag. If you think it's yours, please come to the Lost and Found Center. It is located on the 6th floor and closes at 8:45. Thank you very much.

여: 안내 말씀 드리겠습니다. 여기는 분실물 센터입니다. 방금 남성용 가방이 들어왔는데 검정색 가죽으로 만들어진 것입

39

니다. 앞주머니 하나와 짧은 손잡이가 달려 있습니다. 5층에 있는 ABC Sports Store에서 4시 15분쯤에 발견되었습니다. 가방 속에는 마케팅에 관한 책 두 권과 빨간색 손수건이 들어 있습니다. 본인의 것이라고 생각하시면 분실물 센터로 와 주세요. 이 센터는 6층에 있고 8시 45분에 문을 닫습니다. 대단히 감사합니다.

어휘

Lost and Found 분실물 보관소   leather[léðər] 명 가죽   handle[hǽndl] 명 손잡이   marketing[máːrkitiŋ] 명 마케팅   handkerchief[hǽŋkərtʃi(ː)f] 명 손수건   be located ~에 위치하다

문제 해설

Q: 틀린 정보를 고르시오.

가방이 발견된 시간은 4시 15분쯤이라고 했다.

Listening ★ Practice   p. 40

A 1 ②   2 ③   B 1 ④   2 ②
C 1 ①   2 ④   D 1 ①   2 ③

A [1-2]

M: Do you want to be slim, but don't have much time to work out? Then you should try Magic Solution! Magic Solution looks like a chair, but it is a special piece of exercise equipment. It helps you lose weight easily. You don't have to run or lift anything. All you have to do is to sit in the chair. When you switch the power on, it will shake your whole body. Try it twice a day for 30 minutes and after two weeks, you will notice your body change. Its original price is $200, but we're offering a 40% discount during March only. Order now on our website, or dial 1-800-1234.

남: 날씬해지고 싶은데 운동할 시간이 많지 않으신가요? 그렇다면 Magic Solution을 사용해 보세요! Magic Solution은 의자처럼 생겼지만 특별한 운동 기구입니다. 쉽게 살을 뺄 수 있게 도와 드립니다. 달리거나 무언가를 들어 올릴 필요가 없습니다. 그냥 의자에 앉아 있기만 하면 됩니다. 전원을 켜면 이 기구가 몸 전체를 흔들어 줄 것입니다. 하루에 두 번 30분씩 해 보시면, 2주 후에는 신체의 변화를 확인하게 될 것입니다. 원래 가격은 200달러인데 3월 동안에만 40% 할인을 해 드립니다. 저희 웹사이트에서 지금 주문하시거나 1-800-1234로 전화 주세요.

어휘

slim[slim] 형 날씬한   work out 운동하다   solution[səlúːʃən] 명 해결책   equipment[ikwípmənt] 명 기구, 장비

lose weight 살을 빼다   lift[lift] 동 들어 올리다   switch on 스위치를 켜다   shake[ʃeik] 동 진동시키다, 흔들리게 하다 (shake-shook-shaken)   notice[nóutis] *동 알아채다; 명 통지   original[ərídʒənəl] 형 원래의   offer[ɔ́(ː)fər] 동 제공하다   dial[dáiəl] 동 전화를 걸다

문제 해설

Q1: Magic Solution을 쓰고 있는 사람은?

의자처럼 생긴 기구에 앉아 있으면서 몸 전체가 떨리는 상태인 사람을 고른다.

Q2: 틀린 정보를 고르시오.

원래 가격인 200달러의 40% 할인가는 120달러이다.

B [1-2]

W: Where have you been?
M: I went to a cosmetics store. I bought some Venus Best lotion for my sensitive skin.
W: Oh, no! You shouldn't use it.
M: Why not?
W: I read some reviews on the Internet. People with allergies had some skin problems after using it.
M: Really? But the ad said it passed a skin allergy test.
W: Yes, but I don't think they're telling the truth.
M: That's so wrong. I'll never buy another product from the Venus Company.
W: It's not only the Venus Company. I read an article which said that the government made over twenty companies change their ads.
M: Did they also give wrong information in their ads?
W: Right. We shouldn't always believe advertisements. So before I shop, I read customer reviews to get information.

여: 어디 갔었니?
남: 화장품 가게에 갔었어. 내 민감한 피부를 위해 Venus Best 로션을 좀 샀어.
여: 아, 저런! 그거 쓰면 안 돼.
남: 왜 안 돼?
여: 인터넷에서 사용 후기를 몇 개 읽었어. 알레르기가 있는 사람들이 그걸 쓰고 나서 피부 트러블이 생겼대.
남: 정말? 하지만 광고에선 피부 알레르기 테스트를 거쳤다고 했어.
여: 응, 하지만 사실을 얘기하는 것 같지 않아.
남: 그건 아주 잘못된 거잖아. 난 Venus Company에서 다른 상품을 절대 사지 않을 거야.
여: Venus Company뿐만이 아니야. 정부가 20개가 넘는 회사의 광고를 수정하게 했다는 기사를 읽었어.

남: 그들도 광고에서 잘못된 정보를 준 거야?

여: 맞아. 광고를 항상 믿어서는 안 돼. 그래서 난 쇼핑을 하기
전에 정보를 얻기 위해 고객 후기를 읽어.

어휘

cosmetics [kɑzmétiks] 몡 화장품 sensitive skin 민감성
피부 allergy [ǽlərdʒi] 몡 알레르기 ad [æd] 몡 광고
(= advertisement) government [gʌ́vərnmənt] 몡 정부
[문제] advantage [ədvǽntidʒ] 몡 이점, 장점 strategy
[strǽtədʒi] 몡 전략 effective [iféktiv] 혱 효과적인 trust
[trʌst] 동 신뢰하다 brand-name [brǽndnèim] 혱 유명 상
표가 붙은 compare [kəmpέər] 동 비교하다

문제 해설

Q1: 그들은 주로 무엇에 관해 이야기하고 있나?
잘못된 정보를 주고 있는 광고들이 많아 더 이상 광고를 신
뢰할 수 없다는 내용의 대화이다.

Q2: 현명한 쇼핑을 위한 여자의 조언은?
광고에 나오는 정보를 믿지 않고 상품 후기를 읽는다고 했다.

C [1-2]

W: Attention, please. This is an announcement
for passengers on flight BT 201 to New York.
The departure of the flight is being delayed
because of repair problems. The ground crew
is currently working on it, but the departure
time has been changed to 11 o'clock. The
departure gate may also be changed, so
please check before boarding the plane. And
there's one more notice. The departure gate
of flight TX 1215 to London, leaving at 10:30
a.m., has been changed from Gate 2 to Gate
16. The passengers for this flight should
arrive at Gate 16 by 10 a.m. We apologize for
the inconvenience.

여: 안내 말씀 드리겠습니다. 뉴욕으로 가는 BT 201 항공편 승객
을 위한 안내 방송입니다. 비행편의 출발이 수리 문제로 인해
지연되고 있습니다. 지상 근무원들이 현재 작업 중이지만 출
발 시각은 11시로 변경되었습니다. 출발 게이트 역시 변경될
수 있으니 비행기에 탑승하시기 전에 확인하시기 바랍니다.
그리고 한 가지 더 알려 드립니다. 오전 10시 30분에 출발하
는 런던행 TX 1215편의 출발 게이트는 2번 게이트에서 16번
게이트로 변경되었습니다. 이 항공편의 승객들께서는 오전
10시까지 16번 게이트로 오셔야 합니다. 불편을 드려 죄송합
니다.

어휘

announcement [ənáunsmənt] 몡 공지, 안내 방송
passenger [pǽsəndʒər] 몡 승객 departure [dipáːrtʃər]
몡 출발 delay [diléi] 동 지연시키다 repair [ripέər] 몡 수
리 ground crew 지상 근무원 currently [kə́ːrəntli] 튀

현재 gate [geit] 몡 문, 탑승구 board [bɔːrd] 동 탑승하다
apologize for ~에 대해 사과하다 inconvenience
[ìnkənvíːnjəns] 몡 불편함 [문제] cancel [kǽnsəl] 동 취소하
다 due to ~때문에 destination [dèstənéiʃən] 몡 행선지,
도착지

문제 해설

Q1: BT 201편에 관해 맞는 것은?
① 출발 시간이 변경되었다.
② 기상 조건 때문에 결항되었다.
③ 곧 탑승을 시작할 것이다.
④ 출발 게이트가 16번 게이트로 변경되었다.
BT 201편은 수리 문제로 출발 시간이 11시로 변경되었다고
했다.

Q2: TX 1215편의 도착지와 출발 시간을 고르시오.
런던으로 오전 10시 30분에 출발하는 항공편이다.

D [1-2]

M: Hey, look at this TV commercial. I have no
idea what it is advertising.

W: I heard that's a new car ad.

M: But it only shows a girl swimming in the
sea! What does it have to do with a car?

W: It's a teaser advertisement. It's common
these days.

M: A teaser advertisement?

W: Yes. It doesn't give product information. It
even hides what kind of product it is.

M: That's not good. An advertisement should
describe the product in detail so that
people want it.

W: In most cases, you're right. But teaser ads
can make people very curious about the
product.

M: I see. As you said, it seems to be good for
getting attention.

W: Yes, that's why teaser ads are often used
for new products.

남: 야, 이 TV 광고 좀 봐. 무엇을 광고하는 건지 모르겠어.

여: 그거 새로 나온 자동차 광고라고 들었어.

남: 그렇지만 바다에서 수영하는 여자애만 보여주는걸! 그게 차
랑 무슨 상관이야?

여: 그건 티저 광고야. 요즘 흔한 거야.

남: 티저 광고라고?

여: 응. 티저 광고는 상품 정보를 주지 않아. 심지어 상품의 종류
를 감추기도 하지.

남: 그건 별로다. 광고는 사람들이 사고 싶게끔 상품에 대해서
자세히 설명해 줘야 해.

여: 대부분의 경우 네 말이 맞아. 하지만 티저 광고는 사람들이

상품에 대해 아주 궁금해 하도록 만들 수가 있지.

남: 그렇구나. 네가 말한 대로 관심을 끌기에는 좋을 것 같아.

여: 그래, 신상품에 티저 광고가 자주 사용되는 이유가 그거야.

어휘

commercial[kəmə́ːrʃəl] 몡 TV 광고 advertise
[ǽdvərtàiz] 통 광고하다 have to do with ~와 관련이 있
다 teaser advertisement 티저 광고(궁금증을 일으키는
광고) in detail 자세히 attention[ətènʃən] 몡 주목, 관심
[문제] attract[ətrǽkt] 통 (주의·흥미를) 끌다 positive
[pázitiv] 몡 긍정적인

문제 해설

Q1: 티저 광고의 좋은 점은?

티저 광고는 사람들의 관심을 끌게 되어 신제품의 광고로 많
이 쓰인다고 했다.

Q2: 티저 광고를 고르시오.

구체적인 상품 정보가 없고 무엇을 광고하는지 알 수 없는
광고가 티저 광고이다.

Listening ★ Challenge p. 42

A 1 ③ 2 ④ B 1 ③ 2 ③

A [1-2]

M: Ladies and gentlemen, welcome on board
Star Cruise. Star Cruise is going to travel to
four beautiful Greek islands in seven days.
During this time, you will get to enjoy some
beautiful scenery. Fireworks on Monday
evening, a special dance performance on
Wednesday, and a magic show on Friday – all
of these are waiting for you. And if you want
to taste various foods from all around the
world, just walk down to the Lux Restaurant!
You can also visit our sauna, sports center,
bar, and duty free shops anytime you want.
In ten minutes, however, our safety lesson
will start. I'd like you to gather together in
the main hall with your life jackets on. If you
have any problems, please let our staff know.
Thank you.

남: 신사 숙녀 여러분, Star Cruise에 탑승하신 걸 환영합니다.
Star Cruise는 7일 동안 네 개의 아름다운 그리스의 섬들을
여행하게 됩니다. 이 기간 동안 여러분께서는 아름다운 풍경
을 즐기시게 됩니다. 월요일 저녁에 불꽃놀이, 수요일에 특
별 댄스 공연, 그리고 금요일에 마술쇼 등 이 모든 것들이
여러분을 기다리고 있습니다. 만약 전 세계의 다양한 요리
를 맛보고 싶으시면 Lux Restaurant로 내려가세요! 사우나
와 스포츠 센터, 바, 면세점도 원하시면 언제든지 가실 수 있

습니다. 그런데, 10분 뒤에 안전 교육이 시작될 것입니다. 구
명조끼를 입고 메인 홀에 모두 모여주시기 바랍니다. 문제가
있으시면 저희 스태프에게 알려 주십시오. 감사합니다.

어휘

on board 승선한, 탑승한 cruise[kruːz] 몡 순항; *선박 여
행 scenery[síːnəri] 몡 풍경 firework[fáiərwə̀ːrk] 몡 불
꽃놀이 performance[pərfɔ́ːrməns] 몡 공연 taste[teist]
통 맛보다 sauna[sɔ́ːnə] 몡 사우나 duty free shop 면
세점 safety lesson 안전 교육 gather[gǽðər] 통 모이
다 life jacket 구명조끼 staff[stæf] 몡 스태프, 직원
[문제] feature[fíːtʃər] 통 특집으로 하다, 특별 행사로 보여주
다 deck[dek] 몡 갑판

문제 해설

Q1: Star Cruise 여행에 관해 사실이 아닌 것은?

수요일에는 특별 댄스 공연이 있고 금요일에 마술쇼를 보여
준다고 안내했다.

Q2: 이 안내 방송 이후에 승객들이 할 일은?

10분 후에 바로 안전 교육이 있어 구명조끼를 입고 모이라고
했으므로 승객들은 구명조끼를 입을 것이다.

B [1-2]

W: Welcome to *Issues of the Day*. We're going
to discuss junk food ads tonight. We have
Mr. Williams from the government here.
Hello.

M: Hello, Ms. O'Brien.

W: I heard that due to a new law, some junk
food ads will not be allowed to appear on
TV at a particular time of day. Can you
explain why this is?

M: We believe junk food is harmful for children.
So we've decided to ban those ads when
most kids watch TV.

W: Could you explain when that is?

M: It's for three hours, from 5 to 8 p.m.

W: What kinds of junk food will be affected by
the law?

M: Ads for hamburgers, pizza, chocolate, chips,
and soda will be affected.

W: I guess the junk food companies might
disagree with the law.

M: You're right. However, I believe children's
health should come first. I hope companies
understand this and make their food
healthier.

W: I see. Thank you for coming today.

여: 'Issues of the Day'에 오신 것을 환영합니다. 오늘 밤에
는 정크푸드 광고에 대해 논의해 보겠습니다. 정부에서

Williams 씨가 나와 주셨습니다. 안녕하세요.

남: 안녕하세요, O'Brien 씨.

여: 새로운 법안 때문에 몇몇 정크푸드 광고가 특정 시간대에 TV에 나올 수 없게 될 것이라고 들었습니다. 왜 그런지 설명해 주시겠어요?

남: 우리는 정크푸드가 아이들에게 해롭다고 믿습니다. 그래서 대부분의 아이들이 TV를 보는 시간에 그런 광고를 금지하기로 결정했습니다.

여: 그게 언제인지 설명해 주시겠어요?

남: 오후 5시에서 8시까지 세 시간 동안입니다.

여: 법에 의해 어떤 종류의 정크푸드가 영향을 받게 되나요?

남: 햄버거나 피자, 초콜릿, 감자칩, 탄산음료에 대한 광고에 영향을 미치게 됩니다.

여: 정크푸드 회사는 법안에 동의하지 않을 것 같군요.

남: 맞습니다. 하지만 아이들의 건강이 우선시되어야 한다고 믿습니다. 회사들이 이것을 이해하고 더 건강에 좋은 음식을 만들기를 바랍니다.

여: 알겠습니다. 오늘 나와 주셔서 감사합니다.

어휘

issue[íʃuː] 몡 쟁점, 논쟁 junk food 정크푸드(칼로리는 높으나 영양가가 낮은 즉석 식품) government[gʌ́vərnmənt] 몡 정부 appear[əpíər] 동 나오다 particular[pərtíkjulər] 혱 특정한 harmful[háːrmfəl] 혱 해로운 ban[bæn] 동 금지하다 affect[əfékt] 동 영향을 주다 soda[sóudə] 몡 탄산음료 disagree with ~와 동의하지 않다 [문제] fair [fɛər] 혱 공정한 profit[práfit] 몡 수익, 이익

문제 해설

Q1: 오후 5시에서 8시 사이에 TV에서 금지되지 <u>않는</u> 광고는?

초콜릿, 햄버거, 감자칩이 금지될 광고로 언급되었다.

Q2: Williams 씨와 같은 의견인 사람은?

① TV에서 특정한 종류의 광고를 금지하는 것은 공정하지 않다.

② 정크푸드 광고는 하루 종일 TV에서 금지되어야 한다.

③ 아이들의 건강이 회사의 수익보다 더 중요하다.

Williams 씨는 아이들의 건강이 우선시되어야 하기 때문에 정크푸드 광고 금지에 대해 정크푸드 회사들이 이해해야 한다고 했으므로 아이들의 건강을 회사의 수익보다 중요하게 여기는 의견과 같다.

Critical ★ Thinking   p. 43

1 ③   2 ②

W: Did you like the movie?

M: Not so much. The only thing I can remember is the main actress's cell phone.

W: Yeah, it appeared in so many scenes. The worst part was when the actress suddenly explained how good her phone was.

M: That's product placement. Film directors place some products in movies on purpose, after they receive money from the companies.

W: I know. But I don't think product placement should be used in movies. It is very annoying.

M: But I understand the film directors. To make a good movie, they need a large amount of money.

W: So, do you think it's okay even when there are many unnecessary product placement scenes in movies?

M: No. I don't think product placement should ever lower the quality of the movie. But I think it's okay for directors to use product placement properly.

여: 영화 좋았어?

남: 별로였어. 유일하게 기억나는 거라고는 여자 주인공의 휴대전화야.

여: 맞아, 너무 많은 장면에 나왔지. 가장 최악이었던 부분은 여배우가 갑자기 자기 휴대전화가 얼마나 좋은지 설명했을 때였어.

남: 그게 간접광고야. 영화 감독이 기업으로부터 돈을 받고 나서 영화에 일부러 상품을 배치하는 거지.

여: 알아. 하지만 난 간접광고가 영화에 쓰이지 말아야 한다고 생각해. 정말 거슬려.

남: 하지만 난 영화 감독이 이해가 돼. 좋은 영화를 만들려면 많은 돈이 필요하잖아.

여: 그렇다면 영화에 불필요한 간접광고 장면들이 많이 나오더라도 괜찮다고 생각하니?

남: 아니. 간접광고가 절대 영화의 질을 떨어뜨려서는 안 된다고 생각해. 하지만 감독들이 간접광고를 적당하게 사용한다면 괜찮다고 생각해.

어휘

main actress 주연 여배우 scene[siːn] 몡 장면 product placement 간접광고(상품을 영화, 드라마 속에 사용하는 간접적인 광고) film director 영화 감독 on purpose 일부러, 고의로 annoying[ənɔ́iiŋ] 혱 성가신, 짜증나는 unnecessary[ʌnnésəsèri] 혱 불필요한 lower [lóuər] 동 떨어뜨리다, 낮추다 properly[prápərli] 부 적당히

문제 해설

Q1: 그들은 주로 무엇에 대해 이야기하고 있나?

① 왜 감독들은 간접광고를 쓰는가?

② 간접광고를 쓰는 것이 효과적인가?

③ 영화에서 간접광고를 쓰는 것이 괜찮은가?

④ 간접광고 사용의 나쁜 점은 무엇인가?

영화의 간접광고가 보기에 짜증난다는 의견과 제작비를 위해 간접광고를 하게 되는 상황을 이해한다는 의견 등 간접광

고가 영화에 나와도 괜찮은지에 대한 토론이다.

Q2: 간접광고에 대한 남자의 의견은?

남자는 간접광고를 통해 영화 제작비를 보충할 수 있지만 영화의 질을 떨어뜨리는 정도는 안 된다고 주장했다.

UNIT 07 Technology

Getting ★ Ready p. 44

A 1 ⓔ 2 ⓕ 3 ⓓ 4 ⓑ 5 ⓒ 6 ⓐ
B 1 ⓐ 2 ⓕ 3 ⓒ

B 1 남: 그 기술이 씨앗을 어떻게 변화시켰어?
　　여: 생산성이 증가한 것으로 밝혀졌어.
　2 남: 왜 이 차를 추천하니?
　　여: 멋질 뿐만 아니라 몇 가지 앞선 기능이 있어.
　3 남: 개 통역기가 어떻게 발명되었지?
　　여: 많은 개들의 소리를 분석해서 만들어졌지.

Listening ★ Start p. 45

1 ②, ④ 2 ① 3 ②, ③

1

M: Robots are becoming more and more like humans. Have you heard about the robot called Kobian?
W: No. Is it very similar to a human?
M: Yes. It expresses emotions just like humans do. It shows seven emotions, including happiness and sadness.
W: Wow, how does it do that?
M: Kobian can change the position of its lips, eyelids and eyebrows, as well as make gestures.
W: How interesting!
M: So, when happy, it opens its eyes and mouth widely, lifting its arms above its head. When sad, it drops its head and closes its eyes.
W: Wow, I want to see it. What's the purpose of this robot?
M: It's going to be used to do housework for old people.

남: 로봇이 점점 더 인간처럼 되어가고 있어. Kobian이라는 로봇에 대해서 들어 본 적 있니?

44

여: 아니. 그게 인간과 아주 비슷해?
남: 응. 인간이 하는 것처럼 감정을 표현해. 행복이나 슬픔을 포함해서 7가지 감정을 나타내지.
여: 와, 어떻게 그렇게 하지?
남: Kobian은 제스처를 할 뿐 아니라 입술과 눈꺼풀, 눈썹의 위치를 바꿀 수 있어.
여: 흥미로운걸!
남: 그래서 기쁠 땐 머리 위로 팔을 들면서 크게 눈을 뜨고 입을 벌려. 슬플 땐 머리를 떨구고 눈을 감아.
여: 와, 그거 보고 싶다. 이 로봇의 용도는 뭐야?
남: 고령자들을 위해 집안일을 하는 데 사용될 거야.

어휘
robot[róubət] 몡 로봇　human[hjúːmən] 몡 사람
emotion[imóuʃən] 몡 감정　sadness[sǽdnis] 몡 슬픔
position[pəzíʃən] 몡 위치　eyelid[áilid] 몡 눈꺼풀
eyebrow[áibràu] 몡 눈썹　make a gesture 제스처를
하다, 몸짓을 하다　lift[lift] 통 들다　purpose[pə́ːrpəs] 몡
목적, 의도　[문제] facial expression 표정

문제 해설
Q: Kobian이 감정을 표현하는 방법 두 가지를 고르시오.
　이 로봇은 표정을 바꾸거나 제스처를 해서 감정을 나타낸다고 했다.

2

W: India is a country with a powerful IT industry. How did it create such an industry? First of all, there was the effort of the government. The government encouraged software exports and cut taxes for software companies. Also, although Indian workers have good English and technical skills, labor costs are cheap. Therefore, developed countries began to hire them. The final reason is the 12-hour time difference between India and the world's IT center, the U.S. Indian workers can follow up on projects from U.S. workers while they sleep, allowing IT companies to work 24 hours a day.

여: 인도는 막강한 IT 산업을 가진 나라입니다. 어떻게 그런 산업을 만들어낼 수 있었을까요? 우선, 정부의 노력이 있었습니다. 정부는 소프트웨어 수출을 장려하고 소프트웨어 회사들의 세금을 감해 주었습니다. 또한 인도의 근로자들은 영어를 잘하고 기술력이 있으면서도 인건비가 저렴합니다. 그래서 선진국이 그들을 고용하기 시작했습니다. 마지막 이유는 인도와 세계 IT 중심지인 미국과의 시차가 12시간이라는 것입니다. 인도 근로자들은 미국 근로자들이 자는 동안 프로젝트를 넘겨받아 후속 작업을 할 수 있는데, 이로 인해 IT 회사는 하루 24시간 가동될 수 있습니다.

어휘

IT(information technology) 정보 기술 **industry**
[índəstri] 몡 산업 **effort**[éfərt] 몡 노력 **encourage**
[inkə́:ridʒ] 통 장려하다 **export**[ékspɔːrt] 몡 수출
software company 소프트웨어 회사 **although**[ɔːlðóu]
쩝 비록 ~지만 **technical**[téknikəl] 혱 기술적인 **labor
cost** 인건비, 노동 비용 **developed country** 선진국
hire[haiər] 통 고용하다 **follow up** 계속하여 행하다

문제 해설

Q: 여자는 주로 무엇에 대해 이야기하고 있나?

① 인도의 IT 산업이 어떻게 발달되었는지

② IT 산업에 종사하는 것이 왜 좋은지

③ 어떤 나라들이 막강한 IT 산업을 가지고 있는지

④ 인도 정부가 어떻게 IT 산업을 지원했는지

인도의 IT 산업이 발달하게 된 이유에 대한 내용이다.

3

M: Hello. I'm the CEO of IB Motors. I'm pleased to show you our company's latest vehicle, the Revolution. The Revolution is not only stylish but also has several advanced functions. You may have heard that falling asleep while driving is more dangerous than drunk driving. Well, the Revolution's mirrors have sensors that watch the movement of the driver's eyes. If the driver's eyes stop moving, an alarm sounds. There's also a special function for easy parking. The computer screen in the car lets you know which way to turn the wheel and whether to go forward or backward.

남: 안녕하세요. 전 IB Motors의 최고경영자입니다. 저희 회사의 최신 승용차, Revolution를 소개하게 되어 기쁩니다. Revolution은 멋질 뿐만 아니라 몇 가지 앞선 기능을 가지고 있습니다. 졸음 운전이 음주 운전보다 더 위험하다는 것을 들어본 적이 있을 것입니다. 음, Revolution의 거울에는 운전자의 눈의 움직임을 주시하는 센서가 있습니다. 운전자의 눈이 움직임을 멈추면 경고음이 울립니다. 또한, 주차를 쉽게 할 수 있도록 해 주는 특수 기능도 있습니다. 차 안의 컴퓨터 스크린으로 어느 방향으로 바퀴를 돌려야 하는지, 앞으로 갈지 뒤로 갈지를 알려 줍니다.

어휘

latest[léitist] 혱 최신의 **vehicle**[víːikl] 몡 차량, 승용차
revolution[rèvəljúːʃən] 몡 혁명 **stylish**[stáiliʃ] 혱 멋진,
폼 나는 **advanced**[ædvǽnst] 혱 진보된, 앞선 **function**
[fʌ́ŋkʃən] 몡 기능 **fall asleep** 잠들다 **drunk driving**
음주 운전 **sensor**[sénsər] 몡 센서, 감지기 **alarm**[əláːrm]
몡 경보 **parking**[páːrkiŋ] 몡 주차 **wheel**[hwiːl] 몡 바퀴

forward[fɔ́ːrwərd] 묀 앞으로 **backward**[bǽkwərd] 묀
뒤로 [문제] **automatically**[ɔ̀ːtəmǽtik(ə)li] 묀 자동적으로

문제 해설

Q: Revolution의 앞선 기능 두 가지는?

① 술이 취했을 때는 작동이 되지 않는다.

② 운전하는 동안 깨어 있도록 도와준다.

③ 주차를 쉽게 하도록 도와준다.

④ 자동적으로 과속을 멈추게 해 준다.

운전 중에 졸지 않도록 해 주는 기능과 스크린을 통해 방향을 알려주어 주차를 쉽게 하도록 하는 기능이 있다.

Listening ★ Practice p. 46

A 1 ② 2 (1) T (2) F (3) T B 1 ③ 2 ①
C 1 ① 2 ② D 1 ④ 2 ④

A [1-2]

M: Kate, are you upset about something?

W: Yes. It's my pet dog. He doesn't move an inch or eat anything these days. And he sometimes makes a strange sound.

M: Maybe he's sick. Have you taken him to an animal hospital?

W: Yes, but the doctor said he's totally fine. I don't know how to find out what's wrong.

M: How about using a dog translator, then?

W: A dog translator?

M: Yes. It can tell how your dog feels by the way it sounds. It knows six different feelings, such as happy or sad.

W: Amazing! Does it show you on a monitor or something?

M: Yes. But it can also tell you with a human voice.

W: How was this technology developed?

M: It was made by analyzing the sounds of many different kinds of dogs.

W: Maybe I should buy one today.

남: Kate, 뭐 기분 안 좋은 일이라도 있어?

여: 응. 내 애완견 때문이야. 요즘 꼼짝도 하지 않고 아무것도 먹질 않아. 그리고 때론 이상한 소리를 내.

남: 아픈 모양이다. 동물 병원에 데리고 가 봤어?

여: 응, 하지만 의사 선생님이 모두 정상이래. 무엇이 문제인지 알아낼 방법을 모르겠어.

남: 그럼, 개 통역기를 이용해 보는 게 어때?

여: 개 통역기?

남: 응. 그게 개가 내는 소리로 그 개가 어떤 감정인지 알아낸대.

기쁘거나 슬프거나 하는 6가지의 감정을 알아내.

여: 놀라운데! 화면 같은 데서 보여주는 거니?

남: 응. 하지만 사람 목소리로 말해줄 수도 있어.

여: 이 기술은 어떻게 개발되었어?

남: 많은 종류의 개의 소리를 분석해서 만들어졌어.

여: 오늘 하나 사야 할 것 같다.

어휘

upset[ʌpsét] 휑 근심이 되는, 걱정하는   pet[pet] 명 애완동물   not ~ an inch 조금도 ~ 않는   totally[tóutəli] 틘 완전히, 전적으로   translator[trænsléitər] 명 *통역기; 번역가   technology[teknálədʒi] 명 기술   analyze[ǽnəlàiz] 통 분석하다   [문제] bark[baːrk] 통 짖다   identify[aidéntəfài] 통 인지하다, 감정하다

문제 해설

Q1: 여자가 걱정하고 있는 것은?

여자는 자신의 개가 잘 먹지도, 움직이지도 않고, 이상한 소리를 내는 행동을 보여서 걱정하고 있다.

Q2: 개 통역기에 대해 사실이면 T, 사실이 아니면 F에 √표 하시오.

(1) 여섯 가지 감정을 인지할 수 있다.

(2) 개의 감정을 화면으로만 보여준다.

(3) 많은 개의 소리를 연구해서 만들어졌다.

개의 여섯 가지 감정 상태를 구별할 수 있고, 결과를 화면과 사람 목소리 두 가지로 제시한다고 했으며, 여러 개의 소리를 분석해서 만들어졌다고 했다.

46

B [1-2]

M: An American company is gathering tourists for its new spaceship, the Lynx. Did you hear about it?

W: No. But I heard some companies have been developing space shuttles for a space trip. Spaceship 2 is one of them.

M: Spaceship 2? What does it look like?

W: It looks like three planes put side by side, and it can hold eight people.

M: Wow. I guess it's larger than the Lynx. The Lynx looks like a regular plane, but smaller.

W: How much do tourists have to pay for a space trip on the Lynx?

M: It's $95,000 for thirty minutes.

W: Thirty minutes seems too short. You can travel through space for two hours if you take Spaceship 2.

M: That's quite a long time, but I guess it's more expensive.

W: Right. It costs $200,000.

M: In that case, I'd rather choose the Lynx.

남: 미국의 한 회사가 새로운 우주선, Lynx의 여행객을 모집하

고 있어. 들었니?

여: 아니. 하지만 몇몇 회사들이 우주 여행을 위한 우주 왕복선을 개발하고 있다는 것은 들었어. Spaceship 2가 그 중 하나야.

남: Spaceship 2라고? 어떻게 생겼는데?

여: 세 대의 비행기를 나란히 놓은 것 같이 생겼는데 8명을 수용할 수 있어.

남: 와. 그게 Lynx보다 더 큰가 보다. Lynx는 일반 비행기 같은데, 좀 더 작아.

여: Lynx로 우주 여행을 하려면 여행객들이 얼마를 내야 해?

남: 30분에 95,000달러야.

여: 30분은 너무 짧은 것 같다. Spaceship 2를 타면 2시간 동안 우주를 여행할 수 있어.

남: 그거 꽤 긴 시간이네, 하지만 더 비쌀 것 같은데.

여: 맞아. 200,000달러가 들어.

남: 그렇다면 난 Lynx를 고르겠어.

어휘

gather[gǽðər] 통 모으다   tourist[tú(ː)ərist] 명 여행객   spaceship[spéisʃip] 명 우주선   space shuttle 우주 왕복선   side by side 나란히   regular[régjulər] 휑 평범한, 보통의

문제 해설

Q1: Spaceship 2의 그림을 고르시오.

세 개의 비행기를 나란히 붙여놓은 모양이라고 했다.

Q2: 남자가 Lynx를 선호하는 이유는?

Spaceship 2의 여행 비용이 Lynx보다 훨씬 비싸서, Lynx를 고르겠다고 했다.

C [1-2]

M: Why don't we take part in this year's design competition held by JY Mobile Company?

W: What kind of competition is it?

M: It's a competition to design future cell phones. This is the 3rd year of the competition and the winner gets $20,000 plus the latest cell phone.

W: Sounds interesting. Tell me more about the competition.

M: Well, anyone over the age of 18 can participate. The judges mostly consider whether it will be favorable to consumers.

W: What else?

M: Well, creativity also counts.

W: Did you see last year's winning design?

M: Yes. It was a cell phone which was worn around the wrist. It could be used as an accessory, too.

W: Wow, that's a good idea.

M: But I liked another one more. It looked like a regular cell phone, but it could change into wireless headphones.

W: Wow, that's amazing.

남: JY Mobile Company가 개최하는 올해의 디자인 경연 대회에 나가보는 게 어때?

여: 어떤 대회인데?

남: 미래의 휴대전화를 디자인하는 경연 대회야. 이번이 3년째인데 우승자는 20,000달러와 최신 휴대전화를 받게 되지.

여: 재미있을 거 같다. 대회에 대해 더 알려줘.

남: 음, 18세 이상이면 누구나 참가할 수 있어. 심사 위원은 소비자들이 좋아할 만한 디자인인지를 주로 고려하지.

여: 또 다른 건?

남: 음, 독창성도 중요해.

여: 지난해 우승 디자인을 봤니?

남: 응. 손목에 차는 휴대전화였어. 액세서리로도 쓸 수 있는 거야.

여: 와, 그거 좋은 생각이다.

남: 하지만 난 다른 게 더 좋았어. 보통 휴대전화 모양인데 무선 헤드폰으로 바뀌는 거야.

여: 와, 그거 멋지다.

어휘

take part in ~에 참가하다   competition [kὰmpətíʃən] 뗑 *경연 대회; 경쟁   participate [pɑːrtísəpèit] 뙹 참가하다   judge [dʒʌdʒ] 뗑 심사 위원   favorable [féivərəbl] 뙇 우호적인   consumer [kənsúːmər] 뗑 소비자   creativity [krìːeitívəti] 뗑 독창성   count [kaunt] 뙹 중요하다   wrist [rist] 뗑 손목   wireless [wáiərlis] 뙇 무선의   [문제] annual [ǽnjuəl] 뙇 해마다의   preference [préfərəns] 뗑 선호

문제 해설

Q1: 틀린 정보를 고르시오.

이 디자인 경연 대회는 3회째이며, 18세 이상이면 참가 가능하고, 소비자의 선호와 독창성이 심사 대상이며 부상은 20,000달러와 최신 휴대전화이다.

Q2: 지난해 우승 디자인을 고르시오.

우승한 디자인은 손목에 차는 형태의 휴대전화이다.

D [1-2]

W: There's a very unique cigarette vending machine in Japan. This smart machine can identify a person's age. It was made to prevent teenagers from buying cigarettes from vending machines. In order to use this machine, the person must stare at a digital camera set in the machine. The machine then takes a photo. From this photo, it guesses the person's age by the number of wrinkles, skin condition and bone structure. It then compares the face with 100,000 sets

of facial data saved in the machine. Adults who get rejected because of a younger looking face can put their driver's license into the machine to be checked.

여: 일본에는 매우 독특한 담배 자판기가 있습니다. 이 똑똑한 기계는 사람의 나이를 식별할 수 있습니다. 이것은 십대들이 자동판매기에서 담배를 사는 것을 막기 위해 만들어졌습니다. 이 기계를 사용하려면 기계에 장착된 디지털 카메라를 쳐다보아야만 합니다. 그러면 이 기계는 사진을 찍습니다. 이 사진에서 주름의 수와 피부 상태, 골격을 통해 그 사람의 나이를 추측합니다. 그런 다음 기계에 저장된 100,000개의 얼굴 데이터 세트와 그 얼굴을 비교합니다. 어려 보이는 얼굴 때문에 거부당한 성인은 운전면허증을 기계에 넣어 확인할 수 있습니다.

어휘

unique [juːníːk] 뙇 독특한   cigarette [sìɡərét] 뗑 담배   vending machine 자동판매기   prevent A from v-ing A가 ~ 하는 것을 막다   in order to-v ~하기 위해서   stare [stɛər] 뙹 쳐다보다   digital camera 디지털 카메라   wrinkle [ríŋkl] 뗑 주름   bone structure 뼈 구조, 골격   compare A with B A와 B를 비교하다   set [set] 뙹 설치하다; 뗑 세트   reject [ridʒékt] 거절하다   driver's license 운전면허증   [문제] fingerprint [fíŋɡərprìnt] 뗑 지문

문제 해설

Q1: 이 자동판매기가 만들어진 이유는?

① 노인 흡연자의 수를 줄이기 위해

② 흡연자의 나이를 조사하기 위해

③ 사람들의 얼굴에 대한 정보를 얻기 위해

④ 십대들이 담배를 사지 못하게 하기 위해

사람의 나이를 식별해 내는 자동판매기로 십대가 담배를 사지 못하게 하기 위한 것이다.

Q2: 자동판매기를 사용하기 위해 해야 할 일은?

기계에 장착된 디지털 카메라를 보면 사진이 찍히고 그 사진으로 나이를 판별한다.

Listening ★ Challenge   p. 48

A 1 ③ 2 ④   B 1 ④ 2 ①

A [1-2]

M: China has been sending vegetable seeds into space since the 1980s. For China, where the number of people is huge, this is one way to solve the food shortage problem. You might wonder why they're sending seeds into space. It's because scientists found that seeds' genetic characteristics

47

were changed after a trip to space. When the seeds were planted, it turned out that productivity increased. For example, wheat grew up to 9% more. For tomatoes and cucumbers, both productivity and taste improved. The weight of one green pepper even went up to nearly 750 g. The Chinese scientists are not sure why these changes happen. But if this study keeps going, food shortages won't be a problem in China in the future.

남: 중국은 1980년대 이후로 채소 씨앗을 우주로 보내고 있습니다. 인구의 수가 엄청난 중국으로서는 이것이 식량 부족 문제를 해결하기 위한 한 방법입니다. 왜 우주로 씨앗을 보내는지 궁금하시죠. 그것은 씨앗이 우주에 다녀온 후에 그것의 유전적인 특징이 바뀐다는 것을 과학자들이 알아냈기 때문입니다. 그 씨앗을 심었을 때 생산성이 증가된 것으로 밝혀졌습니다. 예를 들어, 밀은 9% 증가했습니다. 토마토와 오이는 생산성과 맛 모두 개선되었습니다. 피망 한 개의 무게가 거의 750그램까지 늘었습니다. 중국 과학자들은 왜 이런 변화가 생기는지 확신하지 못합니다. 하지만 이 연구가 계속되면 미래에 식량 부족은 중국에서 문제가 되지 않을 것입니다.

어휘

seed [siːd] 명 씨앗 huge [hjuːdʒ] 형 거대한, 막대한 shortage [ʃɔ́ːrtidʒ] 명 부족 genetic [dʒənétik] 형 유전적인 characteristic [kæ̀riktərístik] 명 특징 turn out ~으로 판명이 나다, 드러나다 productivity [pròudəktívəti] 명 생산성 increase [inkríːs] 동 증가하다 cucumber [kjúːkʌmbər] 명 오이 taste [teist] 명 맛 weight [weit] 명 무게 green pepper 피망 [문제] astronaut [ǽstrənɔ̀ːt] 명 우주 비행사

문제 해설

Q1: 중국이 우주로 씨앗을 보내는 이유는?

우주에 다녀온 씨앗의 생산성이 증가된 것을 알아낸 후, 식량 부족 문제를 해결하기 위해 씨앗을 우주로 보낸다고 했다.

Q2: 우주로부터 온 씨앗이 보여준 변화가 아닌 것은?

토마토와 오이는 맛과 생산성이 모두 좋아졌고 피망은 무게가 증가했지만, 성장 속도가 빨라졌다는 언급은 없었다.

B [1-2]

W: Good morning. On today's *Book Club*, we have Peter Adams, the author of *Enjoy Your Life*, as our guest.
M: Thank you for having me here.
W: Could you introduce your book first?
M: Of course. This book helps middle-aged fathers learn how to enjoy high-tech devices like cell phones, digital cameras, PMPs and MP3 players just like teenagers do.
W: I was surprised to learn that you didn't even know how to turn on a computer three years ago. What made you change?
M: It was my daughter. She would play with her computer and cell phone for hours. But I didn't know anything about these devices, so we had less and less to talk about.
W: So how did you learn about them?
M: I started by learning how to use a computer. I took free computer classes at a community center. I strongly recommend these classes to readers of my book.

여: 안녕하세요. 오늘 'Book Club'에서는 〈Enjoy Your Life〉의 저자, Peter Adams 씨를 초대 손님으로 모셨습니다.

남: 초대해 주셔서 감사합니다.

여: 우선 책에 대해서 소개해 주시겠어요?

남: 물론이죠. 이 책은 중년의 아버지들이 십대들처럼 휴대전화나, 디지털 카메라, PMP, MP3 같은 첨단 기기를 즐기는 방법을 가르쳐 줍니다.

여: 선생님이 3년 전까지만 해도 컴퓨터를 켜는 방법조차 모르셨다는 걸 알고 놀랐습니다. 뭐 때문에 바뀌신 거죠?

남: 제 딸 때문이었죠. 그 애가 컴퓨터와 휴대전화로 여러 시간을 놀곤 했죠. 하지만 전 그런 기기들에 대해 전혀 몰라서 우리가 얘기할 거리가 점점 없어졌어요.

여: 그럼 기기들을 어떻게 배우셨나요?

남: 컴퓨터를 사용하는 법을 배우는 것으로 시작했어요. 지역 문화센터의 무료 컴퓨터 강좌에 다녔어요. 제 책의 독자들께 이런 강좌들을 강력히 추천해 드립니다.

어휘

author [ɔ́ːθər] 명 저자 middle-aged [mídléidʒd] 형 중년의 high-tech [háiték] 형 첨단 기술의 device [diváis] 명 기기, 장치 community center 지역 문화센터 recommend [rèkəménd] 동 추천하다 [문제] electronics store 전자제품 가게 publish [pʌ́bliʃ] 동 출판하다

문제 해설

Q1: 〈Enjoy your Life〉에서 다룰 만한 내용은?

① IT 산업에 취직하는 방법

② 십대들과 의사소통하는 방법

③ 중년의 남자들이 즐길 수 있는 취미

④ 디지털 카메라를 사용해서 사진 찍는 법

십대들이 주로 사용하는 첨단 기기들을 즐겨 쓰는 방법에 대한 책이라고 했으므로 디지털 카메라로 사진 찍는 방법이 내용으로 나올 것이다.

Q2: 남자가 최신 기기를 배우기 시작한 이유는?

컴퓨터와 휴대전화을 가지고 노는 딸과 대화하기 위해 컴퓨터를 배우기 시작했다고 했다.

★　★

Critical ★ Thinking   p. 49

1 (1) Against (2) For (3) Against
2 (1) ⓐ (2) ⓑ (3) ⓒ

W1: I'm Christina. Getting the best results by
challenging your body's limits is the true
spirit of sports. But now, wearing a high-tech
swimsuit or running shoes can improve an
athletes' performance. Some athletes are
even breaking records with the help of
technology. This is only the competition of
scientific technology, not of sports.

M: I'm Chris. Technology is used in every area
of our lives. Therefore it doesn't make sense
not to use it in sports. There's no reason
we shouldn't use technology in sports if it
helps athletes get new world records.

W2: I'm Betty. Fair play is the most important
part of sports. That means all players should
have an equal chance. But players who get
help from technology have an advantage
over those who don't. This means that
only players from technically developed
countries will be able to take the lead.

여1: 난 Christina야. 신체의 한계에 도전해서 최고의 결과를 얻
는 게 진정한 스포츠 정신이야. 하지만 지금은 첨단 수영복
이나 운동화를 착용해서 선수들의 성적을 향상시킬 수 있어.
어떤 선수들은 기술의 도움을 받아 기록을 깨고 있기까지 해.
이건 스포츠가 아니라 과학 기술의 경쟁일 뿐이야.

남: 난 Chris야. 기술은 우리 생활의 모든 분야에 사용돼. 그러니
스포츠에서만 사용하지 않는다는 것은 말이 되지 않아. 기술
이 운동 선수가 세계 신기록을 내는 데 도움이 된다면 스포
츠에 기술을 사용하지 말아야 할 이유가 없지.

여2: 난 Betty야. 공정한 경기는 스포츠의 가장 중요한 부분이
야. 그건 모든 선수들이 동등한 기회를 가져야 한다는 거야.
하지만 기술의 도움을 받은 선수들은 그렇지 않은 선수들에
비해 유리한 거잖아. 이것은 기술적으로 발달한 나라의 선수
들만이 선두가 될 수 있다는 걸 의미해.

어휘
result [rizʌ́lt] 몡 결과 challenge [tʃǽlindʒ] 동 도전하다
limit [límit] 몡 한계 spirit [spírit] 몡 정신 swimsuit
[swímsùːt] 몡 수영복 athlete [ǽθliːt] 몡 운동 선수
performance [pərfɔ́ːrməns] 몡 성적, 성과 break a
record 기록을 깨다 scientific [sàiəntífik] 혱 과학의, 과학
적인 make sense 말이 되다. 논리에 맞다 equal [íːkwəl]
혱 동등한, 평등한 advantage [ædvǽntidʒ] 몡 이점, 혜택
technically [téknikəli] 뷔 기술적으로 take the lead 선
두에 서다, 주도권을 잡다 [문제] favor [féivər] 동 ~에게 유
리하다

문제 해설
Q1: 스포츠에서 기술의 도움을 받는 것에 대해 각 인물이 찬성
하는지 반대하는지 ✓표 하시오.
Christina는 스포츠에 기술을 이용하게 되면 과학 기술의 경
쟁에 지나지 않는다며 반대했고, Chris는 선수들이 신기록을
낼 수 있도록 도와준다는 점에서 찬성했으며, Betty는 기술
강국의 선수에게만 유리한 처사라며 반대했다.

Q2: 각 인물의 의견을 고르시오.
ⓐ 스포츠는 자신의 신체만을 이용해 이기는 것이다.
ⓑ 기록을 깨기 위해 스포츠에서 기술이 사용되어야 한다.
ⓒ 기술을 사용하는 것은 선진국 출신의 선수에게 유리하다.
ⓓ 스포츠에서 최고의 성적을 내는 것이 가장 중요한 것은
아니다.
Christina는 신체의 한계에 도전하는 것이 진정한 스포츠 정
신이라고 했고, Chris는 세계 기록을 세우는 데 도움이 된다
면 기술을 사용하는 것이 좋다고 했으며, Betty는 기술이 사
용되면 기술 강국의 선수들만이 유리할 것이라고 했다.

UNIT 08 Animals
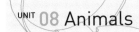

Getting ★ Ready   p. 50

A 1 ⓗ 2 ⓓ 3 ⓔ 4 ⓑ 5 ⓖ 6 ⓐ
B 1 ⓐ 2 ⓔ 3 ⓓ

B 1 여: 돼지가 얼마나 영리한 줄 알아?
남: 응. 개만큼 영리하지.
2 여: 왜 고릴라를 구하기 위해 애써야 하지?
남: 그것들이 멸종 위기에 처해 있어.
3 여: 코끼리들이 더운 여름을 잘 이겨내?
남: 응. 더위에 별로 민감하지 않아.

Listening ★ Start   p. 51

1 (1) ③ (2) ④ 2 ③ 3 ②

1

W: (1) This kind of dog is highly sensitive to
smell and has good sight, so it can easily
find rabbits or foxes which are hiding. When
a hunter shoots a bird, causing it to fall to
the ground, this kind of dog quickly goes
and gets it.

M: (2) This kind of dog is trained to guide
blind people in the streets. It knows how to
deal with many obstacles on the road. At a

corner or crosswalk, this kind of dog stops and waits for an order such as "forward," "stop," "right," or "left."

여: (1) 이 종류의 개는 냄새에 매우 민감하고 시력이 좋아서 숨어 있는 토끼나 여우를 쉽게 찾을 수 있습니다. 사냥꾼이 새를 쏘아 땅에 떨어뜨리면 재빠르게 가서 가져옵니다.

남: (2) 이 종류의 개는 거리에서 시각 장애인들을 안내하도록 훈련을 받습니다. 이 개는 거리의 여러 장애물에 대처하는 방법을 압니다. 모퉁이나 횡단보도에서 이 종류의 개는 멈춰서서 '앞으로', '멈춰', '오른쪽', '왼쪽'과 같은 명령을 기다립니다.

어휘

highly[háili] 뿐 매우 sensitive[sénsətiv] 톙 민감한, 감각이 예민한 sight[sait] 톙 시력 hunter[hántər] 톙 사냥꾼 shoot[ʃuːt] 동 쏘다 (shoot-shot-shot) guide[gaid] 동 안내하다 blind[blaind] 톙 시각 장애의 deal with ~에 대처하다 obstacle[ábstəkl] 톙 장애물 crosswalk [krɔ́(ː)swɔ̀ːk] 톙 횡단보도 order[ɔ́ːrdər] 톙 명령, 지시 forward[fɔ́ːrwərd] 뿐 앞으로

문제 해설

Q: 설명하는 개의 종류를 고르시오.

(1)은 사냥개에 대한 설명이고, (2)는 시각 장애인을 안내하는 맹도견에 관한 설명이다.

50

2

M: Have you heard that animals have a sixth sense?

W: No, what's that?

M: Humans have five senses, which are sight, hearing, taste, touch and smell. But it seems animals have an extra sense.

W: Really?

M: Yes. Do you remember the tsunami that occurred in the Indian Ocean in 2004?

W: Of course. Many people were killed by it.

M: At that time, more than 200 people died in a national park in Sri Lanka. However, none of the animals living there died.

W: How come?

M: Well, they seemed to sense the upcoming natural disaster using a sixth sense, and then moved to higher places.

W: I find that hard to believe.

M: There are many similar cases in which animals seemed to predict earthquakes or volcanoes.

W: How surprising.

남: 동물들에게 제6감이 있다는 말 들어 봤니?

여: 아니, 그게 뭐야?

남: 인간에게는 시각과 청각, 미각, 촉각, 후각이라는 오감이 있잖아. 그런데 동물에게는 추가적인 감각이 있는 것 같아.

여: 정말?

남: 응. 2004년 인도양에서 일어난 쓰나미 기억하지?

여: 물론이지. 수많은 사람들이 그것 때문에 죽었잖아.

남: 그때 스리랑카의 한 국립공원에서 200명 이상의 사람들이 죽었어. 하지만 거기 살던 동물들은 하나도 죽지 않았어.

여: 어떻게 그렇게 되었지?

남: 음, 그들은 제6감을 사용해서 다가오는 자연재해를 감지하고 고지대로 이동했던 것 같아.

여: 믿기가 힘들다.

남: 동물들이 지진이나 화산을 예견했던 것처럼 보이는 비슷한 경우들이 많이 있어.

여: 정말 놀라운걸.

어휘

sixth sense 제6감 touch[tʌtʃ] 톙 촉각 tsunami [tsunáːmi] 톙 쓰나미(지진 해일) occur[əkɔ́ːr] 동 일어나다 Indian Ocean 대서양 sense[sens] 동 알아채다, 느끼다 upcoming[ʌ́pkʌ̀miŋ] 톙 다가오는 natural disaster 자연재해 predict[pridíkt] 동 예견하다 earthquake [ɔ́ːrθkwèik] 톙 지진 volcano[vɑlkéinou] 톙 화산 [문제] enemy[énəmi] 톙 적 approach[əpróutʃ] 톙 접근

문제 해설

Q: 남자에 따르면, 동물의 제6감은 무엇인가?

동물에게는 쓰나미나 지진, 화산과 같은 자연재해를 예견하는 감각이 있다고 했다.

3

M: Animals have various strategies to protect themselves from enemies. Some animals change their body color so as not to be seen. For example, gray tree frogs can turn white, green, or brown, depending on their surroundings. Animals like the blowfish blow up their bodies when they are in danger. It makes them look bigger and stronger, so they can scare away their enemies. Lastly, skunks are well-known for shooting a liquid at their enemies. The liquid smells so terrible that it makes their enemies run away.

남: 동물은 적들로부터 자신을 보호하기 위한 다양한 전략을 가지고 있습니다. 어떤 동물들은 눈에 띄지 않게 하기 위해 몸색깔을 바꿉니다. 예를 들어, 회색 나무 개구리는 주변 환경에 따라 흰색이나 녹색, 갈색으로 변합니다. 팽창어 같은 동물은 위험에 처하면 몸을 부풀립니다. 이는 몸집을 더 크고 강하게 보이도록 해서 적을 겁주어 쫓을 수 있습니다. 마지

막으로 스컹크는 적에게 액체를 쏘는 것으로 유명합니다. 그
액체는 냄새가 너무 지독해서 적들이 도망치도록 만듭니다.

어휘

strategy[strǽtədʒi] 몡 전략   protect[prətékt] 똉 보호하다
gray tree frog 회색 나무 개구리   depending on ~에
따라   surrounding[səráundiŋ] 몡 《~s》 주변, 배경
blowfish[blóufiʃ] 몡 팽창어(복어 등 몸을 부풀리는 물고기)
blow up 부풀리다   scare away 겁주어 쫓아 버리다
skunk[skʌŋk] 몡 스컹크   liquid[líkwid] 몡 액체   [문제]
survival[sərváivəl] 몡 생존을 위한   pretend[priténd] 똉
~인 척 하다   spray[sprei] 똉 뿌리다   smelly[sméli] 휑
고약한 냄새가 나는

문제 해설

Q: 동물의 생존 전략으로 언급된 것이 <u>아닌</u> 것은?

① 몸집을 크게 만들기

② 죽은 척 하기

③ 냄새가 나는 액체를 뿌리기

④ 몸의 색깔을 바꾸기

죽은 척 하는 방법은 언급되지 않았다.

Listening ★ Practice   p. 52

A 1 ①   2 ①   B 1 ③   2 ③
C 1 ②   2 ③   D 1 ②   2 ①

A [1-2]

M: Excuse me. Are you Melrose Brown? I'm
Sam Jackson.

W: Oh, yes. We talked on the phone.

M: Nice to meet you. Well, this is my pet, Betty.
I'll hand her over to you.

W: Wow, she looks much cuter than in the
pictures.

M: She really is a lovely pet. Please take good
care of her.

W: May I ask the reason why you're giving her
away?

M: I'm going abroad to study, and I can't take
her. And everyone in my family is too busy
to take care of her.

W: That's too bad. Is there anything that I
should be particularly careful about?

M: The most important thing is to control the
temperature. A chameleon isn't active if it's
cold or shady.

W: Okay. I'll keep her somewhere sunny.

남: 실례합니다. Melrose Brown 씨이신가요? 전 Sam
Jackson입니다.

여: 아, 네. 통화했었지요.

남: 만나서 반갑습니다. 음, 이쪽은 제 애완동물 Betty입니다. 건
네드릴게요.

여: 와, 사진에서보다 훨씬 더 귀여워요.

남: 정말 사랑스러운 애완동물이죠. 잘 보살펴 주세요.

여: 이 애를 저에게 주시는 이유를 여쭤봐도 될까요?

남: 제가 외국에 공부하러 가서 데리고 갈 수가 없어요. 그리고
제 가족들은 모두 너무 바빠서 돌볼 수가 없어요.

여: 그거 참 안됐네요. 특별히 주의해야 할 일이 있나요?

남: 가장 중요한 것은 온도를 조절하는 것이에요. 카멜레온은 춥
거나 그늘이 지면 활동적이지 않아요.

여: 알겠어요. 햇빛이 드는 곳에다 둘게요.

어휘

hand over 건네주다   give away 남에게 주다   go
abroad 해외에 가다   particularly[pərtíkjulərli] 뜀 특별히
control[kəntróul] 똉 조절하다   temperature
[témpərətʃər] 몡 온도   chameleon[kəmíːliən] 몡 카멜레온
active[ǽktiv] 휑 활동적인   shady[ʃéidi] 휑 그늘이 진
[문제] care for ~을 돌보다   feed[fiːd] 똉 먹이를 주다

문제 해설

Q1: 남자가 더 이상 Betty를 키울 수 없는 이유는?

남자는 외국으로 공부하러 가는데 애완동물을 데리고 갈 수
없다고 했다.

Q2: Betty를 돌볼 때 중요한 것은?

카멜레온인 Betty는 따뜻한 온도에 있어야 하며 그렇지 않으
면 활동을 잘 하지 않는다고 했다.

B [1-2]

W: Jason, let's go to the beach to swim.

M: Didn't you see the headline in today's
newspaper? A boy was attacked by a shark
while surfing.

W: Oh, my god! Is he okay?

M: Fortunately, he didn't get seriously hurt,
though he was bitten on the arm.

W: What a relief.

M: The news said this is the time when sharks
often appear off the coast.

W: We should be careful, then. But is there any
way to avoid a shark attack?

M: The most important thing is not to swim
alone. Also, sharks are most active at night,
so it's better to swim during the day.

W: Okay. Do you know what we should do if
we see a shark?

M: We should stay calm, as sudden movements
may attract its attention.

W: That could be very difficult!

여: Jason, 수영하러 해변에 가자.

남: 오늘 신문의 헤드라인 못 봤어? 한 남자애가 파도타기를 하다가 상어에게 공격을 당했어.

여: 저런! 그 애는 괜찮아?

남: 다행히도, 팔을 물리긴 했어도 심각하게 다치진 않았어.

여: 그거 다행이다.

남: 뉴스에서 지금이 상어가 해변으로 자주 출몰하는 시기라고 했어.

여: 그럼 조심해야겠다. 하지만 상어의 공격을 피하는 방법이 있긴 하니?

남: 가장 중요한 건 혼자 수영하지 않는 거야. 또한, 상어는 밤에 가장 활발하니까 낮에 수영하는 것이 낫지.

여: 알겠어. 상어를 보게 되면 어떻게 해야 하는지 아니?

남: 침착해야 하는데, 갑작스럽게 움직이면 상어의 주의를 끌지도 모르기 때문이야.

여: 그건 아주 어려울 거야!

어휘

headline[hédlàin] 몡 (신문 기사 등의) 큰 표제   attack
[ətǽk] 통 공격하다   shark[ʃɑːrk] 몡 상어   surf[səːrf] 통
파도타기 하다   fortunately[fɔ́ːrtʃənitli] 뷔 다행스럽게도
seriously[sí(ː)əriəsli] 뷔 심각하게   bite[bait] 통 물다 (bite
-bit-bitten)   What a relief. 다행이다.   off the coast
해안 가까이에   calm[kɑːm] 형 침착한   sudden[sʌ́dn] 형
급작스런   attract[ətrǽkt] 통 (주의·흥미를) 끌다
attention[əténʃən] 몡 주의   [문제] survive[sərváiv] 통 살
아남다   remain[riméin] 통 ~인 상태로 머물다

문제 해설

Q1: 남자가 읽은 신문의 헤드라인이었을 것은?

신문 기사는 한 소년이 파도타기를 하던 중 상어를 만났지만 상처만 입고 살아났다는 내용이다.

Q2: 상어의 공격을 피하는 방법이 아닌 것은?

혼자 수영하거나 밤에 수영하는 것을 피하고 상어를 봤을 때 침착하라고 했으나, 짙은 색깔의 수영복을 입으라는 말은 없었다.

C [1-2]

M: I'm considering getting a pet, but I can't decide what kind.

W: Why don't you get a pet pig? I have one, and he's really cute.

M: You're raising a pig in your house? Aren't pigs dirty animals?

W: Not at all. That's a common misunderstanding.

M: But I've seen pigs rolling in mud many times.

W: That's because they can't control their body temperature by themselves. They keep themselves cool by rolling in mud.

M: I see. But I want a smart animal like a dog.

W: Well, you know what? Pigs are just as

smart as dogs.

M: Really? That's unbelievable.

W: Besides, pigs are not greedy about food. They eat just the amount of food that their bodies need.

M: Wow, I'm learning many things about pigs.

남: 애완동물을 키울까 생각 중인데 종류를 결정하지 못하겠어.

여: 애완 돼지를 키우는 게 어때? 나 한 마리 키우는데 아주 귀여워.

남: 집 안에서 돼지를 키운다고? 돼지는 더러운 동물 아니니?

여: 전혀. 그건 흔한 오해야.

남: 하지만 진흙에서 돼지가 뒹구는 거 많이 봤는데.

여: 그건 돼지가 스스로 체온을 조절할 수 없기 때문이야. 그들은 진흙에서 뒹굴면서 몸을 시원하게 만드는 거야.

남: 그렇구나. 하지만 난 개처럼 영리한 동물을 원해.

여: 음, 그거 알아? 돼지는 개만큼이나 영리해.

남: 정말? 믿을 수 없어.

여: 게다가, 돼지는 식탐이 강하지도 않아. 몸이 필요로 하는 양의 음식만 먹어.

남: 와, 돼지에 관해서 많은 걸 배우네.

어휘

common[kάmən] 형 흔한   misunderstanding
[mìsʌndərstǽndiŋ] 몡 오해   roll[roul] 통 뒹굴다   mud
[mʌd] 몡 진흙   by oneself 혼자서   unbelievable
[ʌ̀nbəlíːvəbl] 형 믿을 수 없는   greedy[gríːdi] 형 탐욕스러운
[문제] lower[lóuər] 통 낮추다

문제 해설

Q1: 그들은 주로 무엇에 관해 이야기하고 있나?

돼지가 더럽다거나 식탐이 강하다거나 하는 돼지에 대한 일반적인 오해에 관한 내용이다.

Q2: 돼지가 진흙에서 뒹구는 이유는?

스스로 체온 조절을 할 수 없기 때문에 진흙에서 뒹굴어 몸을 차게 만든다고 했다.

D [1-2]

W: What are you doing? What is that strange costume?

M: This is a gorilla costume that I'll wear for the "Great Gorilla Run" this evening.

W: What's that?

M: It's an event to raise money to save gorillas. They are in danger of extinction now.

W: What do you do in the event?

M: We're supposed to walk or run 7 km, dressed up like a gorilla.

W: That sounds very funny. How did you find out about such a wonderful event?

M: When I went to Africa last year, I joined a

tour to watch gorillas. During the tour, I learned that their numbers are decreasing fast.

W: So you wanted to do something for them.

M: Right. And I found out about this event online.

W: Do you mind if I go to watch you?

M: Of course not.

W: Great. I'll take pictures.

여: 뭐 하니? 그 이상한 의상은 뭐야?

남: 이건 오늘 저녁에 있을 'Great Gorilla Run'에서 입을 고릴라 의상이야.

여: 그게 뭔데?

남: 고릴라를 구하기 위한 돈을 모금하는 행사야. 지금 멸종 위기에 있거든.

여: 그 행사에서 넌 뭘 하는데?

남: 우린 고릴라처럼 옷을 입고 7킬로미터를 걷거나 달릴거야.

여: 아주 재미있겠는걸. 그런 멋진 행사는 어떻게 찾았니?

남: 작년에 아프리카에 갔을 때 고릴라를 관람하는 투어에 참가했어. 투어 중에 고릴라의 수가 빠르게 감소하고 있다는 걸 알게 됐지.

여: 그래서 그들을 위해 뭔가 하고 싶었구나.

남: 맞아. 그리고 온라인에서 이 이벤트를 발견했지.

여: 너 보러 가도 괜찮겠니?

남: 물론 괜찮지.

여: 좋아. 사진을 찍어야지.

어휘

costume[kάstjuːm] 몡 의상 gorilla[gərílə] 몡 고릴라 raise money 모금하다 save[seiv] 동 구하다 extinction[ikstíŋkʃən] 몡 멸종 be supposed to-v ~하기로 되어 있다 dress up ~로 분장하다, ~의 복장을 하다 decrease[dikríːs] 동 감소하다 Do you mind if ~? ~해도 괜찮겠니? [문제] campaign[kæmpéin] 몡 캠페인 journal[dʒə́ːrnəl] 몡 신문, 잡지 documentary[dὰkjuméntəri] 몡 다큐멘터리

문제 해설

Q1: 오늘 저녁에 남자가 할 일은?

남자는 고릴라 의상을 입고 걷거나 달리기를 하는 행사에 참여할 것이라고 했다.

Q2: 남자가 고릴라가 위험에 처해 있다는 것을 알게 된 때는?

남자는 작년 아프리카에서 고릴라를 관람하는 투어에 참가해서 그 사실을 알게 되었다.

Listening ★ Challenge   p. 54

A 1 (1) ⓑ (2) ⓐ (3) ⓒ 2 ②
B 1 ③ 2 (1) T (2) T (3) F

A [1-2]

W: Hello, viewers. This is Cindy Simpson at California Zoo. Today, I'll explain how animals endure the hot summer weather. Hello.

M: Hello. I'm Samuel Wilford.

W: What are you doing?

M: I'm preparing food for polar bears. It's frozen fruit and fish.

W: It looks like a big ice cube. I'm sure they like it.

M: Sure. They spend time eating these delicious ice cubes in the pool.

W: I see. How do other animals beat the heat?

M: Rhinoceros don't feel the summer heat when somebody brushes their skin. So we brush them for about 10 minutes every day.

W: That's very interesting.

M: In the case of elephants, they are not very sensitive to heat, because they come from hot countries.

W: That makes sense.

M: However, when it's very hot during the day, we spray cold water on them.

W: That's great. Thanks to your efforts, animals can keep cool.

53

여: 안녕하세요, 시청자 여러분. California Zoo에 나와 있는 Cindy Simpson입니다. 오늘은 동물들이 어떻게 더운 여름 날씨를 견디는지 설명해 드리겠습니다. 안녕하세요.

남: 안녕하세요. 전 Samuel Wilford입니다.

여: 뭐 하시던 중이었나요?

남: 북극곰에게 줄 먹이를 준비하고 있어요. 얼린 과일과 생선입니다.

여: 커다란 각얼음처럼 보이네요. 분명 북극곰들이 좋아할 것 같군요.

남: 물론이죠. 물 웅덩이 안에서 이 맛있는 각얼음을 먹으면서 시간을 보내지요.

여: 그렇군요. 다른 동물들은 더위를 어떻게 이겨내죠?

남: 코뿔소는 피부를 솔질해 주면 여름 더위를 느끼지 않아요. 그래서 저희가 매일 10분 정도씩 솔질해 주죠.

여: 그거 아주 흥미로운데요.

남: 코끼리의 경우에는 더운 나라에서 왔으니까 더위에 그다지 민감하지 않아요.

여: 말이 되네요.

남: 하지만, 낮에 아주 더울 때는 차가운 물을 뿌려 줍니다.

여: 좋군요. 선생님의 노력 덕분으로 동물들이 시원하게 지낼 수 있네요.

어휘

viewer[vjúːər] 명 시청자　endure[indʒúər] 동 견디다, 참
다　polar bear 북극곰　frozen[fróuzən] 형 냉동된, 얼린
cube[kjuːb] 명 육면체, 육면체 모양의 것　beat[biːt] 명 이
기다　heat[hiːt] 명 열, 더위　rhinoceros[rainásərəs] 명
코뿔소, 무소 (복수 rhinoceros)　brush[brʌʃ] 동 솔질하다
make sense 이해가 되다, 이치에 맞다　effort[éfərt] 명
노력　[문제] zookeeper[zúːkìːpər] 명 동물원 관리인, 사육사

문제 해설

Q1: 각 동물과 그들이 더운 날씨에 대처하는 방법을 연결하시오.
북극곰은 물에서 얼린 과일과 생선을 먹으면서 더위를 피하
게 해 주고, 코뿔소는 피부를 솔질해 주며 코끼리는 찬물로
씻겨준다.

Q2: 화자 간의 관계는?
리포터와 동물원 사육사가 동물들이 더위를 피하는 방법에
대해 나누는 대화 내용이다.

B [1-2]

M: May I help you?

W: I found this dog near the Union Square
Theater. It seems to be abandoned.

M: Does it have a name tag?

W: No, it doesn't.

M: Let me see. It looks like a female dog. What
happened to its legs?

W: She was not walking well when I found her.
It seems like she broke her leg.

M: Okay. This Dog Center will provide a shelter
for her for a month.

W: What will happen after a month?

M: If we can't find her owner and she is not
adopted during the period, we'll have her
put to sleep.

W: Are you saying she'll be killed? No way!

M: We can't help it. Our center can only hold
100 dogs. But more dogs than that are
brought in.

W: Oh, no. Well, I'll try to find a person who
can adopt her. Is there an adoption fee?

M: No, it's free. You can show people the dog's
picture on our website.

W: Great.

남: 뭘 도와드릴까요?

여: Union Square Theater 근처에서 이 개를 발견했어요. 버
려진 것 같아요.

남: 이름표가 있나요?

여: 아니요, 없어요.

남: 어디 봅시다. 암컷 강아지인 것 같군요. 다리는 어떻게 된 건

가요?

여: 제가 발견했을 때 제대로 걷지 못하고 있었어요. 다리가 부
러진 것 같아요.

남: 알겠어요. 저희 Dog Center는 이 개에게 한 달 동안 지낼
곳을 제공할 거예요.

여: 한 달 후엔 어떻게 되는데요?

남: 그 기간에 주인을 찾지 못하고 입양되지 않으면 안락사를 시
켜야 해요.

여: 죽게 될 거란 말인가요? 안 돼요!

남: 어쩔 수 없답니다. 저희 센터는 100마리의 개만 수용할 수
있어요. 그런데 그보다 많은 수의 개들이 들어오죠.

여: 아, 저런. 음, 입양할 사람을 찾도록 해 볼게요. 입양료가 있
나요?

남: 아니요, 무료입니다. 저희 웹사이트에서 개의 사진을 사람들
에게 보여주실 수 있어요.

여: 좋아요.

어휘

abandon[əbǽndən] 동 버리다　name tag 이름표
female[fíːmeil] 형 암컷의　shelter[ʃéltər] 명 임시 수용소,
피난처　adopt[ədápt] 동 입양하다　put to sleep 안락사
시키다　adoption[ədápʃən] 명 입양　fee[fiː] 명 요금
[문제] male[meil] 형 수컷

문제 해설

Q1: 틀린 정보를 고르시오.
남자가 개는 암컷인 것 같다고 했다.

Q2: Dog Center에 관해 사실이면 T, 사실이 아니면 F를 쓰시오.
(1) 버려진 개들을 한 달 동안 보호해 준다.
(2) 동시에 100마리의 개를 수용할 수 있다.
(3) 개를 싼 값에 판매한다.
Dog Center는 개를 판매하지는 않고 주인을 찾아주거나 입
양을 시키는 일을 하고 있다.

Critical ★ Thinking　p. 55

1 (1) For　(2) Against　(3) Against
2 (1) ⓑ　(2) ⓐ　(3) ⓒ

M1: I'm Mike. Animal testing is a necessary
process when making new medicines. We
can't test new drugs on people when we're
not sure about their possible side effects.
Many drugs have been developed after
experiments on animals, and these drugs
have saved millions of people from diseases.

W: I'm Mary. Animals are living things just like
humans. They can feel pain and have
feelings. Who can decide that animals are
less precious than humans? We have to stop
cruel experiments using living creatures.

M2: I'm Bill. No animal species has the exact same DNA as humans. Even if a new drug doesn't harm an animal, this doesn't mean that it is safe for humans. That means that animals are killed for nothing. So we have to develop another way to test new drugs.

남1: 난 Mike야. 동물 실험은 신약을 만들 때 꼭 필요한 과정이야. 어떤 부작용이 있을지 확신할 수 없는 상황에서는 사람에게 신약을 실험해 볼 수 없어. 많은 약들이 동물 실험을 한 후에 개발되어 수백만 명의 사람들을 질병으로부터 구해 왔어.

여: 난 Mary야. 동물들은 인간과 똑같은 생명체야. 고통을 느낄 수 있고 감정이 있어. 동물이 인간보다 덜 귀하다고 누가 결정할 수 있지? 생명체를 이용하는 잔인한 실험을 그만두어야 해.

남2: 난 Bill이야. 어떤 동물 종도 인간과 정확히 같은 DNA를 가지고 있지 않아. 신약이 동물에 아무런 해를 미치지 않는다고 하더라도 그것이 인간에게 안전하다는 걸 뜻하지는 않아. 그러니까 동물은 아무 의미 없이 죽게 되는 거지. 그러니 신약을 실험하는 다른 방법을 개발해야 해.

어휘

animal testing 동물 실험 necessary[nésəsèri] 혱 필요한 process[práses] 몡 과정 medicine[médəsin] 몡 약 test[test] 통 실험하다 drug[drʌg] 몡 약 possible[pásəbl] 혱 가능한, 있을 수 있는 side effect 부작용 develop[divéləp] 통 개발하다 experiment[ikspérəmənt] 몡 실험 disease[dizíːz] 몡 질병 pain[pein] 몡 고통 precious[préʃəs] 혱 귀한, 소중한 cruel[krúː(ə)l] 혱 잔인한 creature[kríːtʃər] 몡 생물, 피조물 species[spíːʃiːz] 몡 (생물) 종 exact[igzǽkt] 혱 정확한 [문제] effective[iféktiv] 혱 효과적인

문제 해설

Q1: 각 인물이 동물 실험에 찬성하는지 반대하는지 ✓표 하시오.
Mike는 사람 대신 동물에 실험을 해서 신약의 안전성을 확인해야 한다고 생각하므로 찬성하고, Mary는 동물 또한 인간과 같은 소중한 생명체이므로 실험을 그만두어야 한다고 했고, Bill은 인간과 DNA가 다른 동물에 실험을 하는 것이 무의미하므로 다른 방법을 찾아야 한다고 반대하고 있다.

Q2: 각 인물과 해당 의견을 연결하시오.
ⓐ 동물은 인간과 똑같이 귀하다.
ⓑ 동물 실험을 거친 약이 많은 사람을 구했다.
ⓒ 동물 실험은 인간과 동물이 다른 DNA를 가지고 있으므로 효과적이지 않다.
Mike는 동물 실험을 통해 개발된 약이 많은 사람의 질병을 고쳤다고 생각하고, Mary는 인간과 동물은 동등하게 귀하다고 생각하며, Bill은 인간과 다른 DNA를 가진 동물에게 실험하는 것이 효과가 없다고 생각한다.

UNIT 09 Psychology

Getting ★ Ready p. 56

A 1 ⓐ 2 ⓔ 3 ⓑ 4 ⓗ 5 ⓕ 6 ⓓ
B 1 ⓕ 2 ⓑ 3 ⓔ

B 1 남: 왜 많이 먹지 않니?
여: <u>남자 친구와 헤어진 후로 입맛을 잃었어.</u>

2 남: 네 방을 왜 그 색깔로 칠했니?
여: <u>그게 사람들을 차분하게 해 주는 색이거든.</u>

3 남: 이 사진 속 우리 부모님을 봐봐. 두 분이 닮지 않으셨니?
여: 응, 그러네. <u>결혼한 부부는 서로 닮는 경향이 있지.</u>

Listening ★ Start p. 57

1 ③ 2 (1) ⓑ (2) ⓐ (3) ⓓ 3 ②

1

W: How was your blind date yesterday?
M: It didn't go well. She said I wasn't her type.
W: What did you wear on the date?
M: The yellow T-shirt and black pants that I often wear. Is something wrong?
W: You should've dressed carefully. You look far from stylish when you wear those clothes.
M: You mean the girl didn't like me because I wasn't well-dressed?
W: I'm saying that clothes are important for making a good first impression. She didn't know about you, so she might have judged you on a first impression.
M: I see.
W: And once a first impression is made, it's difficult to change it.
M: Okay. I'll pay more attention to my clothes from now on.

여: 어제 소개팅은 어땠니?
남: 잘 안 되었어. 그 여자애가 내가 자기 취향이 아니라고 하더라.
여: 데이트할 때 뭘 입었는데?
남: 내가 자주 입는 노란 티셔츠랑 검은 바지. 뭐 잘못된 거 있니?
여: 주의해서 입었어야지. 너 그 옷을 입으면 멋져 보이는 거랑 거리가 멀어.
남: 내가 옷을 잘 입지 못해서 그 여자애가 날 좋아하지 않았단 말이니?

여: 내 말은 옷이 좋은 첫인상을 주는 데 중요하단 거야. 그 여자
애는 너에 대해 모르니까 첫인상으로 널 판단했을지도 모르지.

남: 그렇구나.

여: 그리고 일단 첫인상이 형성되면 바꾸기 힘들어.

남: 알았어. 지금부터 옷에 더 많이 신경을 쓸게.

어휘

blind date 소개팅 type[taip] 명 취향 far from 조금도
~ 않다 stylish[stáiliʃ] 형 맵시 있는, 멋진 well-dressed
[wéldrést] 형 옷을 잘 입은 impression[impréʃən] 명 인상,
느낌 judge[ʤʌʤ] 동 판단하다 pay attention to ~에
주의하다 [문제] appearance[əpí(:)ərəns] 명 외모

문제 해설

Q: 여자의 요점은?

처음 만나는 사람에게 좋은 첫인상을 주려면 옷차림도 잘 갖
추어야 한다는 조언을 하고 있다.

2

M: When you buy wallpaper for your house,
it's important to choose the right color. For
example, green can help people concentrate.
Students can focus on their studying better
in a green room. Blue is used to reduce
stress and appetite. On the other hand,
orange improves appetite. It would be the
best color to use in a kitchen. Pink is the color
that makes people feel calm. After a prison
in the US painted its walls pink, there was
less violence.

남: 집의 벽지를 살 때 적절한 색을 고르는 것이 중요합니다. 예
를 들어, 녹색은 집중하는 데 도움이 됩니다. 학생은 녹색 방
에서 공부에 더 잘 집중할 수 있습니다. 파란색은 스트레스
나 식욕을 줄이는 데 사용됩니다. 반면에 오렌지색은 식욕을
증진시킵니다. 부엌에 쓰기 가장 좋은 색입니다. 분홍색은
사람을 차분하게 해 주는 색입니다. 미국의 한 감옥에서 벽
을 분홍색으로 칠한 후 폭력이 줄었습니다.

어휘

wallpaper[wɔ́ːlpèipər] 명 벽지 concentrate
[kánsəntrèit] 동 집중하다 reduce[ridjúːs] 동 줄이다
appetite[金pətàit] 명 식욕 on the other hand 다른 한
편, 반면에 improve[imprúːv] 동 증진하다 prison
[prízən] 명 감옥 violence[váiələns] 명 폭력 [문제]
uneasy[ʌníːzi] 형 불안한, 걱정되는 calm down 진정하다

문제 해설

Q: 각 인물에게 알맞은 벽지를 고르시오.

식욕을 억제해주는 색은 파란색이고, 집중을 도와주는 색은
녹색이며, 마음을 차분하게 하는 색은 분홍색이다.

3

W: Who are the people in this picture? Are they
your parents?

M: Yes. This is when my family went to France.

W: Wow, your mother and father look so much
alike. It might be true that married couples
tend to resemble each other.

M: That's been scientifically proven. I've read
an article about it.

W: Really? Why does it happen?

M: Married couples go through many things
together, both good and bad, don't they?

W: Of course.

M: Because they share the same experiences,
they begin to have similar facial expressions.
This makes them have similar wrinkles on
their faces.

W: I see.

M: Also, people tend to like others who look
like themselves. Maybe that's another
reason.

여: 이 사진 속 사람들은 누구야? 너희 부모님이니?

남: 응. 우리 가족이 프랑스에 갔을 때야.

여: 와, 너희 어머니와 아버지께서는 정말 많이 닮으셨다. 결혼
한 부부는 서로 닮는 경향이 있다는 게 사실일지도 모르겠어.

남: 그거 과학적으로 증명되었어. 그것에 관한 기사를 읽었어.

여: 정말? 왜 그런 일이 생긴대?

남: 결혼한 부부는 좋은 일이건 나쁜 일이건 많은 일들을 함께
겪어나가잖아, 그렇지 않니?

여: 물론이지.

남: 같은 경험을 공유하기 때문에 비슷한 표정을 갖기 시작하는
거야. 그게 얼굴에 비슷한 주름을 만들게 되지.

여: 알겠어.

남: 또, 사람은 자신과 닮은 사람을 좋아하는 경향이 있어. 아마
도 그게 또 하나의 이유일 거야.

어휘

look alike 닮아 보이다, 같아 보이다 tend to-v ~하는 경
향이 있다 resemble[rizémbl] 동 닮다 scientifically
[sàiəntífikəli] 부 과학적으로 prove[pruːv] 동 입증하다, 증
명하다 (prove-proved-proven) go through 겪다, 경험
하다 share[ʃɛər] 동 공유하다 facial[féiʃəl] 형 얼굴의
wrinkle[ríŋkl] 명 주름

문제 해설

Q: 그들은 주로 무엇에 대해 이야기하고 있나?

결혼한 부부가 닮아가는 이유에 대한 내용의 대화이다.

Listening ★ Practice p. 58

A 1 ② 2 ② B 1 ④ 2 ④
C 1 ④ 2 ①, ③ D 1 ③ 2 ①

A [1-2]

M: Ms. Smith, have you noticed that Jeff is doing better these days?
W: Oh, yes. He was a troublemaker, but he changed a lot. What happened to him?
M: Well, I changed the way I reacted to his bad behavior.
W: Tell me more.
M: I used to punish him in class when he did something wrong. But it didn't help.
W: You're right. I had the same experience.
M: So I decided to change my approach. I tried to show a lot of interest in him. And I praised him whenever he did something good.
W: So did that work?
M: At first, he seemed embarrassed. But soon he started making an effort to be praised.
W: That's amazing. I'll try that with my class, too.

남: Smith 선생님, Jeff가 요즘 나아지고 있는 거 눈치채셨나요?
여: 아, 네. 그 애가 문제아였는데 많이 바뀌었어요. 그 애에게 무슨 일이 있었죠?
남: 음, 제가 그 애의 나쁜 행동에 대처하는 방식을 바꿨어요.
여: 더 말씀해 주세요.
남: 그 애가 잘못을 하면 교실에서 벌을 주곤 했거든요. 하지만 그게 도움이 안 되더군요.
여: 맞아요. 저도 같은 경험을 했어요.
남: 그래서 접근 방식을 바꾸기로 결정했죠. 그 애에게 많은 관심을 보여주려고 했어요. 그리고 좋은 일을 했을 때마다 칭찬했죠.
여: 그래서 그게 효과가 있었어요?
남: 그 애가 처음엔 당황하는 것 같더군요. 하지만 곧 칭찬을 받으려고 노력하기 시작했어요.
여: 그거 놀랍네요. 우리 반에서도 해 봐야겠어요.

어휘
notice[nóutis] [동] 알아차리다 troublemaker[trʌ́blmèikər] [명] 문제아, 말썽꾸러기 react[riǽkt] [동] 대응하다, 반응하다 behavior[bihéivjər] [명] 행동 punish[pʌ́niʃ] [동] 벌하다 approach[əpróutʃ] [명] 접근법 praise[preiz] [동] 칭찬하다; [명] 칭찬 embarrassed[imbǽrəst] [형] 당황한 make an effort 노력하다 [문제] attitude[ǽtitjùːd] [명] 태도 concern[kənsə́ːrn] [명] 관심 reward[riwɔ́ːrd] [명] 보상 proper[prápər] [형] 적절한 principal[prínsəpəl] [명] 교장

문제 해설
Q1: Jeff의 태도를 바꾸어 놓은 것은?
남자가 Jeff에게 많은 관심을 보이고 칭찬을 해 준 후로 Jeff가 바뀌게 되었다고 했다.

Q2: 화자 간의 관계는?
Jeff의 수업을 담당하고 있는 교사들이 Jeff가 달라진 이유를 묻고 답하는 대화이다.

B [1-2]

M: One day in 1964, a woman was killed on a street in New York. There were about 30 people at the crime scene, but nobody helped her. Why did it happen? When people decide to help someone, they consider whether there are other people around or not. If there are other people around them, they might think someone else can do something instead of them. However, if there's nobody else around, people tend to feel more responsible and try to help. Now what should you do to get help when you face a dangerous situation? You should pick one specific person to ask for help. For example, you can shout "You in the blue T-shirt! Please help me!"

남: 1964년의 어느 날, 뉴욕에서 한 여성이 길에서 살해당했습니다. 범죄 현장에 약 30명의 사람이 있었지만 아무도 그녀를 도와주지 않았습니다. 왜 그런 일이 생겼을까요? 사람들은 누군가를 돕기로 결정할 때 주변에 다른 사람들이 있는지 없는지를 고려합니다. 다른 사람들이 주변에 있으면 자기 대신 다른 누군가가 도울 수 있다고 생각할 수도 있습니다. 그러나 주변에 아무도 없으면 책임감을 더 많이 느끼고 도움을 주려는 경향이 있습니다. 그럼 위험한 상황을 맞을 때 도움을 구하기 위해서 무엇을 해야 할까요? 도움을 부탁할 특정한 사람을 지정해야 합니다. 예를 들어, "청색 티셔츠 입은 분! 도와주세요!"라고 외치면 됩니다.

어휘
crime[kraim] [명] 범죄 scene[siːn] [명] 장면; *현장 instead of ~의 대신에 responsible[rispánsəbl] [형] 책임이 있는 face[feis] [동] 직면하다 situation[sìtʃuéiʃən] [명] 상황 specific[spisífik] [형] 특정한 shout[ʃaut] [동] 외치다 [문제] be scared of ~을 두려워하다 urgent[ə́ːrdʒənt] [형] 긴급한 loudly[láudli] [부] 크게, 시끄럽게 call for 청하다, 요구하다 tear[tiər] [명] 눈물

문제 해설
Q1: 사람들이 여자를 도와주지 않은 이유는?
① 무엇을 해야 할지 몰랐다.
② 살인자를 두려워했다.

③ 급박한 상황이라고 생각하지 않았다.

④ 다른 사람이 그녀를 도와줄 거라 생각했다.

약 30명의 사람들이 있었지만 서로 누군가가 나설 거라고 생각해서 아무도 돕지 않았다고 했다.

Q2: 곤경에 빠진 사람이 다른 사람들에게서 도움을 얻기 위한 최선의 방법은?

특정한 사람을 선택해서 도와달라고 부탁하면 도움을 받기가 쉽다고 했다.

C [1-2]

W: Sellers use many different strategies to sell their products. One of the most common strategies is having prices end with 99 cents. Most people feel that a $9.99 T-shirt is much cheaper than a $10 T-shirt, even though it's only a one cent difference. Another common strategy is using fake prices. Suppose there is a $70 bag. Sellers put a fake price tag on it that says it's $100, not $70. Then, they tell customers it's on sale at 30% off. Customers pay $70 for the bag, which is its real price. However, because they think it used to cost $100, they feel that they have found a bargain.

여: 판매자는 자신의 상품을 팔기 위해 여러 다른 전략들을 사용합니다. 가장 흔한 전략 중 하나는 가격의 끝자리를 99센트로 하는 것입니다. 대부분의 사람들은 단 1센트 차이임에도 불구하고, 10달러짜리 티셔츠보다 9.99달러짜리 티셔츠가 훨씬 싸다고 느낍니다. 또 다른 흔한 전략은 가짜 가격을 사용하는 것입니다. 70달러짜리 가방이 있다고 가정해 봅니다. 판매자는 거기에 70달러가 아닌 100달러라고 써 있는 가짜 가격표를 붙입니다. 그리고 고객들에게 그 가방이 30% 세일 중이라고 말합니다. 고객들은 가방의 실제 가격인 70달러를 냅니다. 하지만 그것이 100달러였다고 생각하기 때문에 물건을 싸게 샀다고 생각합니다.

어휘

seller[sélər] 몡 판매자   strategy[strǽtədʒi] 몡 전략
product[prάdəkt] 몡 상품   fake[feik] 몡 가짜의
suppose[səpóuz] 동 가정하다   bargain[bάːrgən] 몡 싸게 산 물건, 특가품

문제 해설

Q1: 여자는 주로 무엇에 대해 이야기하고 있나?

① 물건을 싸게 사는 방법

② 가짜 가격표를 사용하는 이유

③ 정말 싸게 물건을 구입하는 것의 어려움

④ 고객을 끌기 위한 가격 전략

고객을 유인하기 위한 판매자들의 가격 전략에 대한 내용이다.

Q2: 설명된 두 가지 전략을 고르시오.

가격의 끝을 99센트로 하는 전략과 정가를 조작하여 세일가인 것처럼 만드는 전략이 설명되었다.

D [1-2]

M: How's your preparation for the performance going? It's next Thursday night, right?

W: Yes. But there is a problem. I have to give a presentation in science class next Friday.

M: That's too bad. You have to take care of two things at the same time.

W: Right. So I'm considering asking Peter to switch presentation times with me.

M: That's a good idea.

W: But I'm afraid he might say no.

M: I'll let you know how you should do it. Before asking him a favor, do something nice first.

W: I don't get it.

M: For example, buy him a Coke or help him with his homework. It will make him feel like he owes you something.

W: I see. Then he is less likely to refuse my request for a favor, because he thinks he owes me one.

M: Exactly!

남: 공연 준비는 잘 되고 있니? 다음 주 목요일 밤이지, 그렇지?

여: 응. 그런데 문제가 있어. 다음 주 금요일 과학 시간에 발표를 해야 해.

남: 그거 안됐구나. 동시에 두 가지 일을 처리해야 하네.

여: 그러게 말이야. 그래서 Peter에게 나랑 발표 시간을 바꿔달라고 부탁할까 생각 중이야.

남: 그거 좋은 생각이다.

여: 하지만 그 애가 안 된다고 할까 봐 걱정이야.

남: 어떻게 해야 할지 내가 알려 줄게. 그에게 부탁을 하기 전에 좋은 일을 먼저 해 줘.

여: 무슨 말인지 모르겠어.

남: 예를 들어, 콜라를 사주거나 숙제를 도와줘. 그러면 그 애가 너에게 빚을 졌다고 느끼게 될 거야.

여: 알겠어. 그럼 나에게 빚을 졌다고 생각하니까 내가 부탁하는 요청을 거절할 확률이 더 적다는 거구나.

남: 바로 그거야!

어휘

preparation[prèpəréiʃən] 몡 준비   presentation
[prìːzəntéiʃən] 몡 발표   at the same time 동시에
switch[switʃ] 동 바꾸다, 교환하다   favor[féivər] 몡 호의, 도움   owe[ou] 동 빚지다   be likely to-v ~할 것 같다
refuse[rifjúːz] 동 거절하다   request[rikwést] 몡 요청
exactly[igzǽktli] 됨 정확하게

문제 해설

Q1: 여자가 Peter에게 부탁할 일은?

과학 발표 시간을 Peter와 바꾸고 싶어 부탁하겠다고 했다.

Q2: 남자의 충고를 따르고 있는 사람은?

① Amy에게 부탁을 하기 전에 저녁을 사 줄 거야.

② 부탁을 하는 동안 계속 미소를 지을 거야.

③ 다른 친구들과 함께 있을 때 John에게 부탁할 거야.

부탁을 하기 전에 좋은 일을 해주면 빚을 졌다는 느낌이 들어서 부탁을 거절하지 않게 된다고 했으므로 저녁을 사 준 다음 부탁을 하는 경우가 이에 해당한다.

Listening ★ Challenge **p. 60**

A 1 (1) T (2) F (3) T 2 ③ B 1 ④ 2 ②, ③

A [1-2]

M: Susan, you look tired today. What's the matter?

W: I stayed up all night reading a very interesting book.

M: What was it about?

W: It was a book about Münchausen syndrome.

M: What's that? I've never heard about it.

W: It's a kind of mental illness. People pretend to have an illness although they're actually fine.

M: That sounds really strange.

W: The patients even hurt themselves to make others believe they're sick.

M: Really? Why do people act like that?

W: It's because they want love and attention. You know, we pay more attention to sick people.

M: I see. By the way, why is it called Münchausen syndrome?

W: It's named after a German who lived in the 18th century.

M: Is he the one who discovered the illness?

W: No. He was a great liar. Because lying is the main symptom of the syndrome, it was given his name.

남: Susan, 너 오늘 피곤해 보인다. 무슨 일이야?

여: 아주 재미있는 책을 읽느라 밤을 새웠거든.

남: 뭐에 대한 거였는데?

여: 뮌하우젠 신드롬에 대한 책이었어.

남: 그게 뭐니? 들어본 적이 없는데.

여: 정신병의 일종이야. 실제로 몸이 멀쩡한데도 질병이 있는 척하는 거야.

남: 아주 이상하네.

여: 그 환자들은 남들이 자신이 아프다는 것을 믿게 하려고 자해를 하기까지 하지.

남: 정말? 왜 그런 행동을 하는 거야?

여: 그들이 사랑과 관심을 원하기 때문이야. 너도 알다시피, 아픈 사람에게 더 많은 관심을 갖게 되잖아.

남: 그렇구나. 그런데 왜 뮌하우젠 신드롬이라고 불리는 거지?

여: 18세기에 살았던 독일인의 이름을 따서 지은 거야.

남: 그 질병을 발견한 사람이니?

여: 아니. 그는 엄청난 거짓말쟁이였어. 거짓말이 그 증후군의 주요 증상이라서 그의 이름으로 지어진 거야.

어휘

syndrome [síndroum] 몡 증후군 mental [méntəl] 혱 정신의, 심적인 illness [ílnis] 몡 병 pretend [priténd] 동 ~인 체하다 patient [péiʃənt] 몡 환자 attention [əténʃən] 몡 관심 German [dʒə́ːrmən] 몡 독일 사람 discover [diskʌ́vər] 동 발견하다 liar [láiər] 몡 거짓말쟁이 lie [lai] 동 거짓말하다 symptom [símptəm] 몡 증상 [문제] suffer from 앓다

문제 해설

Q1: 뮌하우젠 신드롬을 앓는 사람에 관해 사실이면 T, 사실이 아니면 F를 쓰시오.

(1) 아픈 체한다.

(2) 상처를 입을까 봐 두려워한다.

(3) 다른 사람의 관심을 바라기 때문에 증후군이 생긴다.

아픈 것처럼 가장하고, 아프게 보이려고 자해를 하기도 하는 이 증후군은 다른 사람의 관심을 받고 싶어하는 정신병이라고 했다.

Q2: 뮌하우젠 신드롬은 무엇을 따라 이름이 지어졌나?

거짓말을 하는 것이 이 신드롬의 주요 증상이기 때문에 18세기에 거짓말로 유명했던 사람의 이름에서 유래했다.

B [1-2]

W: I visited a fortune teller today. I was so surprised because she knew so many things about me.

M: What did she say?

W: She said I'm worried about something now. And I've had a hard time because of love.

M: Um... what else?

W: She also said I sometimes feel lonely. Isn't that amazing?

M: Do you really believe her?

W: Why not? What she said about me was completely true.

M: She only talked about general things. Who doesn't worry about something? Who doesn't feel lonely from time to time?

W: Oh... that makes sense.

M: I read a book about fortune tellers' tricks. It said that when people are told a fact that everybody shares, they often believe it's their own story.

W: Just like me.

M: That's right. Also, if people are told good things about them, they tend to trust them.

W: I didn't know that. I won't waste my time and money again.

여: 오늘 점쟁이에게 갔었어. 그 여자가 나에 대해 너무나 많은 걸 알고 있어서 아주 놀라웠어.

남: 그 여자가 뭐라고 했는데?

여: 내가 지금 뭔가를 걱정하고 있다고 했어. 그리고 사랑 때문에 힘든 시간을 보낸 적이 있었대.

남: 음… 또 다른 건?

여: 내가 종종 외로움을 느낀다고 했어. 놀랍지 않니?

남: 너 정말 그 여자 말을 믿니?

여: 왜 아니겠니? 나에 대해 한 얘기가 완벽하게 맞잖아.

남: 그 여자는 일반적인 것들만 말했을 뿐이야. 뭔가를 걱정하지 않는 사람이 있니? 때로로 외롭다고 느끼지 않는 사람이 있어?

여: 아… 말이 되네.

남: 점쟁이들의 속임수에 대한 책을 읽었어. 누구나 공유하는 사실을 얘기하면 사람들은 자신만의 얘기라고 믿는다고 거기 써 있더라.

여: 꼭 나처럼.

남: 맞아. 또, 자신에 대해 좋은 말을 들으면 그 말을 신뢰하는 경향이 있대.

여: 그건 몰랐어. 다신 시간과 돈을 낭비하지 않을 거야.

어휘

fortune teller 점쟁이, 점술가 lonely[lóunli] 휑 외로운 completely[kəmplíːtli] 뿐 완전히 general[dʒénərəl] 휑 일반적인 from time to time 때때로 make sense 일리가 있다, 말이 되다 trick[trik] 똉 속임수 trust[trʌst] 동 믿다, 신뢰하다 waste[weist] 동 낭비하다 [문제] origin[ɔ́(ː)rədʒin] 똉 기원 form[fɔːrm] 똉 형태 term[təːrm] 똉 용어

문제 해설

Q1: 남자가 읽었을 책은?

점쟁이들의 속임수에 관한 책이라고 했으므로 〈점술의 숨겨진 비밀〉이라는 책 제목이 가장 적절하다.

Q2: 점쟁이들이 쓰는 두 가지 속임수는?

점쟁이들은 일반적인 얘기를 하여 듣는 사람으로 하여금 그것을 자신만의 얘기로 받아들이게 하는 수법을 쓰고, 긍정적인 말을 들으면 믿고 싶어지는 심리를 이용한다고 했다.

1 ① 2 ①, ②

M: Why have you stopped eating? Have some more.

W: I lost my appetite after I broke up with Mark. I want to forget him and move on, but it's difficult.

M: That's why you look so depressed. Cheer up. How about eating some chocolate?

W: No, I don't want any.

M: Hey, just try it. Chocolate can make us feel better. Research has shown that eating chocolate for a couple of months is good for overcoming depression.

W: Sorry, but I don't feel like eating anything.

M: Then let's go jogging or bike riding. It's also proven that working out helps change our mood.

W: Really? Does it need to be for a long time?

M: Just move your body for 20 minutes. Then you'll feel much better for the next 12 hours.

W: How come?

M: While we're working out, our brains produce a material called beta-endorphin. It relieves pain and stress.

W: Okay. Then let's go bike riding.

남: 왜 그만 먹는 거니? 좀 더 먹어.

여: Mark와 헤어진 후로 입맛을 잃었어. 그를 잊고 살아가고 싶은데 그게 어려워.

남: 그래서 네가 아주 우울해 보이는구나. 기운 내. 초콜릿 좀 먹는 게 어때?

여: 아니, 먹고 싶지 않아.

남: 야, 한 번 먹어 봐. 초콜릿이 기분을 더 좋게 만들어 주거든. 연구에서 초콜릿을 몇 달 동안 먹으면 우울증을 극복하는 데 좋다고 했어.

여: 미안해, 하지만 아무것도 먹고 싶지가 않네.

남: 그럼, 조깅이나 자전거를 타러 가자. 운동을 하는 것도 기분을 전환하는 데 도움이 된다는 게 증명되었거든.

여: 정말? 오랫동안 해야 할 필요가 있어?

남: 단 20분 동안이라도 몸을 움직여 봐. 그럼 그 후 12시간 동안 훨씬 기분이 좋을 거야.

여: 왜?

남: 운동을 하는 동안 우리 뇌가 베타 엔도르핀이라는 물질을 만들어내. 그게 통증과 스트레스를 줄여주지.

여: 좋아. 그럼 자전거 타러 가자.

어휘

break up with ~와 헤어지다 move on 앞으로 나아가다
depressed[diprést] 형 우울한, 낙담한 research[risə́ːrtʃ]
명 연구 overcome[òuvərkʌ́m] 동 극복하다
depression[dipréʃən] 명 우울증 jog[dʒɑg] 동 조깅하다
work out 운동하다 mood[muːd] 명 기분 produce
[prədjúːs] 동 생성하다 material[mətí(ː)əriəl] 명 물질
beta-endorphin[béitəendɔ́ːrfin] 베타 엔도르핀(뇌하수체에
서 방출되는 고통 억제 호르몬) relieve[rilíːv] 동 줄이다, 해
소하다

문제 해설

Q1: 그들은 주로 무엇에 대해 이야기하고 있나?

남자 친구와 헤어져 우울한 여자에게 기분을 좋게 만드는 여
러 방법에 대해 말해 주고 있다.

Q2: 인간의 감정에 대한 남자의 두 가지 설명은?

① 운동은 기분을 좋게 해 준다.

② 초콜릿을 먹는 것은 우울증에 도움이 된다.

③ 조깅은 스트레스를 해소하는 가장 좋은 운동이다.

④ 베타 엔도르핀은 사람을 우울하게 만든다.

남자는 운동을 하면 우울한 감정과 스트레스를 해소할 수 있
다고 이야기했고, 초콜릿을 먹으면 우울증을 극복하는 데 도
움이 된다고 한 연구에 대해 언급했다.

UNIT 10 Social Issues

Getting ★ Ready p. 62

A 1 ⓓ 2 ⓕ 3 ⓑ 4 ⓒ 5 ⓔ 6 ⓐ
B 1 ⓑ 2 ⓔ 3 ⓐ

B 1 남: 왜 처음에 총기 소지가 가능했던 거지?
   여: 처음에는 자기 방어용으로 총기 소지가 허락되었어.

  2 남: 초등학교 때 외국에서 공부하는 것에 대해 어떻게 생
     각해?
   여: 난 반대야. 아이들이 다른 문화를 접하기엔 너무 일러.

  3 남: 왜 요즈음 가족이 함께 식사하기가 어렵게 된 거지?
   여: 맞벌이 부부의 증가 때문이지.

Listening ★ Start p. 63

1 ③ 2 ① 3 (1) F (2) T (3) F

1

M: How often does your family have a meal
together? Due to an increase in double-
income couples and family members' busy
schedules, it's hard to have a family meal.
However, according to various studies,
there are many advantages to family meals.
First, it's good for developing children's
brains. Surprisingly, children learn ten times
more new words during family meals than
when reading books. Also, children get to
eat healthier food like fruits and vegetables
rather than junk food. Moreover, children
who take part in regular family meals are
less likely to smoke, drink alcohol, or take
drugs.

남: 여러분의 가족은 얼마나 자주 함께 식사를 하나요? 맞벌이
부부의 증가와 가족 구성원들의 바쁜 스케줄 때문에 가족 식
사를 하기가 힘듭니다. 그러나 다양한 연구에 따르면, 가족
식사에는 좋은 점이 많이 있습니다. 우선, 아이들의 두뇌 발
달에 좋습니다. 놀랍게도 아이들은 책을 읽을 때보다 가족 식
사 동안에 10배나 많은 새 단어를 배웁니다. 또한 아이들은
정크푸드보다 과일이나 채소와 같은 건강에 더 좋은 음식을
먹게 됩니다. 게다가, 정기적으로 가족 식사에 참여하는 아이
들은 흡연을 하거나 술을 마시거나 마약을 복용할 가능성이
더 적어집니다.

어휘

meal[miːl] 명 식사 due to ~때문에 double-income
couple 맞벌이 부부 advantage[ədvǽntidʒ] 명 이점, 이득
rather than ~라기 보다 junk food 정크푸드(열량은 높고
영양가는 낮은 인스턴트 음식) moreover[mɔːróuvər] 부 게
다가, 더욱이 take part in ~에 참여하다 regular
[régjulər] 형 정기적인 alcohol[ǽlkəhɔ̀(ː)l] 명 알코올, 술
drug[drʌg] 명 약; *마약

문제 해설

Q: 남자는 주로 무엇에 대해 이야기하고 있는가?

① 아이들이 얼마나 자주 정크푸드를 먹는지

② 왜 사람들이 가족 식사를 덜 하는지

③ 왜 가족 식사가 아이들에게 중요한지

④ 요즘 아이들이 어떤 종류의 식사를 하는지

가족 식사를 하면 아이들의 두뇌가 발달하고 건강에 좋은 음
식을 먹게 되며, 나쁜 일을 하지 않게 된다는 점을 들고 있으
므로 아이들에게 가족식사가 왜 중요한지에 대한 내용임을
알 수 있다.

2

W: Johnny, let's go shopping for milk and fruit.
M: All right. Are you going to Joe's Groceries
near the house?
W: No. I'm going to the large discount store
which just opened.

M: Has another large discount store opened? I heard that many small groceries are going out of business because of big discount stores.

W: It's natural for people to go to big discount stores. They have a wide selection and bigger discounts.

M: But if everybody goes to them, small grocery stores will shut down. It can affect our local economy.

W: Oh, I've never thought about that.

M: In the long run, only large discount stores owned by big companies will survive.

W: I get it. Then let's go to Joe's Groceries today.

여: Johnny, 우유와 과일 사러 가자.

남: 좋아. 집에서 가까운 Joe's Groceries로 갈 거야?

여: 아니. 막 개점한 대형 할인점에 가려고 해.

남: 대형 할인점이 또 생겼어? 대형 할인점 때문에 작은 식품점들이 많이 망하고 있다고 들었는데.

여: 사람들이 대형 할인점에 가는 건 당연해. 선택의 폭이 넓고 할인을 많이 해 주잖아.

남: 하지만 모두 거기로 가면 작은 식품점은 문을 닫게 돼. 그건 우리 지역 경제에 영향을 줄 수 있지.

여: 아, 그건 생각하지 못했어.

남: 결국에는 대기업 소유의 대형 할인점만 남게 될 거야.

여: 알았어. 그럼 오늘은 Joe's Groceries에 가자.

어휘

grocery[gróusəri] 명 식품점, 잡화점; 식료 잡화류 large discount store 대형 할인점 go out of business 도산하다, 망하다 selection[silékʃən] 명 선택 shut down 문을 닫다, 폐업하다 affect[əfékt] 동 영향을 주다 local[lóukəl] 형 지역의 economy[ikánəmi] 명 경제 in the long run 결국에는 own[oun] 동 소유하다 survive[sərváiv] 동 살아남다

문제 해설

Q: 남자가 여자에게 제안한 것은?

대형 할인점으로 가면 작은 식품점은 망하게 되고 지역 경제에 영향을 주게 되므로 작은 식품점에 가는 것이 좋겠다고 했다.

3

W: Lately, the "working poor" have become a serious problem around the world. This term first appeared in the US in the mid 90's. It refers to people who work hard but still remain poor. These people have low income jobs which could be lost at any time.

If they lose their jobs or become sick, they can directly fall into the poorest class. The number of working poor around the world has been increasing since the year 2000. The main reason is that the number of full-time jobs is decreasing, while the number of part-time jobs is increasing.

여: 최근에 '근로 빈곤층'은 세계적으로 심각한 문제가 되었습니다. 이 용어는 90년대 중반에 미국에서 처음으로 나타났습니다. 이것은 열심히 일하지만 여전히 가난한 사람들을 가리킵니다. 이들은 언제 잃을지 모르는 저임금 직업을 가지고 있습니다. 이들이 직장을 잃거나 아프게 되면 바로 최빈곤층으로 떨어질 수 있습니다. 세계적으로 근로 빈곤층의 수는 2000년 이후로 증가하고 있습니다. 주된 이유는 시간제 일자리의 수는 증가하는 반면 정규직의 수가 줄어들고 있기 때문입니다.

어휘

lately[léitli] 부 최근에 term[təːrm] 명 용어 mid[mid] 형 중반의, 중간의 refer to ~를 가리키다 remain[riméin] 동 ~인 상태로 남다 income[ínkʌm] 명 수입, 소득 directly[diréktli] 부 곧장, 바로 class[klæs] 명 계층 full-time job 정규직 decrease[diːkríːs] 동 줄다 part-time job 시간제 일자리

문제 해설

Q: '근로 빈곤층'에 관해 사실이면 T, 사실이 아니면 F에 ✓표 하시오.

(1) 그들은 부유해지기 위해 열심히 일하지 않는다.

(2) 그들은 직업이 있지만 낮은 임금을 받는다.

(3) 그들의 수는 2002년 이후로 빠르게 증가해 왔다.

근로 빈곤층은 열심히 일하지만 낮은 임금을 받으며 빈곤층에 머물러 있는 사람들이며 2000년 이후로 증가하고 있다고 했다.

Listening ★ Practice p. 64

A 1 ④ 2 ①   B 1 ② 2 ①
C 1 ③ 2 ③   D 1 ② 2 ③

A [1-2]

M: Jenny, how have you been doing?

W: Great, thanks. I'm working part-time in a coffee shop to save money.

M: For what? Are you going to travel abroad?

W: No. I'm not satisfied with my small eyes. So I want to get plastic surgery this summer.

M: What? You look fine as you are. And what if there are side effects?

W: The technology has been upgraded, so

there are fewer side effects nowadays.

M: Still, I'm not for plastic surgery. Women with self-confidence look more beautiful to me.

W: That's why I've decided to do it. I think I can get self-confidence by changing my eyes.

M: If you were my sister, I would persuade you not to do it. Please think about it again.

W: Anyway, thanks for your concern.

남: Jenny, 어떻게 지냈니?

여: 잘 지내지, 고마워. 난 돈을 모으기 위해서 커피숍에서 아르바이트를 하고 있어.

남: 뭐 때문에? 해외로 여행 가려고?

여: 아니. 내 작은 눈에 만족을 못하겠어. 그래서 이번 여름에 성형 수술을 받고 싶어.

남: 뭐? 너 지금 그대로도 괜찮아. 그리고 부작용이 있으면 어떻게 해?

여: 기술이 향상되어서 요즘은 부작용이 거의 없대.

남: 그래도 성형 수술은 찬성할 수 없어. 자신감이 있는 여자들이 나에겐 더 아름답게 보이던데.

여: 그래서 내가 수술을 하기로 결정한 거야. 내 눈을 바꿈으로써 자신감을 얻을 수 있다고 생각해.

남: 네가 내 여동생이면 하지 말라고 설득할 텐데. 제발 다시 생각해라.

여: 어쨌든, 걱정해줘서 고마워.

어휘

travel abroad 해외 여행가다　be satisfied with ~에 만족하다　plastic surgery 성형 수술　side effect 부작용 self-confidence [sélfkάnfidəns] 명 자신감　persuade [pərswéid] 동 설득하다　concern [kənsə́ːrn] 명 걱정, 관심 [문제] medical [médikəl] 형 의학의　consult with ~와 상의하다, 상담하다

문제 해설

Q1: 그들은 주로 무엇에 관해 이야기하고 있는가?

　　돈을 모아 성형 수술을 하겠다는 여자와 부작용에 대해 걱정하며 하지 말라는 남자의 대화 내용이므로 성형 수술을 해야 하는지 하지 말아야 하는지에 대한 내용이다.

Q2: 남자와 같은 의견을 가진 사람은?

　　① John: 네 자신에 대해 자신감을 가져.

　　② Kate: 새로운 의학 기술은 믿을 수 있어.

　　③ Ted: 수술을 받기 전에 의사와 상의해.

　　남자는 성형 수술을 하지 말고 자신의 모습에 자신감을 가지라고 말하고 있다.

B [1-2]

W: A low birthrate is a serious social problem in Singapore. To increase the birthrate, the Singapore government has been trying various policies for a long time. The

Singapore government founded a wedding consulting agency in 1984. This agency has held many events such as cooking classes and blind dating on a riverboat. Also, the government encouraged colleges to open "dating classes" to teach dating techniques. After the average birthrate per woman dropped from 1.24 in 2003 to 1.04 in 2004, the government decided to provide financial support. It gives some money to families with children and cuts taxes for them. With these efforts, Singapore's birthrate reached 1.08 in 2008.

여: 낮은 출산율은 싱가포르의 심각한 사회문제입니다. 출산율을 높이기 위해 싱가포르 정부는 오랫동안 다양한 정책을 시도해왔습니다. 싱가포르 정부는 1984년에 결혼 정보 회사를 설립했습니다. 이 회사는 요리 강좌와 유람선 소개팅과 같은 많은 행사를 열었습니다. 또한, 정부는 대학들이 연애 기법을 가르치는 '데이트 강좌'를 개설하도록 권장했습니다. 여성당 평균 출산율이 2003년 1.24명에서 2004년 1.04명으로 떨어진 후로, 정부는 재정적인 후원을 제공하기로 결정했습니다. 아이들이 있는 가정에 약간의 돈을 제공하고 세금을 감면해 줍니다. 이러한 노력으로 싱가포르의 출산율은 2008년 1.08명에 이르렀습니다.

어휘

birthrate [bə́ːrθrèit] 명 출산율　policy [pάləsi] 명 정책 found [faund] 동 설립하다　wedding consulting agency 결혼 정보 회사　riverboat [rívərbòut] 명 강배, 유람선　encourage [inkə́ːridʒ] 동 권장하다　technique [tekníːk] 명 기술, 기법　average [ǽvəridʒ] 형 평균의 drop [drɑp] 동 떨어지다　financial [fainǽnʃəl] 형 재정적인 tax [tæks] 명 세금　reach [riːtʃ] 동 도달하다, 이르다

문제 해설

Q1: 출산율을 늘리기 위해 싱가포르 정부가 한 일이 아닌 것은?

　　① 결혼 정보 회사를 만들었다.

　　② 결혼식장을 무료로 제공했다.

　　③ 대학에서 연애 기법을 가르치도록 했다.

　　④ 자녀가 있는 가족에게 세금을 줄여 주었다.

　　결혼식장을 무료로 제공했다는 언급은 없었다.

Q2: 싱가포르의 출산율을 보여주는 그래프를 고르시오.

　　2003년에는 1.24, 2004년에는 1.04로 떨어졌다가, 2008년에는 1.08로 다시 상승했다.

C [1-2]

M: Julie, how was your trip to California?

W: Well... there was a problem at the airport. I had to wait for four hours before the departure.

M: What happened? Was there some kind of weather problem?

W: No. A man called the airline and said there was a bomb on the flight.

M: Oh, my god!

W: All the passengers on board had to get off. Then the police searched the plane.

M: So did they find it?

W: No. It turned out to be a false bomb threat.

M: I can't believe it.

W: The worst part is he did it for no reason. That kind of behavior is no longer a joke. Bomb threats are a serious issue around the world.

M: People who make false bomb threats should be punished heavily so that they won't do it again.

W: Right. People should realize how much trouble their behavior can cause for others.

남: Julie, 캘리포니아로의 여행은 어땠니?

여: 음… 공항에서 문제가 있었어. 출발하기까지 4시간을 기다려야 했어.

남: 무슨 일이 있었는데? 날씨에 문제라도 있었던 거야?

여: 아니. 어떤 남자가 항공사에 전화해서 비행기에 폭탄이 있다고 했대.

남: 세상에!

여: 탑승한 승객들이 전부 내려야 했어. 그리고 나서 경찰이 비행기를 수색했어.

남: 그래서 찾았어?

여: 아니. 허위 폭탄 협박이었던 걸로 드러났어.

남: 믿을 수가 없구나.

여: 최악인 것은 그 사람이 아무 이유도 없이 그랬다는 거야. 그런 종류의 행동은 더 이상 장난이 아니야. 폭탄 협박은 세계적으로 심각한 문제야.

남: 다시는 그런 일을 하지 않도록 허위 폭탄 협박을 하는 사람들을 강력히 처벌해야 해.

여: 맞아. 사람들은 자신들의 행동이 얼마나 남에게 피해를 줄 수 있는지 깨달아야 해.

어휘

departure[dipáːrtʃər] 명 출발 bomb[bɑm] 명 폭탄 passenger[pǽsəndʒər] 명 승객 on board 탑승한 search[səːrtʃ] 동 수색하다, 찾다 turn out ~로 드러나다 false[fɔːls] 형 가짜의, 허위의 threat[θret] 명 협박 behavior[bihéivjər] 명 행동 no longer 더 이상 ~이 아닌 punish heavily 중죄로 처벌하다 [문제] storm[stɔːrm] 명 폭풍 out of order 고장 난 apologize for ~에 대해 사과하다 deal with ~에 대처하다, ~을 다루다

문제 해설

Q1: 여자의 비행기가 지연된 이유는?

폭탄 협박 때문에 비행기를 수색하느라 출발 시간이 지연되었다.

Q2: 남자의 의견은?

① 항공사는 지연에 대해 사과해야 한다.

② 항공사는 비행기 사고에 대해 주의해야 한다.

③ 허위 폭탄 협박에 대해 중한 처벌이 필요하다.

④ 경찰은 폭탄 협박에 더 빨리 대처해야 한다.

남자는 허위 폭탄 협박을 강력히 처벌해야 한다고 주장하고 있다.

D [1-2]

M: Have you heard about "helicopter parents"? They are parents who are always around their children, and who care too much about everything their children do. They frequently call the school, showing concern about things like homework or lunch menus. Even after their children become adults, they insist on telling them what to do when it comes to jobs, dating, and even marriage. This is to prevent their kids from making mistakes or failing at something. But helicopter parents are not helpful for their children. These children don't learn problem solving abilities and have a hard time dealing with failures. As a result, they can't be successful in society.

남: '헬리콥터 부모'에 대해서 들어본 적이 있으세요? 아이들 주변에 항상 붙어있고 아이들이 하는 모든 일에 지나치게 관심을 보이는 부모들을 말합니다. 그들은 숙제나 점심 메뉴 같은 일에 관심을 보이면서 자주 학교에 전화를 겁니다. 심지어 아이들이 성인이 된 이후에도 직장과 데이트, 결혼에 대해서까지 어떻게 해야 할지 얘기해주는 것을 고집합니다. 이것은 아이들이 실수를 하거나 어떤 일에 실패하지 않도록 하기 위한 것입니다. 그러나 헬리콥터 부모는 그들의 아이들에게 도움이 되지 않습니다. 이런 아이들은 문제 해결 능력을 배우지 못하고 실패에 대처하는 것을 힘들어 합니다. 결과적으로 그들은 사회에서 성공할 수 없습니다.

어휘

care[kɛər] 동 걱정하다, 마음을 쓰다 frequently[fríːkwəntli] 부 자주 adult[ədʌ́lt] 명 성인 insist on v-ing ~하는 것을 고집하다, 주장하다 when it comes to ~에 대해서 marriage[mǽridʒ] 명 결혼 fail[feil] 동 실패하다 problem solving ability 문제 해결 능력 have a hard time v-ing ~하는 것을 힘들어 하다 failure[féiljər] 명 실패 as a result 결과적으로 successful[səksésfəl] 형

성공적인 [문제] keep an eye on ~을 주시하다, 살피다
responsible[rispánsəbl] [형] 책임감이 있는

문제 해설

Q1: 헬리콥터 부모는?

① John & Tina: 우리는 아들에게 자주 조언을 하지만 결정은 아이 스스로 합니다.

② Joe & Cindy: 우리는 아들을 항상 살피고 그 애가 하는 모든 일을 걱정합니다.

③ Mike & Jill: 우리는 우리 애가 무엇을 하는지 걱정하지 않습니다.

헬리콥터 부모는 아이들의 곁에서 모든 일을 걱정하고 문제들을 대신 해결해 주는 부모를 가리킨다.

Q2: 헬리콥터 부모를 가진 아이들을 설명한 것은?

헬리콥터 부모를 둔 아이들은 실패에 대처하는 것을 힘들어 한다고 했다.

Listening ★ Challenge p. 66

A 1 ③ 2 ①, ② B 1 (1) T (2) F (3) T 2 ④

A [1-2]

W: You've donated more blood than anyone this year. How do you feel?

M: I feel very good about myself.

W: Recently, blood shortages have become a serious problem. When did you start donating blood?

M: In 1984. I've donated blood every three months since then.

W: How did you start? Did someone suggest you do it?

M: Well... I have a special story. When my wife had surgery, it was hard to get extra blood. That's when I realized the importance of blood donation.

W: I see. Could you tell our viewers about the benefits of blood donation?

M: Well, best of all, you can save people's lives with little effort.

W: Anything else?

M: Yes. I became healthier. Because it's not possible to donate blood if I'm sick, I pay more attention to my body by working out and eating a healthy diet.

W: I see. We hope many viewers will donate blood after watching this program.

여: 당신은 올해 누구보다도 많은 혈액을 기증하셨어요. 기분이 어떠세요?

남: 제 자신에 대해 뿌듯합니다.

여: 최근에 혈액 부족이 심각한 문제가 되었어요. 언제부터 헌혈을 시작하셨나요?

남: 1984년이요. 그 이후로 3개월마다 헌혈했어요.

여: 어떻게 시작하셨나요? 누가 하라고 제의했었나요?

남: 음… 특별한 사연이 있어요. 제 아내가 수술을 받을 때 추가 혈액을 구하기가 어려웠어요. 그 때 헌혈의 중요성을 깨달았어요.

여: 알겠습니다. 시청자들에게 헌혈의 이점에 대해 말씀해 주시겠어요?

남: 음, 가장 좋은 점은 작은 노력으로 사람의 생명을 살릴 수 있다는 겁니다.

여: 또 다른 게 있나요?

남: 네. 저는 더 건강해졌어요. 아프면 헌혈을 할 수가 없어서 운동하고 건강한 식사를 하면서 몸에 더 많은 주의를 기울이게 됩니다.

여: 알겠습니다. 많은 시청자들이 이 프로그램을 보고 나서 헌혈을 하시길 바랍니다.

어휘

donate[dóuneit] [동] 기증하다 shortage[ʃɔ́:rtidʒ] [명] 부족
surgery[sə́:rdʒəri] [명] 수술 blood donation 헌혈
benefit[bénəfit] [명] 이점, 혜택 pay attention to ~에 주의를 기울이다 work out 운동하다 healthy diet 건강한 식단 [문제] medical checkup 건강검진

문제 해설

Q1: 남자가 헌혈을 시작하게 된 이유는?

① 그의 친구가 하라고 제안했다.

② 그의 의사가 혈액 부족에 대해 얘기했다.

③ 그의 아내가 수술을 받을 때 혈액이 필요했다.

④ 헌혈에 관한 다큐멘터리를 봤다.

아내가 수술을 받을 때 추가 혈액을 구하기가 힘들었던 이후로 혈액을 기증하기 시작했다고 했다.

Q2: 남자에 따르면, 헌혈의 좋은 점 두 가지는?

자신의 건강에 더 주의를 기울이게 되어 더 건강해지고, 다른 사람의 생명을 살릴 수 있다는 점을 들었다.

B [1-2]

W: Hello, everyone. Today, we'll be talking about gun control with Professor Jackson. Hello, professor.

M: Thank you for having me.

W: Shootings are increasing these days. Yesterday, 12 students lost their lives because of campus shootings.

M: Yes. And about 30,000 people are killed by guns every year in America.

W: What could be the reason?

M: The main reason is that people can get guns

too easily. After the age of 21, people can buy guns with a simple identification check.

W: At first, people were allowed to keep guns for self-defense, right?

M: Right. But now it has caused many problems.

W: What's more, it seems there's been a sudden increase in the number of shootings recently.

M: Shootings tend to increase when the economy is bad.

W: I see. Surprisingly, some of these shootings are carried out by teenagers.

M: I think it's mainly because of the media. They copy shooting scenes from movies and TV shows.

여: 여러분, 안녕하세요. 오늘은 Jackson 교수님과 총기 규제에 대해 얘기를 나누겠습니다. 안녕하세요, 교수님.

남: 초대해 주셔서 감사합니다.

여: 총기 사고가 요즘 증가하고 있습니다. 어제, 12명의 학생들이 교내 총기사고 때문에 목숨을 잃었습니다.

남: 네. 미국에서 총기 때문에 매년 약 30,000명의 사람들이 죽습니다.

여: 이유가 뭘까요?

남: 주된 이유는 사람들이 너무 쉽게 총을 구할 수 있기 때문입니다. 21세 이후면 간단한 신분 확인만으로 총을 살 수 있습니다.

여: 처음에는 자기 방어용으로 총을 소지하도록 허락되었던 거였죠?

남: 맞습니다. 하지만 지금은 많은 문제를 일으키고 있죠.

여: 게다가 최근 총기 사고가 급작스럽게 증가하는 것 같습니다.

남: 총기 사고는 경제가 안 좋을 때 증가하는 경향이 있습니다.

여: 그렇군요. 놀랍게도 이 총기 사고들 중 몇몇은 십대들에 의해 벌어지고 있습니다.

남: 그것은 대중 매체가 주원인이라고 봅니다. 그들은 영화나 TV 쇼의 총기 장면을 모방합니다.

어휘

gun control 총기 규제 professor[prəfésər] 명 교수 shooting[ʃúːtiŋ] 명 총기 발사 identification [əidèntəfikéiʃən] 명 신분 확인 self-defense[sélfdiféns] 명 자기 방어 what's more 게다가, 뿐만 아니라 sudden [sʌ́dn] 형 급작스런 carry out 수행하다 teenager [tíːnèidʒər] 명 십대 copy[kápi] 동 모방하다 [문제] be related to ~와 관계가 있다 illegal[ilíːgəl] 형 불법적인 access[ǽksès] 명 접근성

문제 해설

Q1: 사실이면 T, 사실이 아니면 F에 ✓표 하시오.

  (1) 매년 미국에서 약 30,000명의 사람들이 총기 사고로 죽는다.

  (2) 미국에서는 19세가 넘으면 총을 소지할 수 있다.

  (3) 총기 사고 건수의 증가는 경제와 관련이 있을 수 있다.
  미국에서 매년 약 30,000명의 사람들이 총기 사고로 죽고, 21세가 되면 총기 소지가 허락되며, 총기 사고는 경제가 안 좋을 때 증가한다고 했다.

Q2: 남자에 따르면, 십대 총기 사고의 주된 이유는?
  십대들이 대중 매체에 나오는 총기 장면을 모방하기 때문이라고 말했다.

Critical ★ Thinking p. 67

1 (1) Against (2) For (3) Against
2 (1) ⓐ (2) ⓓ (3) ⓒ

M1: I'm Nick. Lately, many elementary school students are going abroad alone to learn foreign languages. But how hard will it be for such small children to live without their parents? Because their parents aren't there to guide them, these kids can be led in the wrong direction.

W: I'm Anna. Children can learn foreign languages fast by studying abroad at an early age. It may be difficult at first, but children usually get used to a new environment quickly. The language ability that they get through studying abroad will be useful when they look for a job in the future.

M2: I'm Jay. The problem is that elementary school is too early for children to face different cultures. They will feel confused about their identity since they haven't fully learned their own culture and language yet. What's the point of being good at foreign languages without first establishing your own identity?

남1: 난 Nick이야. 최근에 많은 초등학교 학생들이 외국어를 배우기 위해 혼자 외국에 가고 있어. 그런데 그렇게 어린 아이들이 부모도 없이 사는 게 얼마나 어렵겠어? 지도해 줄 부모가 거기 없기 때문에 이런 아이들은 잘못된 방향으로 나아갈 수 있어.

여: 난 Anna야. 아이들은 어린 나이에 외국에서 공부함으로써 외국어를 빠르게 배울 수 있어. 처음에는 어려울 지도 모르지만 아이들은 보통 새로운 환경에 빠르게 적응하게 돼. 그 애들이 유학을 통해 얻은 언어 능력은 미래에 취직을 할 때 유용할 거야.

남2: 난 Jay야. 문제는 초등학교 때는 아이들이 다른 문화를 접하기에 너무 이르다는 거야. 그들은 아직 자신의 문화와 언어도 완전히 익히지 않았기 때문에 정체성에 대해 혼란을

느끼게 될 거야. 먼저 자신의 정체성을 확립하지 않고 외국어를 잘하는 게 무슨 의미가 있겠어?

어휘

lately[léitli] 부 최근에   guide[gaid] 통 지도하다
direction[dirékʃən] 명 방향   get used to ~에 적응하다
environment[inváiərənmənt] 명 환경   confused
[kənfjúːzd] 형 혼란스러운   identity[aidéntəti] 명 정체성
establish[istǽbliʃ] 통 확립하다   [문제] misguide[misgáid]
통 잘못 지도하다

문제 해설

Q1: 아이들이 외국에서 공부하는 것에 대해 각 인물이 찬성인지 반대인지 √표 하시오.
　　Nick은 어린 아이들이 외국에서 혼자 생활하는 것이 힘들기 때문에 반대하고, Anna는 아이들은 새 환경에 빨리 적응하여 외국어를 배우므로 찬성하며, Jay는 외국어보다는 정체성의 확립이 더 중요하기 때문에 반대하는 입장이다.

Q2: 각 인물의 의견을 고르시오.
　　ⓐ 부모 없이는 아이들이 쉽게 잘못된 방향으로 나아갈 수 있다.
　　ⓑ 아이들은 새로운 문화에 적응하는 데 오랜 시간이 걸린다.
　　ⓒ 자신의 정체성을 확립한 후에 외국에 나가서 공부하는 것이 더 좋다.
　　ⓓ 어린 나이에 외국어를 배우는 것은 장래 직업에 도움이 된다.
　　Nick은 부모가 옆에 없으면 아이들이 나쁜 길로 빠질 수 있다고 생각하고, Anna는 외국어를 배워 놓으면 나중에 취직할 때 도움이 된다고 믿으며, Jay는 정체성을 확립하는 일이 중요하다고 생각한다.

UNIT 11 Sports

Getting ✶ Ready   p. 68

A 1 ⓓ   2 ⓔ   3 ⓗ   4 ⓐ   5 ⓑ   6 ⓕ
B 1 ⓒ   2 ⓐ   3 ⓑ

B 1 여: Tom Green은 100미터 경주에서 어떻게 됐니?
　　남: 1차전에서 탈락했어.
　2 여: 당신의 우승 전략은 뭐죠?
　　남: 그들을 이기기 위해 강한 블로킹을 할 거예요.
　3 여: 왜 Manchester United로 이적하지 않았나요?
　　남: 그 팀은 충분한 이적료를 제안하지 않았어요.

1 ④   2 ③   3 ③

1

M: Julie, what happened to your head? Did you fall down?
W: No. I went to a baseball stadium and got hit in the head by a foul ball.
M: Oh, no! Are you okay?
W: Yes. I went to the hospital right away, and I'm fine now.
M: So that baseball team paid your hospital bills, right?
W: Surprisingly no. They said it was our responsibility to avoid foul balls.
M: What? That's not fair.
W: But if a parked car outside of the stadium is damaged by a home run, the home team pays for it.
M: Why?
W: Because a parked car can't avoid a ball.

남: Julie, 네 머리에 무슨 일이 있었던 거니? 넘어졌어?
여: 아니. 야구장에 갔다가 파울 볼에 머리를 맞았어.
남: 저런! 괜찮아?
여: 응. 바로 병원에 가서 이젠 괜찮아.
남: 그럼 그 야구팀이 병원비를 내줬겠다, 그렇지?
여: 놀랍게도 아니야. 파울 볼을 피하는 건 우리 책임이라고 그러더라.
남: 뭐? 그건 정당하지 않아.
여: 하지만 경기장 밖에 주차된 차가 홈런 때문에 손상이 되면 홈팀이 지불해 준대.
남: 왜?
여: 주차된 차는 공을 피할 수 없기 때문이지.

어휘

fall down 넘어지다   stadium[stéidiəm] 명 경기장
foul ball 파울 볼   right away 당장   bill[bil] 명 청구서
responsibility[rispὰnsəbíləti] 명 책임   avoid[əvɔ́id] 통
피하다   fair[fɛər] 형 공정한   parked[pɑːrkt] 형 주차된
damage[dǽmidʒ] 통 손상을 입히다

문제 해설

Q: 여자에게 일어난 일은?
　　여자는 야구 경기를 보러 갔다가 파울 볼에 머리를 맞았다고 했다.

2

W: This is Jamie Christine. I'm here with George Jackson.

M: Hello.

W: George, you led your team to victory with the goal in the second half. How did you feel?

M: As you might guess, I was really happy.

W: After scoring the goal, you made a heart shape with your arms. Was it for your girlfriend?

M: Yes, it was. I kissed my ring last time I scored, and she liked it. So this time I prepared another celebration.

W: How sweet! Anyway, London United is only one game away from winning the Champions League.

M: That's right. I'll try to score a goal in the finals. Then I'll carry the coach on my back.

W: I'm looking forward to seeing that celebration.

여: 저는 Jamie Christine입니다. George Jackson과 함께 하고 있습니다.

남: 안녕하세요.

여: George, 후반전에 골을 넣어 팀을 승리로 이끄셨는데요. 기분이 어땠나요?

남: 추측하시는 대로, 아주 기뻤습니다.

여: 골을 넣고 나서 팔로 하트 모양을 만드셨는데요. 여자 친구를 위한 것이었나요?

남: 네, 그래요. 지난번 득점 때는 반지에 키스를 했는데 여자 친구가 좋아했어요. 그래서 이번엔 다른 세리머니를 준비했죠.

여: 다정하시네요! 어쨌든, London United는 Champions League에서 우승하기까지 한 경기만 남았네요.

남: 맞아요. 결승전에서 득점하기 위해 노력할 거예요. 그러면 코치님을 등에 업을 겁니다.

여: 그 세리머니를 보게 되길 고대할게요.

어휘
victory[víktəri] 명 승리   second half 후반전   score [skɔːr] 동 득점하다   celebration[sèləbréiʃən] 명 축하; *축하의식, 축하 세리머니   final[fáinəl] 명 ((~s)) 결승전   coach[koutʃ] 명 코치   look forward to v-ing ~하기를 고대하다   [문제] celebrate[séləbrèit] 동 축하하다

문제 해설
Q: 남자는 결승전에서 득점하면 어떤 세리머니를 할 것인가?
남자는 득점하면 코치를 등에 업을 것이라고 했다.

3

M: Do you know who won the most gold medals at the Olympics? It is American swimming hero Michael Phelps. He won a total of 14 gold medals, six of them in the 2004 Olympics, and eight more in the 2008 Olympics. And he set seven world records in the 2008 Olympics. This amazing record could be achieved mainly because Michael has a suitable body for swimming. He's 193 cm tall, which is similar to other swimmers. But the length of his open arms is longer than other swimmers. Also, his big feet help him swim faster.

남: 올림픽에서 가장 많은 금메달을 딴 사람이 누구인지 아세요? 미국의 수영 영웅 Michael Phelps입니다. 그는 총 14개의 금메달을 땄는데 2004년 올림픽에서 6개, 2008년 올림픽에서 8개를 더 땄습니다. 그리고 2008년 올림픽에서는 7개의 세계 기록을 수립했습니다. 이 놀라운 기록이 이루어질 수 있었던 주된 이유는 Michael의 몸이 수영에 적합하기 때문입니다. 그는 키가 193센티미터로, 다른 수영 선수들과 비슷합니다. 하지만 팔을 벌렸을 때의 길이는 다른 수영선수들보다 더 깁니다. 또, 발이 큰 것도 빠르게 수영하는 데 도움이 됩니다.

어휘
medal[médəl] 명 메달   hero[hí(ː)ərou] 명 영웅   set[set] 동 수립하다 (set-set-set)   record[rékərd] 명 기록   achieve[ətʃíːv] 동 이루다   suitable[súːtəbl] 형 적합한   length[leŋkθ] 명 길이

문제 해설
Q: Michael Phelps에 관해서 사실이 아닌 것은?
키는 다른 수영선수들과 비슷하다고 했다.

Listening ★ Practice   p. 70

A 1 ② 2 ①   B 1 (1) T (2) F (3) T   2 ④
C 1 ④ 2 ①   D 1 ④ 2 ②

A [1-2]

W: Henry, I heard you got accepted onto the school soccer team.

M: Yes. I received my uniform today. I'm anxious to wear it to practice.

W: You look really happy.

M: Of course. And I can't believe I can wear number 9.

W: What's so special about the number 9?

M: The number 9 usually represents the team's No. 1 striker.

W: Really? I thought the players just chose whatever number they like.

M: No. Each number has a symbolic meaning in soccer. For example, the number 7 goes to the team's most famous player.

W: Oh, I remember David Beckham wore the number 7.

M: Right. And the number 1 is only for the goalkeeper. Field players can't wear that number.

W: Interesting. Anyway, when is your first practice?

M: This Friday. I wish it would come soon.

여: Henry, 네가 학교 축구팀에 들어가게 되었다고 들었어.

남: 응. 오늘 유니폼을 받았어. 얼른 유니폼을 입고 연습하고 싶다.

여: 너 아주 행복해 보여.

남: 물론이지. 그리고 내가 9번 옷을 입을 수 있다는 게 믿기지 않아.

여: 9번이 뭐가 그렇게 특별한 건데?

남: 9번은 대개 그 팀의 최고의 스트라이커를 나타내.

여: 그래? 난 선수들이 그냥 자신이 좋아하는 번호를 고른다고 생각했는데.

남: 아니야. 축구에서 각 번호는 상징적인 의미가 있어. 예를 들어, 7번은 팀의 가장 유명한 선수에게 주어지지.

여: 아, David Beckham이 7번을 입었던 게 기억나.

남: 맞아. 그리고 1번은 골키퍼만을 위한 거야. 필드 플레이어들은 그 번호 옷을 입을 수 없어.

여: 흥미로운걸. 어쨌든, 첫 연습이 언제니?

남: 이번 금요일. 빨리 금요일이 됐으면 좋겠어.

어휘

soccer[sάkər] 명 축구 uniform[júːnəfɔ̀ːrm] 명 유니폼 be anxious to-v ~하기를 열망하다 represent[rèprizént] 동 나타내다 striker[stráikər] 명 스트라이커(공격수) whatever[hwʌtévər] 대 ~이면 무엇이든 symbolic [simbάlik] 형 상징적인 goalkeeper[góulkìːpər] 골키퍼 [문제] captain[kǽptən] 명 주장 relieved[rilíːvd] 형 안심한 disappointed[dìsəpɔ́intid] 형 실망한

문제 해설

Q1: 축구에서 유니폼 번호의 잘못된 의미를 고르시오.

번호 9번은 최고의 스트라이커, 7번은 가장 유명한 선수, 1번은 골키퍼를 의미한다.

Q2: 남자의 현재 기분은?

축구팀에 들어가게 되어 아주 기쁘고 연습이 기다려지는 상태이므로 들뜨고 흥분된 기분이다.

B [1-2]

W: Usain Bolt was born in Jamaica in 1986. When he was a high school student, his cricket coach discovered his talent and recommended that he become a runner. He ran in the 2004 Olympics in Athens, but dropped out in the first round because of a leg injury. However, four years later, in the 2008 Beijing Olympics, he showed his great ability. He won a gold medal in the 100 meter event. Surprisingly, he slowed down before the finish line to celebrate, but he still broke the world record. His left shoelace was even untied! He also won the 200 meter race and the 400 meter team relay, setting new world records.

여: Usain Bolt는 1986년 자메이카에서 태어났습니다. 고등학교 학생이었을 때 크리켓 코치가 그의 재능을 발견하고 달리기 선수가 될 것을 권했습니다. 그는 2004년 아테네 올림픽에서 뛰었지만 다리 부상으로 1차전에서 탈락하고 말았습니다. 그러나 4년 뒤인 2008년 베이징 올림픽에서 훌륭한 능력을 보여주었습니다. 그는 100미터 경기에서 금메달을 땄습니다. 놀랍게도 그는 결승선 전에 (자신의 우승을) 축하하기 위해 속력을 늦췄으면서도 세계 기록을 깼습니다. 심지어 왼쪽 신발끈은 풀려 있었죠! 그는 200미터 경기와 400미터 계주에서도 세계 신기록을 수립하면서 우승했습니다.

어휘

Jamaica[ʤəméikə] 명 자메이카 cricket[kríkit] 크리켓(야구와 비슷한 구기 경기) runner[rʌ́nər] 명 달리기 선수 drop out 탈락하다 first round 1차전, 1회전 injury [índʒəri] 명 부상 ability[əbíləti] 명 능력 event[ivént] 명 행사; *종목 slow down 늦추다 finish line 결승선 shoelace[ʃúːlèis] 명 신발끈 untied[ʌntáid] 형 묶이지 않은 team relay 계주 [문제] be about to-v 막 ~하려고 하다

문제 해설

Q1: Usain Bolt에 관해 사실이면 T, 사실이 아니면 F를 쓰시오.

Usain Bolt는 그의 달리기 선수로서의 재능을 발견한 크리켓 코치의 추천에 따라 달리기 선수가 되었고, 아테네 올림픽에서는 1차전에 탈락했고, 베이징 올림픽에서 세 개의 금메달을 땄다.

Q2: 2008년 올림픽의 100미터 경기에서 Usain Bolt가 속력을 늦춘 이유는?

그는 결승선을 통과하기 전 자신의 승리를 축하하기 위해 일부러 속력을 늦췄다.

C [1-2]

W: What did you do yesterday?

M: I stayed home and watched the Olympics.

W: Me, too. I watched the women's fencing semifinal. It was such an exciting match.

M: Oh, I missed that one. I was watching women's weightlifting.

W: What were the results?

M: Sarah Wilkins only won a silver medal. She

failed to lift 95 kg in her final attempt. I was really disappointed.
W: Why were you disappointed? She won a silver medal!
M: But athletes practice hard for four years to win a gold medal. Winning a gold medal is the most important thing.
W: Being second best in the world at something is pretty great too, though.
M: I guess I agree with that.
W: In my opinion, winning any medal in the Olympics is a great achievement. Whether it's gold, silver or bronze, it should be celebrated.

여: 어제 뭐 했니?
남: 집에 있으면서 올림픽을 봤지.
여: 나도야. 난 여자 펜싱 준결승전을 봤어. 아주 재미있는 경기였어.
남: 아, 그건 못 봤어. 난 여자 역도를 보고 있었거든.
여: 결과가 어떻게 되었어?
남: Sarah Wilkins가 은메달밖에 못 땄어. 마지막 시기에서 95킬로그램을 드는 데 실패했어. 아주 실망스럽더라.
여: 왜 실망해? 은메달을 땄잖아!
남: 하지만 운동선수들은 금메달을 따려고 4년 동안 열심히 연습하잖아. 금메달을 따는 게 가장 중요한 일이지.
여: 그래도 무언가에서 세계에서 상위 두 번째가 되는 것 역시 상당히 훌륭한 거잖아.
남: 그 말엔 동감인 것 같다.
여: 내 생각으로는 올림픽에서 어떤 메달이든 딴다는 건 대단한 업적이야. 그게 금이든, 은이든, 동이든 축하를 받아야 해.

어휘
fencing[fénsiŋ] 명 펜싱 semifinal[sèmifáinəl] 명 준결승전 match[mætʃ] 명 경기 weightlifting[wéitlìftiŋ] 명 역도 result[rizʌ́lt] 명 결과 attempt[ətémpt] 명 시도, 시기 athlete[ǽθliːt] 명 운동선수 second best 2위 achievement[ətʃíːvmənt] 명 업적 bronze[brɑnz] 명 청동

문제 해설
Q1: 남자가 어제 본 스포츠는?
남자는 여자 역도 경기를 봤다고 했다.

Q2: 여자와 같은 의견을 가진 사람은?
① 어떤 올림픽 메달을 따더라도 축하를 받을 일이다.
② 운동선수의 유일한 목표는 금메달을 따는 것이다.
③ 운동선수에게 올림픽에 참가하는 것은 대단한 영광이다.
여자는 올림픽에서 어떤 메달을 따든 그것은 대단한 업적이고 축하를 받아야 할 일이라고 했다.

D [1-2]

M: Did you hear David Adams is joining the LA Galaxy?
W: Really? I thought he would transfer to Chelsea FC in the Premier League.
M: Me, too.
W: Maybe Chelsea didn't offer a big enough transfer fee.
M: No, they offered a lot.
W: Then, why did he reject it? It's every soccer player's dream to play in the Premier League.
M: He said there was no guarantee of being a main player in Chelsea because there are so many stars. But on the LA Galaxy, the left-wing position is open.
W: I see. But I think he should've taken the risk.
M: Well, he could go to the Premier League after gaining experience in America.
W: This kind of opportunity doesn't come often. I'm disappointed with his decision.
M: David Adams is a great soccer player, so a Premier League team will take him eventually.

남: David Adams가 LA Galaxy에 들어간다는 거 들었어?
여: 정말? 그가 프리미어 리그의 Chelsea FC로 이적할 거라 생각했는데.
남: 나도야.
여: 아마 Chelsea가 이적료를 충분히 제시하지 않았나 보다.
남: 아니, 많이 제시했대.
여: 그럼 왜 거절했지? 프리미어 리그에서 경기하는 건 모든 축구 선수의 꿈이잖아.
남: Chelsea에는 스타 선수들이 많아서 자신이 주전 선수가 될 보장이 없다고 말했대. 하지만 LA Galaxy에는 레프트 윙 포지션이 남아 있거든.
여: 알겠다. 하지만 위험을 감수했어야 한다고 봐.
남: 음, 미국에서 경험을 쌓은 뒤에 프리미어 리그로 갈 수 있잖아.
여: 이런 기회가 자주 오는 건 아니지. 난 그의 결정에 실망했어.
남: David Adams는 훌륭한 축구 선수니까 결국엔 프리미어 리그의 팀이 그를 데려갈 거야.

어휘
transfer[trænsfɚr] 동 이적하다, 옮기다 offer[ɔ́(ː)fər] 동 제안하다 transfer fee 이적료 reject[ridʒékt] 동 거절하다 the Premier League (잉글랜드 축구의) 1부 리그, 프리미어 리그 guarantee[gæ̀rəntíː] 명 보장 main player 주전 선수 left-wing[léftwìŋ] 형 레프트 윙의, 왼쪽 공격수의 position[pəzíʃən] 명 포지션, 위치 risk[risk] 명 위험, 모험 gain[gein] 동 얻다 opportunity[ɑ̀pərtjúːnəti] 명 기회 decision[disíʒən] 명 *결정; 판정 eventually[ivéntʃuəli]

[부] 결국 [문제] respect[rispékt] [동] 존경하다 attitude [ǽtitjùːd] [명] 태도 favorable[féivərəbl] [형] 호의적인 indifferent[indífərənt] [형] 무관심한

문제 해설

Q1: David Adams가 LA Galaxy로 이적한 이유는?
그는 Chelsea FC에는 유명한 선수들이 많아서 주전이 될 확률이 낮기 때문에 LA Galaxy를 선택했다고 했다.

Q2: David Adams의 결정에 대한 여자의 태도는?
여자는 그의 결정이 실망스럽다고 말하고 있으므로 부정적인 태도를 보이고 있다.

Listening ★ Challenge p. 72

A 1 ④ 2 ① B 1 ③ 2 ③

A [1-2]

W: Hello, Mr. Black. First of all, congratulations on tonight's victory.
M: Thank you very much.
W: Including today's match, the last three games were all very tight.
M: Yes, that's true.
W: But the semifinal against Russia is only two days away. The players must be very tired.
M: I'm worried about that. But we'll do our best to win the game with Russia and make the finals.
W: The record shows your team has won 10 times and lost 14 against Russia. Could you tell us what your strategy will be?
M: As you know, the Russia team has many tall players with good blocking techniques.
W: And they're also very powerful spikers.
M: Yes. But we'll use our quickness to beat them. I believe in my players.
W: I see. Well, I hope I get to see your team play in the finals.
M: Thanks.

여: 안녕하세요, Black 씨. 우선, 오늘 밤 승리를 축하드립니다.
남: 정말 감사합니다.
여: 오늘의 경기를 포함해서 지난 세 경기가 정말 접전이었어요.
남: 네, 그렇죠.
여: 그런데 러시아와의 준결승이 이틀밖에 안 남았네요. 선수들이 아주 피곤할 텐데요.
남: 그걸 걱정하고 있습니다. 하지만 러시아와의 경기를 이기기 위해 최선을 다할 거고 결승전에 진출할 것입니다.
여: 러시아를 상대로 10승 14패를 기록하고 있는데요. 전략이 어떤 것인지 말씀해 주시겠어요?
남: 아시다시피, 러시아 팀은 블로킹 기술이 좋은 장신 선수들이 많죠.
여: 그리고 아주 강한 스파이크를 구사하는 선수들이기도 하죠.
남: 네. 하지만 그들을 이기기 위해 우리의 민첩성을 사용할 것입니다. 전 저희 선수들을 믿습니다.
여: 알겠습니다. 음, 결승전에서 당신의 팀의 경기를 보게 되길 바랍니다.
남: 감사합니다.

어휘

tight[tait] [형] 꼭 끼는; *접전의 make the finals 결승전에 오르다 strategy[strǽtədʒi] [명] 전략 blocking[blákiŋ] [명] 블로킹 powerful[páuərfəl] [형] 강한, 센 spiker [spáikər] [명] 스파이크하는 사람 quickness[kwíknis] [명] 민첩성 beat[biːt] [동] 이기다 (beat-beat-beaten) [문제] sportscaster[spɔ́ːrtskæ̀stər] [명] 스포츠 방송 중계자 volleyball[válibɔ̀ːl] [명] 배구 referee[rèfəríː] [명] 심판 head coach 감독 spike[spaik] [명] 스파이크 accurate [ǽkjurət] [형] 정확한 serve[səːrv] [명] 서브

문제 해설

Q1: 남자의 직업은?
경기 후 선수들의 상태, 다음 경기 전략에 대해 설명하는 것으로 볼 때 배구팀의 감독임을 알 수 있다.

Q2: 러시아 팀에 대한 이 팀의 승리 전략은?
상대 선수들의 블로킹과 스파이크 기술에 맞서 빠른 속도를 이용하겠다고 설명했다.

B [1-2]

M: Do you know that you can't see some of the events from the last Olympics in the next Olympics? That's because the official Olympic events are not set. The International Olympic Committee meets every four years to set the events for the next Olympics. For example, mixed doubles ping pong was removed from the 2008 Beijing Olympics. Instead, the women's 3000-meter hurdles and 10 km swimming marathon were added. Also, 2008 was the last Olympics for baseball and softball. They are not official events of the 2012 London Olympics. Taekwondo was selected for the 2012 Olympics, but there's a high chance of it not being included in 2016. On the other hand, karate, golf and rugby might be included in 2016.

남: 다음 올림픽에서 지난 올림픽의 일부 종목을 볼 수 없다는 것을 아세요? 그것은 공식 올림픽 종목이 정해져 있지 않기 때문입니다. 국제 올림픽 위원회는 4년마다 다음 올림

픽 종목을 정하기 위해 모입니다. 예를 들어, 혼합 복식 탁구는 2008년 베이징 올림픽부터 폐지되었습니다. 대신 여자 3000미터 장애물 경기와 10킬로미터 수영 마라톤이 추가되었습니다. 또한 2008년은 야구와 소프트볼이 있던 마지막 올림픽이었습니다. 그것들은 2012년 런던 올림픽의 공식 종목이 아닙니다. 태권도는 2012년 올림픽에 채택되었지만 2016년에는 포함되지 않을 확률이 높습니다. 한편, 가라테와 골프, 럭비는 2016년에 포함될지도 모릅니다.

어휘
official [əfíʃəl] 혱 공식적인　International Olympic Committee 국제 올림픽 위원회　mixed [mikst] 혱 혼성의　doubles [dʌ́blz] 몡 복식 경기　ping pong 탁구　remove [rimúːv] 동 없애다　hurdle [hə́ːrdl] 몡 《~s》 장애물 경주　marathon [mǽrəθɑ̀n] 몡 마라톤　add [æd] 동 추가하다　softball [sɔ́(ː)ftbɔ̀ːl] 몡 소프트볼　on the other hand 다른 한편　karate [kərɑ́ːti] 몡 가라테　rugby [rʌ́gbi] 몡 럭비

문제 해설
Q1: 남자는 주로 무엇에 대해 이야기하고 있나?
　올림픽 종목 중에 없어지거나 추가되는 경기에 대한 내용이다.

Q2: 2012년 올림픽에 채택된 스포츠는?
　태권도는 2012년 종목으로 채택되었지만 2016년에 없어질지도 모른다고 설명했다.

72

Critical ★ Thinking　　p. 73

1 ③　2 ①

M: Did you watch the soccer game between the US and Spain yesterday? It was really exciting.
W: Yes. But the US lost the game because of a referee's mistake.
M: Are you talking about when Spain got a penalty kick because of the US's foul?
W: Yes. Obviously, it wasn't a foul. The US players appealed, but the referee didn't change his decision.
M: Well, I understand why he didn't change his decision, even though it was wrong.
W: Why not? His wrong decision changed the game's result.
M: Think about it. If referees start to change their decisions, all the coaches and players will always complain until they do.
W: I don't think that is likely to happen. They'll protest only when the decision is clearly wrong.
M: Do you really think so?

W: Yes. And even if they often protest, making the correct decision is more important.
M: Well, it's hard to say what's right.

남: 어제 미국과 스페인의 축구 경기 봤니? 정말 재미있었는데.
여: 응. 하지만 심판의 실수로 미국이 경기에 졌어.
남: 미국의 파울로 스페인이 페널티 킥을 얻은 것에 대해 말하는 거니?
여: 응. 분명히 그건 파울이 아니었어. 미국 선수들은 항의했지만 심판이 판정을 바꾸지 않았잖아.
남: 음, 잘못된 것이라 해도 왜 그가 판정을 바꾸지 않았는지는 이해가 돼.
여: 왜지? 그의 잘못된 결정으로 경기의 결과가 바뀌었잖아.
남: 생각해 봐. 심판이 자기 결정을 바꾸기 시작하면 모든 코치와 선수들은 항상 심판이 판정을 바꿀 때까지 불만을 제기할 거야.
여: 그런 일이 생길 것 같지는 않은데. 결정이 확연히 잘못되었을 때만 항의하겠지.
남: 정말 그렇게 생각해?
여: 응. 그리고 자주 항의를 하게 된다고 해도 정확한 결정을 내리는 것이 더 중요해.
남: 음, 무엇이 맞다고 얘기하기 어렵다.

어휘
penalty kick 페널티 킥　foul [faul] 몡 파울, 반칙　obviously [ɑ́bviəsli] 분 분명히　appeal [əpíːl] 동 항의하다　complain [kəmpléin] 동 불평하다　protest [prətést] 동 항의하다　correct [kərékt] 혱 정확한; 바로잡다　[문제] cheat [tʃiːt] 동 속이다　situation [sìtʃuéiʃən] 몡 상황

문제 해설
Q1: 그들은 주로 무엇에 대해 이야기하고 있나?
　① 왜 심판이 자주 잘못된 결정을 내리는지
　② 한 축구팀이 경기를 이기려고 어떻게 속임수를 썼는지
　③ 심판이 자신의 실수를 바로잡아야 하는지
　④ 코치가 어떻게 심판의 결정에 항의할 수 있는지
　심판이 자신의 잘못된 결정을 바로잡아야 하는지, 그냥 첫 번째 판정을 고수해야 하는지에 대한 내용이다.

Q2: 여자의 의견을 고르시오.
　① 심판은 잘못된 판정을 내렸을 때 바로잡아야 한다.
　② 심판의 판정이 결과를 바꾸지 않는다면 수정할 필요가 없다.
　③ 심판은 어떤 상황에서든 판정을 바꾸면 안 된다.
　여자는 잘못된 판정인 경우 심판이 바로잡아야 정확한 판정이 가능하다고 생각한다.

UNIT 12 Environment

Getting ★ Ready p. 74

A 1 ⓕ 2 ⓒ 3 ⓐ 4 ⓑ 5 ⓓ 6 ⓔ
B 1 ⓑ 2 ⓐ 3 ⓓ

B 1 남: 재활용은 우리 환경에 어떤 영향을 줄까?
　　여: 그걸 함으로써 천연 자원을 절약할 수 있지.
　2 남: 북극에서 어떤 환경적인 변화가 일어나고 있지?
　　여: 얼음이 녹고 얇아지고 있어.
　3 남: 물이 왜 더러운 쓰레기로 오염된 거지?
　　여: 공장에서 폐수를 버렸어.

Listening ★ Start p. 75

1 ③ 2 (1) ⓐ (2) ⓒ (3) ⓑ 3 (1) F (2) T (3) F

1

M: Hey, let's throw the garbage here.
W: Wait! Are you going to throw all the garbage into one trash bin?
M: Yeah. What's wrong?
W: It should be separated!
M: I know that. But it's too annoying.
W: Peter! We should think about the future of the environment.
M: How does that affect the future of our environment?
W: We can save natural resources by recycling. And we can reduce waste, too.
M: I heard that there isn't enough space for waste nowadays.
W: You're right. And if you separate garbage, it can be turned into other things. Plastic bottles can be used to make toys, T-shirts, and even park benches.
M: I see. I promise I'll be more careful when I throw away the garbage from now on.

남: 이봐, 여기에다 쓰레기를 버리자.
여: 기다려! 모든 쓰레기를 한 쓰레기통에 버리려는 거야?
남: 응. 뭐가 잘못됐니?
여: 분리해야지!
남: 알아. 하지만 너무 귀찮아.
여: Peter! 환경의 미래에 대해서 생각해야 해.
남: 그게 우리 환경의 미래에 어떻게 영향을 주는 건데?

여: 재활용을 통해 천연 자원을 절약할 수 있어. 그리고 쓰레기를 줄일 수도 있지.
남: 요즘 쓰레기를 위한 공간이 충분하지 않다고 들었어.
여: 맞아. 그리고 쓰레기를 분리하면 그것들이 다른 것으로 바뀔 수가 있어. 플라스틱 병은 장난감이나 티셔츠, 심지어 공원 벤치를 만드는 데 쓰일 수 있어.
남: 알겠어. 지금부턴 쓰레기를 버릴 때 좀 더 신중하겠다고 약속할게.

어휘
garbage[ɡáːrbidʒ] 몡 쓰레기 trash bin 쓰레기통
separate[sépərèit] 통 분리하다 annoying[ənɔ́iiŋ] 혱 성가신, 짜증나는 environment[inváiərənmənt] 몡 환경
affect[əfékt] 통 영향을 주다 resource[ríːsɔːrs] 몡 자원
recycle[riːsáikl] 통 재활용하다 reduce[ridjúːs] 통 줄이다
waste[weist] 몡 쓰레기 bench[bentʃ] 몡 벤치, 의자
[문제] process[práses] 몡 과정 environmental
[invàiərənméntəl] 혱 환경의

문제 해설
Q: 그들은 주로 무엇에 관해 이야기하고 있나?
　쓰레기를 아무렇게나 버리지 않고 분리하여 재활용을 하면 환경을 보호할 수 있다는 내용이다.

2

W: The earth is getting warmer and warmer. Because of global warming, unusual things are happening around the world. In Spanish mountain areas, bears are awake instead of sleeping during winter. Higher temperatures made it possible for them to stay active longer. In the Alps of France, you can see the buds of chestnut trees already during winter. In the past, they were only seen in spring. In New York in the US, it didn't snow during the winter of 2007. It was the first time since 1877.

여: 지구가 점점 더 따뜻해지고 있습니다. 지구 온난화 때문에 세계 곳곳에서 기이한 일이 일어나고 있습니다. 스페인의 산악 지역에서는 곰이 겨울 동안 잠을 자는 대신 깨어 있습니다. 높은 기온이 그들을 더 오랫동안 활동하도록 만들었습니다. 프랑스의 알프스 산맥에서는 겨울에 이미 밤나무의 싹을 볼 수 있습니다. 과거에는 봄에만 볼 수 있었던 것입니다. 미국의 뉴욕에서는 2007년 겨울에 눈이 오지 않았습니다. 1877년 이래 처음 있는 일이었습니다.

어휘
global warming 지구 온난화 unusual[ʌnjúːʒuəl] 혱 드문, 비범한 area[ɛ́əriə] 몡 지역 awake[əwéik] 혱 깨어 있는 Alps[ælps] 몡 알프스 산맥 bud[bʌd] 몡 (식물의) 눈, 싹 chestnut[tʃésnʌt] 몡 밤, 밤나무

문제 해설

Q: 각 나라에 맞는 상황을 고르시오.

온난화로 인해 스페인의 산악 지역에서 곰이 겨울잠을 안 자고, 프랑스의 알프스 산맥에서 밤나무의 싹이 때 이르게 나고, 미국 뉴욕에 눈이 전혀 오지 않는 겨울이 있었다고 했다.

3

M: Hello. This is reporter Chris Jones at Richmond Middle School near the International Airport. As you see, a plane is flying overhead and it's making serious noise. Students at this school hear such noise several times a day. Students complain that it's difficult to focus on studying during class. Because of the noise, they can't open the windows even during the summer. The noise from airplanes can cause a lot of stress and hurt the students' hearing ability. Furthermore, it can have bad effects on their academic achievements. The government needs to do something immediately.

남: 안녕하세요. 국제 공항 근처 Richmond 중학교에 나와 있는 Chris Jones 기자입니다. 보시다시피, 머리 위로 비행기가 날면서 심각한 소음을 내고 있습니다. 이 학교의 학생들은 하루에 몇 번씩 이러한 소음을 듣습니다. 학생들은 수업 시간에 학업에 집중하기 힘들다고 불평합니다. 이 소음 때문에 심지어 여름에도 창문을 열 수가 없습니다. 비행기에서 나오는 소음은 많은 스트레스를 일으키고 학생들의 청력을 손상시킬 수 있습니다. 나아가, 학생들의 학업 성취도에 나쁜 영향을 미칠 수 있습니다. 정부는 즉각 조치를 취할 필요가 있습니다.

어휘

reporter[ripɔ́ːrtər] 명 기자, 통신원 overhead[óuvərhèd] 부 머리 위에, 하늘 높이 cause[kɔːz] 동 일으키다 hearing ability 청력 furthermore[fə́ːrðərmɔ̀ːr] 부 게다가, 나아가 academic achievement 학업 성취도 government[ɡʌ́vərnmənt] 명 정부 immediately[imíːdiətli] 부 즉시 [문제] lower[lóuər] 동 낮추다, 저하시키다

문제 해설

Q: 사실이면 T, 사실이 아니면 F에 ✓표 하시오.

(1) 기자는 지금 국제 공항에 있다.

(2) 비행기 소음은 학생들의 학업 성적을 낮출 수 있다.

(3) 정부는 공항 근처의 소음이 얼마나 심각한지 조사하는 중이다.

기자는 국제 공항이 아니라 공항 근처의 Richmond 중학교에 있고, 비행기 소음이 학생들의 성적에 나쁜 영향을 끼칠 수 있다고 했으며, 정부의 조치를 촉구하는 말로 볼 때 현재 소음의 심각성에 대한 조사가 진행 중이라는 내용은 맞지 않는다.

A 1 ③ 2 ① B 1 ① 2 ④
C 1 ③ 2 ② D 1 ③ 2 ②

A [1-2]

W: Did you watch that documentary about environmental pollution yesterday?

M: Yes. I didn't know that environmental pollution was that serious.

W: After watching it, I decided to join the environment club at our school.

M: Good idea! What do people do in that club?

W: They make guidebooks about protecting the environment. They hand them out to students for free.

M: What else do they do?

W: They sell recycled products. By doing so, they show people that waste can be made into useful items. Plus, they hold lots of events like painting contests based on the environment.

M: I think I'd like to join the environment club, too. How about going to the student office and applying?

W: Great. But can I drop by a bookstore first? I'd like to buy a book about the environment first.

M: No problem. I'll go with you.

여: 어제 환경 오염에 관한 다큐멘터리 봤니?

남: 응. 환경 오염이 그렇게 심각한지 몰랐어.

여: 그걸 보고 나서 우리 학교 환경 동아리에 가입해야겠다고 결심했어.

남: 좋은 생각이다! 그 동아리에서 뭘 해?

여: 환경 보호에 대한 안내 책자를 만들어. 학생들에게 그걸 무료로 나눠주지.

남: 또 어떤 일을 해?

여: 재활용품을 팔아. 그렇게 함으로써 쓰레기가 유용한 제품이 될 수 있다는 것을 사람들에게 보여주는 거지. 또, 환경을 주제로 한 그림 경연 대회 같은 많은 행사를 주최해.

남: 나도 그 환경 동아리에 들고 싶다는 생각이 든다. 학과 사무실에 가서 신청을 하는 게 어때?

여: 좋아. 하지만 우선 서점에 들러도 될까? 먼저 환경에 대한 책을 사고 싶어.

남: 물론이지. 같이 갈게.

어휘

pollution[pəlúːʃən] 명 오염 guidebook[ɡáidbùk] 명 안내 책자 protect[prətékt] 동 보호하다 hand out 나눠주다 recycled product[item] 재활용품 contest

[kántest] 명 경연 대회   based on ~에 기반을 둔   apply
[əplái] 동 지원하다   drop by ~에 들르다   [문제]
campaign[kæmpéin] 명 캠페인   protection[prətékʃən]
명 보호   participate in ~에 참가하다

문제 해설

Q1: 환경 동아리의 활동이 <u>아닌</u> 것은?

　에너지 절약 캠페인에 관한 언급은 없었다.

Q2: 그들이 다음에 할 일은?

　동아리 가입 신청을 하러 가기 전에 환경에 관한 책을 사러
　서점에 같이 가기로 했다.

B [1-2]

M: Hello, everyone. Our school is going to hold a poster painting contest next Saturday, June 4th. The purpose of this event is to show you how to protect our environment. You can paint anything that shows ways to protect the environment. The best posters will be exhibited in the local art gallery. It will give you the chance to think about saving the earth. The contest is going to be held from 9:00 a.m. at the school gym. If you want to join, you must visit the teacher's room by next Friday. Bring an application form and hand it in to Mr. Jones. Everyone is welcome to join!

남: 안녕하세요, 여러분. 우리 학교에서 다음 주 토요일인 6월 4일에 포스터 그리기 경연 대회를 엽니다. 이 행사의 목적은 우리의 환경을 보호하는 방법을 보여주는 것입니다. 환경을 보호하는 방법을 보여주는 것이면 무엇이든 그릴 수 있습니다. 최고의 포스터는 지역 미술관에 전시될 것입니다. 이것은 여러분에게 지구를 보존하는 것에 대해 생각해 볼 기회를 줄 것입니다. 이 경연 대회는 학교 체육관에서 오전 9시부터 열릴 것입니다. 참가하기를 원하면 다음 주 금요일까지 교무실로 오십시오. 신청서를 가져와서 Jones 선생님께 제출하세요. 누가 참가하시든지 환영입니다!

어휘

poster[póustər] 명 포스터, 벽보   purpose[pə́ːrpəs] 명 목적   exhibit[igzíbit] 동 전시하다   local[lóukəl] 형 인근의, 지역의   art gallery 미술관, 화랑   application form 신청서   hand in 제출하다   [문제] inform[infɔ́ːrm] 동 알리다

문제 해설

Q1: 이 경연 대회의 목적은?

　① 지구를 보호하는 방법을 학생들에게 알려 주려고

　② 오염이 얼마나 심각한지 학생들에게 알리려고

　③ 학생들이 그들의 재능을 보여줄 기회를 주려고

　④ 환경 캠페인을 위한 돈을 모금하려고

환경을 보호하는 방법을 보여주는 것이 이번 행사의 목적이라고 했다.

Q2: 틀린 정보를 고르시오.

　신청서는 이번 주 금요일이 아니라 다음 주 금요일까지 제출하면 된다.

C [1-2]

W: Ted, are you looking for a photo of environmental pollution on the Internet?

M: Yes. Did you find a good one? The homework is due tomorrow.

W: Not yet. I'm going to search for one now. Is the seat next to you taken?

M: No, sit here and search.

W: Okay.

M: Susan, look at this photo of a bird floating on water! I'm going to use it.

W: Is it a photo of a dead bird?

M: No, the bird is alive, but the water is polluted with black waste.

W: That's terrible. Anyway, it's a great photo.

M: I'm finished. Do you want me to help you?

W: No thanks. I've found one too.

M: Which one is it?

W: A photo of three birds in the water.

M: Oh my god! Waste water is pouring out of pipes next to them.

W: That's right. I feel sorry for them.

여: Ted, 인터넷에서 환경 오염에 대한 사진을 찾는 중이니?

남: 응. 좋은 거 찾았니? 숙제가 내일까지잖아.

여: 아직. 지금 찾아보려고 해. 네 옆 자리에 사람 있는 거니?

남: 아니, 여기 앉아서 검색해.

여: 좋아.

남: Susan, 이 물 위에 떠 있는 새의 사진 좀 봐! 이걸 써야겠다.

여: 죽은 새의 사진이니?

남: 아니, 새는 살아 있는데 물이 더러운 쓰레기로 오염되어 있어.

여: 끔찍하다. 어쨌든, 훌륭한 사진이야.

남: 난 다했어. 내가 좀 도와줄까?

여: 고맙지만 괜찮아. 나도 하나 찾았어.

남: 어떤 건데?

여: 물 속에 있는 세 마리 새의 사진이야.

남: 저런! 그들 바로 옆에 있는 파이프에서 폐수가 쏟아져 나오고 있구나.

여: 맞아. 새들이 참 안쓰럽다.

어휘

due[djuː] 형 (언제) ~하기로 되어 있는, 기일이 된   search for ~을 검색하다, 찾다   float[flout] 동 떠다니다   dead [ded] 형 죽은   alive[əláiv] 형 살아 있는   black[blæk] 형

검은; *오염된, 더러운 waste water 폐수 pour[pɔːr] 동
붓다, 쏟아내다 [문제] brochure[brouʃúər] 명 소책자, 전단
지 exhibition[èksəbíʃən] 명 전시(회)

Q1: 그들이 지금 하고 있는 것은?

숙제로 제출할 환경 오염과 관련된 사진을 인터넷에서 찾아
보는 중이다.

Q2: Susan이 고른 사진을 고르시오.

Susan은 세 마리의 새가 폐수가 쏟아지는 파이프 옆에 있는
사진을 골랐다.

D [1-2]

W: A hybrid car is a special car made to protect the environment. The biggest difference between a hybrid car and a regular car is that a hybrid car uses two power sources. It gets its driving power from both a gasoline engine and an electric motor. When the car starts to move, it only uses the electric motor. When it speeds up, it uses both the electric motor and the gasoline engine. But, when it slows down, the engine turns off and only the electric motor works. By using both a gasoline engine and an electric motor effectively, hybrid cars use less gasoline and reduce the amount of harmful pollution.

여: 하이브리드 자동차는 환경을 보호하기 위해 만들어진 특수한
차입니다. 하이브리드 자동차와 일반 자동차의 가장 큰 차이
점은 하이브리드 자동차가 두 개의 동력원을 사용한다는 것
입니다. 하이브리드 자동차는 가솔린 엔진과 전기 모터로부
터 구동력을 얻습니다. 차가 움직이기 시작할 때는 전기 모터
만을 사용합니다. 속도가 올라가면 전기 모터와 가솔린 엔진
두 가지를 모두 사용합니다. 그러나 속력을 늦출 때는 엔진은
꺼지고 전기 모터만 작동합니다. 하이브리드 자동차는 가솔
린 엔진과 전기 모터 두 개 모두를 효율적으로 사용함으로써
더 적은 가솔린을 사용하여 해로운 오염의 양을 줄입니다.

어휘

hybrid car 하이브리드 자동차 power source 동력원
driving power 구동력(동력 기구를 움직이는 힘)
gasoline[gǽsəlìːn] 명 가솔린, 휘발유 engine[éndʒin] 명
엔진 electric[iléktrik] 형 전기의 motor[móutər] 명 모터
speed up 속도를 올리다 turn off 끄다 effectively
[iféktivli] 부 효율적으로 harmful[háːrmfəl] 형 해로운
[문제] kph(kilometer per hour) 시속

문제 해설

Q1: 여자는 주로 무엇에 대해 이야기하고 있나?

① 하이브리드 자동차를 운전하는 법

② 하이브리드 자동차를 사야 하는 이유

③ 하이브리드 자동차가 어떻게 환경을 돕는지

④ 하이브리드 자동차가 어떤 동력을 주로 사용하는지

환경을 보호하기 위해 만들어진 하이브리드 자동차가 어떻
게 작동하는지를 설명하고 있다.

Q2: 하이브리드 자동차는 일반 차와 어떻게 다른가?

하이브리드 자동차는 동력원으로 가솔린 엔진과 전기 모터
를 둘 다 사용한다는 점이 일반 자동차와의 가장 큰 차이점
이라고 했다.

Listening ★ Challenge p. 78

A 1 ④ 2 ③ B 1 ④ 2 ③

A [1-2]

W: Hello, everyone. Today, our guest is an environmental expert, Dr. J. He is going to tell us about the changing environment of the Arctic and the problems it's causing. Good morning, Dr. J.

M: Thank you for inviting me.

W: First, let's talk about environmental change in the Arctic. What's happening there?

M: Average temperatures in the Arctic are rising very fast. The ice is melting and getting thinner.

W: How does that affect the Arctic area?

M: If this trend continues, all the ice will melt by 2040. It means animals will lose their homes and die out.

W: Will melting Arctic ice influence other areas?

M: Sure. If the entire ice cover melts, the sea level will rise all over the world. Then, people living in coastal areas and islands may lose their homes.

W: Sounds tragic.

M: Yes. The problem happening in the Arctic may affect our lives as well. That's why we need to work on it.

여: 안녕하세요, 여러분. 오늘의 초대 손님은 환경 전문가이신 J
박사님입니다. 북극의 변화하는 환경과 이것이 일으키는 문
제점들에 관해서 말씀해 주시겠습니다. 좋은 아침입니다, J
박사님.

남: 초대해 주셔서 감사합니다.

여: 우선, 북극의 환경적인 변화에 대해 이야기해 보죠. 북극에
서 어떤 일이 일어나고 있나요?

남: 북극의 평균 기온이 아주 빠르게 오르고 있습니다. 얼음이
녹으면서 점점 얇아져 가고 있어요.

여: 그게 북극 지방에 어떻게 영향을 끼치나요?

남: 이런 추세가 계속된다면 2040년이면 모든 얼음이 녹을 것입니다. 그것은 동물이 서식지를 잃고 멸종하게 된다는 의미죠.

여: 북극 얼음이 녹는 것이 다른 지역에도 영향을 줄까요?

남: 물론이죠. 전체 얼음층이 녹는다면 전 세계적으로 해수면이 상승할 것입니다. 그러면 해안 지역과 섬에 사는 사람들이 집을 잃게 될 수도 있죠.

여: 비극적이겠군요.

남: 네. 북극에서 일어나는 문제는 우리의 삶에도 영향을 줄 지 모릅니다. 그것이 우리가 이 문제에 노력을 기울일 필요가 있는 이유죠.

어휘

guest[gest] 명 손님 expert[ékspə:rt] 명 전문가 Arctic [ɑ́:rktik] 명 《the ~》북극; 형 북극의 average[ǽvəridʒ] 형 평균의 rise[raiz] 동 오르다 melt[melt] 동 녹다 trend [trend] 명 추세, 경향 die out 멸종하다 influence [ínfluəns] 동 영향을 주다 entire[intáiər] 형 전체의 sea level 해수면 coastal[kóustəl] 형 근해의, 연안의 island [áilənd] 명 섬 tragic[trǽdʒik] 형 비극적인 [문제] wildlife[wáildlàif] 명 야생 생물 underwater [ʌ̀ndərwɔ́:tər] 부 물 속에 increase[inkrí:s] 동 증가하다

문제 해설

Q1: 그들은 주로 무엇에 대해 이야기하고 있나?

① 북극의 야생 생물을 보호하는 방법

② 왜 북극의 얼음이 빨리 녹고 있는지

③ 해수면의 상승이 사람들에게 어떻게 영향을 줄 것인지

④ 북극의 얼음이 녹는 것의 영향

북극의 얼음이 녹아서 생기게 되는 영향으로 동물의 멸종과 해수면 상승을 설명하고 있다.

Q2: J 박사에 따르면, 북극의 얼음이 모두 녹으면 어떤 일이 생길 것인가?

해수면이 상승하게 되면 섬과 해안 지역이 물에 잠길 수 있다고 했다.

B [1-2]

W: Do you know that cell phones are harmful to our environment? They have dangerous chemicals inside them. So when they are buried, they pollute the land. They can even affect the water we drink. And once they're buried, the chemicals last for a long time. But recycling can turn them into useful resources, while protecting the environment. To make this happen, we conduct a campaign called "Save the Earth!" every year. It was planned to encourage cell phone recycling. The goal for this year is to collect 4,000 cell phones. From June 1 to July 31, bring your old cell phones to ABC Service Center. We'll sell the phones to a certain cell phone recycling company. By donating your cell phones, you can save the environment. Call 3142-0357 to join us!

여: 휴대전화가 우리 환경에 해롭다는 거 알고 계시나요? 그 안에는 위험한 화학물질이 있습니다. 그래서 매립되면 땅을 오염시킵니다. 심지어 우리가 마시는 물에도 영향을 줄 수 있습니다. 그리고 한번 매립되면 화학물질이 오랫동안 잔류합니다. 그러나, 휴대전화를 재활용하면 환경을 보호하는 동시에 그것을 유용한 자원으로 바꿀 수 있습니다. 이를 실현하기 위해 '지구를 구하자!'라는 캠페인을 매년 실시하고 있습니다. 이는 휴대전화 재활용을 장려하기 위해 계획되었습니다. 올해의 목표는 4,000개의 휴대전화를 수집하는 것입니다. 6월 1일부터 7월 31일까지 ABC 서비스 센터로 여러분의 오래된 휴대전화를 가지고 오세요. 저희는 그 휴대전화들을 특정 휴대전화 재활용 회사에 팔 것입니다. 여러분의 휴대전화를 기증함으로써 환경을 구할 수 있습니다. 3142-0357로 전화해서 참가하세요!

어휘

dangerous[déindʒərəs] 형 위험한 chemical[kémikəl] 명 화학물질 bury[béri] 동 매립하다, 묻다 pollute[pəlú:t] 동 오염시키다 last[læst] 동 오래 가다, 지속하다 conduct [kándʌkt] 동 수행하다 donate[dóuneit] 동 기증하다 [문제] benefit[bénəfit] 명 이점

문제 해설

Q1: 여자는 사람들이 캠페인에 참가하도록 어떻게 장려하고 있나?

① 재활용의 장점을 언급함으로써

② 휴대전화 안에 있는 화학물질에 대해 열거함으로써

③ 휴대전화 매립으로 인해 생기는 질병에 대해 논함으로써

④ 휴대전화로 인해 생기는 유해한 영향을 설명함으로써

휴대전화에 들어 있는 유해한 화학물질이 매립되면서 땅과 물을 오염시킨다며 휴대전화로 인한 유해한 영향을 설명하고 있다.

Q2: 틀린 정보를 고르시오.

40,000개가 아니라 4,000개의 휴대전화를 수집하는 것이 올해의 목표라고 했다.

Critical ★ Thinking p. 79

1 ④ 2 (1) T (2) F (3) T

W: These days, yellow dust is so serious that I don't even want to go out.

M: Right. It's getting worse every year.

W: China is causing most of the yellow dust. China should be held responsible for the problem and pay money for the damages it causes.

M: But as long as the wind blows in desert

areas, they can't stop it.

W: The problem is that the Chinese government doesn't pay much attention to the environment.

M: That's true.

W: The government doesn't try hard to stop people from cutting down trees. It can increase the size of the desert and worsen yellow dust.

M: You have a point. Still, it's hard for China to solve the problem alone. We need to work on it together.

W: Then, what do you think we should do?

M: We should help China bring water to dry areas and plant strong vegetables there. We can prevent the desert from becoming wider that way.

여: 요즘 황사가 너무 심해서 밖에 나가기조차 싫어.

남: 맞아. 매년 더 악화되고 있어.

여: 중국이 대부분의 황사를 일으키고 있어. 중국은 그 문제에 대해서 책임을 지고 황사로 인한 피해에 대해 돈을 지불해야 해.

남: 하지만 사막 지역에서 바람이 부는 한, 그들이 그걸 막을 수는 없잖아.

여: 문제는 중국 정부가 환경에 주의를 많이 기울이지 않는다는 거야.

남: 그건 사실이야.

여: 중국 정부는 나무를 베어버리는 사람들을 막으려고 열심히 노력하지 않아. 그게 사막의 크기를 증가시키고 황사를 악화시킬 수 있는데 말이야.

남: 일리가 있는 말이야. 그래도 중국이 혼자 그 문제를 해결하기는 어려워. 우리가 함께 노력해야 할 필요가 있어.

여: 그럼, 우리가 무엇을 해야 한다고 생각하니?

남: 중국이 건조 지역에 물을 대고 거기에 튼튼한 식물들을 심을 수 있게 도와야 해. 그런 식으로 사막이 더 넓어지는 걸 예방할 수 있어.

어휘

yellow dust 황사   hold ~ responsible for ~에게 …에 대해 책임을 지우다   damage[dǽmidʒ] 몡 손해, 피해 as long as ~하는 한   desert[dézərt] 몡 사막 cut down 자르다   worsen[wə́ːrsən] 통 악화시키다 You have a point. 일리가 있다.   plant[plænt] 통 심다 [문제] mostly[móustli] 凰 대부분   strictly[stríktli] 凰 엄격하게   ban[bæn] 통 금지하다

문제 해설

Q1: 그들은 주로 무엇에 관해 이야기하고 있나?

　① 왜 황사를 줄여야 하나?

　② 황사는 사람들의 삶에 어떤 영향을 주나?

　③ 중국은 황사를 예방하기 위해 무엇을 해야 하나?

　④ 중국이 황사를 줄이는 데 책임을 져야 하나?

　황사를 줄여야 하는 책임을 중국이 져야 한다는 주장과 중국 혼자서는 어렵고 함께 해결해야 한다는 주장이 대립하고 있는 내용이다.

Q2: 사실이면 T, 사실이 아니면 F에 ✓표 하시오.

　(1) 황사는 대부분 중국의 사막 지역에서 온다.

　(2) 중국 정부는 벌목을 엄격하게 금지한다.

　(3) 식물을 심는 것은 황사를 줄이는 데 도움이 될 수 있다.

　중국에서 대부분의 황사가 일어나는데, 이는 사막 지역에서 바람이 불 때 생긴다고 했다. 또한 중국 정부가 벌목을 철저히 막지 않고, 환경 문제에 대해 많은 관심을 보이지 않고 있어 문제라고 했고, 황사를 줄이기 위해 할 수 있는 일로 건조 지역에 식물을 심도록 도와야 한다고 했다.

JUNIOR
READING EXPERT

A Theme-Based Reading Course for Young EFL Learners

Level **1**

Word Book

UNIT *01* *Food*

tasty	형 맛있는
snack	명 간식
dessert	명 후식
wetland	명 습지
marsh	명 습지
heal	동 치유하다, 낫게 하다
injury	명 부상, 상처
medicine	명 약
mix A with B	A와 B를 섞다
nut	명 견과류
owner	명 주인
root	명 (식물의) 뿌리
gelatin	명 젤라틴
instead of	~ 대신에
nowadays	부 오늘날
roast	동 굽다
origin	명 기원
spread	동 퍼지다
season	명 계절
get rid of	~을 제거하다
produce	동 생산하다
by accident	우연히

past	몡 과거
traditional	휑 전통적인
usually	흳 보통, 대개
flavored	휑 ~의 맛[향기]이 나는
typically	흳 보통, 일반적으로
pumpkin	몡 호박
gingerbread	몡 생강 쿠키[케이크]
certainly	흳 틀림없이, 분명히
treat	몡 특별한 것[선물]; 간식
unusual	휑 특이한, 흔치 않은
legend	몡 전설
yell	둉 소리치다
whoopee	캄 야호, 우아
receive	둉 받다
official	휑 공식적인
beloved	휑 인기 많은
recipe	몡 조리법

UNIT 02 *Places*

vacation	몡 휴가
be made out of	~으로 만들어지다
piece	몡 조각

2

million	형 백만의
inside	전 ~ 안에
tiny	형 아주 작은
brick	명 벽돌; (장난감용) 벽돌
perfectly	부 완벽하게
giant	명 거인
grass	명 풀, 잔디
sunshine	명 햇빛
wild	형 야생의
take one's picture	~의 사진을 찍다
enough	부 충분히
carry	동 운반하다, 들고 다니다
go on a ride	놀이기구를 타다
ride	명 놀이기구
stand in line	줄을 서다
finally	부 마침내
reach	동 ~에 이르다
front	명 앞
excited	형 흥분한
through	전 ~을 통과하여
castle	명 성
thousands of	수천의
travel	동 여행하다; 움직이다
scream	동 비명을 지르다

forget	통 잊다
trip	명 여행
theme park	테마파크[유원지]
tour	명 관광
popular	형 인기가 많은
joyful	형 즐거운
bored	형 지루한
scared	형 무서운
interested	형 흥미를 가진
successful	형 성공적인
history	명 역사
choose	통 선택하다
century	명 세기
perhaps	부 아마
put together	조립하다
own	형 자기 자신의, 고유한
creation	명 창작물
Danish	형 덴마크 (사람, 말)의
since	접 ~한 이후로
more than	~ 이상의
billion	형 10억의
let	통 ~하게 하다
imagination	명 상상력

graffiti	똉 (공공장소에 하는) 낙서, 그라피티
artist	똉 예술가
fence	똉 울타리
spray paint	스프레이식 페인트
stencil	똉 스텐실
neighborhood	똉 근처, 이웃
studio	똉 (방송국) 스튜디오; 작업실
artwork	똉 작품
fake	똉 가짜의
like	쩐 ~와 같이, ~처럼
social	똉 사회의
form	똉 형태
modern art	현대 예술
gallery	똉 미술관
express	똥 표현하다
thought	똉 생각
show off	자랑하다
public	똉 공공의
private	똉 사적인
fabric	똉 직물, 천
bring	똥 가져오다
piece	똉 조각; (작품의) 한 점

print	몡 판화
sculpture	몡 조각
entire	혱 전체의
celebrate	동 기념하다
growth	몡 성장
museum	몡 박물관
entry	몡 입장
information	몡 정보
experience	몡 경험
hold	동 잡다; (회의, 시합 등을) 열다

UNIT 04 Animals

prairie	몡 초원
squirrel	몡 다람쥐
underground	혱 지하의 昷 지하에(서)
tunnel	몡 굴, 터널
social	혱 사교적인
curious	혱 궁금한
area	몡 지역
flat	혱 평평한
grassy	혱 풀이 많은
bark	동 짖다

eagle	명 독수리
coyote	명 코요테
danger	명 위험
loudly	부 큰 소리로
warn	동 경고하다
name A after B	B의 이름을 따서 A의 이름을 짓다
lifestyle	명 생활방식
be made up of	~으로 이루어져 있다
purpose	명 목적
entrance	명 입구
nearby	부 근처에
owl	명 올빼미
share	동 공유하다

UNIT 05 Entertainment

diary	명 일기
animated	형 애니메이션으로 된
journey	명 여행, 여정
million	형 백만의
among	전 ~ 중의 하나인
performance	명 공연
perform	동 공연하다

simply	⊕ 단순히; 아주
amazing	⊜ 놀라운, 굉장한
be full of	~으로 가득 차다
costume	⊜ 의상
acting	⊜ 연기
count	⊜ (수를) 세다
insect	⊜ 곤충
surprising	⊜ 놀라운
useful	⊜ 유용한
fantastic	⊜ 환상적인, 멋진
worry	⊜ 걱정
someday	⊕ 언젠가
audition	⊜ 오디션
include	⊜ 포함하다
appearance	⊜ 모습
director	⊜ 감독
designer	⊜ 디자이너
design	⊜ 디자인 ⊜ 디자인하다
successful	⊜ 성공적인
win	⊜ (상 등을) 수상하다
award	⊜ 상
original	⊜ 독창적인
actor	⊜ 배우
hide	⊜ 숨다

task	몡 일, 과제
discover	통 발견하다
unpaid	혱 아직 돈을 내지 않은, 미납의
order	몡 주문
forget	통 잊다
experiment	몡 실험
a series of	일련의
suddenly	뿐 갑자기
force	통 ~하게 만들다
stay	통 그대로 있다
instead of v-ing	~하는 대신에
schedule	통 일정을 잡다
break	몡 휴식 (시간)
improve	통 개선하다, 나아지다
tip	몡 끝; 조언
manner	몡 방식; (~s) 예의
behavior	통 행동
affect	통 영향을 미치다
at once	한꺼번에
information	몡 정보
relate	통 관련시키다
brain	몡 뇌

store	[동] 저장하다
prove	[동] 입증[증명]하다
adjective	[명] 형용사
describe	[동] 묘사하다
personality	[명] 성격
connect	[동] 연결하다

UNIT 07 *Science*

roommate	[명] 룸메이트 (방을 같이 쓰는 사람)
chewing gum	껌
breath	[명] 숨, 호흡
embarrassed	[형] 당황스러운
pretty	[부] 매우, 아주
common	[형] 흔한, 보통의
cause	[동] 유발하다
smelly	[형] (고약한) 냄새가 나는
onion	[명] 양파
garlic	[명] 마늘
bacteria	[명] 세균 (bacterium의 복수형)
increase	[동] 증가하다
billion	[형] 10억의
regularly	[부] 규칙적으로

clean away	~을 청소해 없애다
tongue	명 혀
wash away	~을 씻어 없애다
excuse	동 용서하다
share	동 함께 나누다
refresh	동 상쾌하게 하다
fall asleep	잠들다
brush one's teeth	이를 닦다
soda	명 탄산음료
luckily	부 다행히도
taste	명 맛, 입맛
stay	동 머물다; ~인 채로 있다
awake	형 깨어 있는
have to do with	~와 관계가 있다
overnight	부 밤새도록
result	명 결과
toothbrush	명 칫솔

UNIT 08 Sports

invent	동 발명하다
century	명 세기(100년)
shepherd	명 양치기

push	[동] 밀다
hole	[명] 구멍, 굴
stick	[명] 막대기
throughout	[전] ~의 도처에
introduce	[동] 소개하다
such as	~와 같은
nowadays	[부] 오늘날
golf course	골프장
natural	[형] 자연의
relaxing	[형] 편안한
crowded	[형] 붐비는, 복잡한
swing	[동] 흔들다, 휘두르다
club	[명] (골프, 하키 등의) 채
upper	[형] 위쪽의
explain	[동] 설명하다
suggest	[동] 제안하다
clear	[형] 명백한
tiring	[형] 피곤하게 하는, 힘든
exercise	[명] 운동
travel	[동] 여행하다; 이동하다
feather	[명] 깃털
leather	[명] 가죽
farther	[부] 더 멀리 (far의 비교급)
factory	[명] 공장

rubber	몡 고무
scratch	통 긁다
up to	~까지
dimple	몡 보조개; 움푹 들어간 곳

UNIT 09 Society

habitat	몡 (동물들의) 서식지; 거주지
humanity	몡 인류, 인간
charity	몡 자선 단체
volunteer	혱 자원하는 몡 자원봉사자
rule	몡 규칙
free	혱 자유로운; 무료의
homeowner	몡 집주인
price	몡 가격, 값
pleased	혱 즐거운
proud	혱 자랑스러워하는
in the end	결국
thanks to	~ 덕분에
lesson	몡 수업; 교훈
move	통 움직이다; 이사하다
right	혱 올바른
usual	혱 보통의, 통상의

spend	동 (시간을) 보내다
while	접 ~하는 동안
match	동 ~와 어울리다
energy	명 에너지, 기운

UNIT 10 Literature

point to	~을 가리키다
cousin	명 사촌
brat	명 장난꾸러기
tie	동 매다
mean	형 비열한, 못된
picture	동 상상하다
take a walk	산책하다
moment	명 순간
hateful	형 미운
shout	동 소리치다
smack	명 찰싹하는 소리
mad	형 미친; 몹시 화가 난
punishment	명 벌
explain	동 설명하다
matter	동 중요하다
miss	동 그리워하다; 빠지다

play a trick on	~을 놀리다
fault	몡 잘못
bother	동 괴롭히다
daydream	동 몽상하다
nickname	몡 별명
death	몡 사망
still	부 여전히
childhood	몡 어린 시절
imagination	몡 상상력
outdoors	부 야외에서
dream of v-ing	~하는 것을 꿈꾸다
character	몡 등장인물
publisher	몡 출판사[업자]
publish	동 출판하다
disappoint	동 실망시키다
put away	치워두다
finally	부 마침내
century	몡 세기
touch	동 감동시키다
worldwide	부 전 세계에
imaginative	형 상상력이 풍부한
make up	(이야기 등을) 지어[만들어] 내다

UNIT 11 *Culture*

be famous for	~로 유명하다
exactly	皁 정확히
original	혤 원래의
native	혤 태생의; 원주민의
round	혤 둥근
leave	동 떠나다; 남기다
national	혤 국가의
overseas	皁 해외로
probably	皁 아마도
grow	동 자라다; 재배하다, 기르다
look like	~처럼 보이다
cover	동 덮다
that way	그런 식으로
natural	혤 자연의
beauty	명 미, 아름다움
curious	혤 호기심이 많은
confused	혤 혼란스러운, 헷갈리는
weird	혤 기이한, 이상한
related	혤 관련된
sail	동 항해하다
survive	동 살아남다
culture	명 문화

16

language	몡 언어
develop	동 발달시키다
control	동 지배하다
agreement	몡 일치; 협정
leader	몡 지도자
protect	동 보호하다
a way of life	생활 방식
though	분 그러나
disease	몡 질병
as well	~도 역시

Issues

vegan	몡 완전 채식주의자 혱 완전 채식주의자의
diet	몡 식단
popular	혱 인기 있는
recently	분 최근에
improve	동 개선하다, 향상시키다
health	몡 건강
benefit	몡 혜택, 이득
decrease	동 감소시키다
risk	몡 위험
serious	혱 심각한

researcher	몡 연구원
low	혱 낮은 (비교급 lower)
weight	몡 몸무게
offer	동 제공하다
iron	몡 철분
meat	몡 고기
farm	몡 농장
environment	몡 환경
produce	동 생산하다
amount	몡 양
greenhouse gas	온실가스
global warming	지구 온난화
diligent	혱 부지런한
label	몡 표, 라벨, 상표
all the time	항상
information	몡 정보
necessary	혱 필수적인
pill	몡 알약
calorie	몡 열량
loss	몡 손실; 줄임, 감량
lower	동 낮추다, 내리다
impact	몡 영향
give up	포기하다
favorite	혱 가장 좋아하는

taste	통 맛이 ~하다, ~ 맛이 나다
soy milk	두유
type	명 종류
contain	통 포함하다
protein	명 단백질
instead of	~ 대신에
certain	형 어떤
vegetable	명 채소
mushroom	명 버섯
replace	통 대체하다
give it a try	시도하다, 한번 해보다
wheat	명 밀

UNIT 13 *History*

president	명 대통령
politician	명 정치인
intelligent	형 똑똑한, 지성을 갖춘
advice	명 충고
run for	~에 출마하다
win	통 이기다
shadow	명 그림자
skinny	형 깡마른

beard	명 턱수염
grow	동 (수염, 손톱 등을) 기르다
elect	동 선출하다
before long	머지 않아
have no idea	전혀 모르다
by mistake	실수로
relationship	명 관계
slim	형 날씬한 (비교급 slimmer)
freedom	명 자유
upset	동 화나게 하다
in the end	결국
honest	형 정직한
honesty	명 정직
well-known for	~으로 잘 알려진
personality	명 성격
count	동 (수를) 세다
customer	명 고객
change	명 잔돈
return	동 돌려주다
carry	동 들고 가다
lie	명 거짓말
fortune	명 행운
earn	동 (돈을) 벌다; 얻다
overcome	동 극복하다

| truthful | 혱 정직한 |
| bring about | ~을 일으키다, 생기게 하다 |

The Economy

coin	몡 동전
pocket	몡 주머니
closely	뷰 자세히
first of all	우선
sharp	혱 뾰족한
corner	몡 모서리
hurt	동 다치게 하다
in addition	게다가
regularly	뷰 정기[규칙]적으로
roll	동 굴러가다
vending machine	자판기
sort	동 분류하다, 구분하다
get stuck	꼼짝 못하게 되다
wear down	닳다, 마모되다
last	동 오래가다, 지속되다
rub	동 문지르다
shape	몡 모양
at the same time	동시에

invent	동 발명하다
hardly	부 거의 ~않는
function	동 기능하다
credit card	신용 카드
debit card	직불 카드
reason	명 이유
cash	명 현금
accept	동 받아들이다
seller	명 판매자
device	명 기구
payment	명 지불
pay	동 지불하다
common	형 흔한
spend	동 (돈을) 쓰다
buyer	명 구매자
discount	명 할인

UNIT 15 *Festivals*

balloon	명 풍선; 기구
hot air balloon	열기구
describe	동 묘사하다
fiesta	명 축제 (= festival)

22

floating	혱 떠있는
wonder	몡 놀라운 물건; 경이
unforgettable	혱 잊을 수 없는
lift off	이륙하다
burner	몡 버너
roar	통 큰 소리를 내다
rise	통 솟아오르다
take one's breath away	~을 놀라게 하다
glow	몡 (불꽃 없이 타는 물체의) 빛 통 빛나다
firefly	몡 반딧불이
farthest	垈 가장 멀리 (far의 최상급)
in addition to	~ 외에도
discovery	몡 발견
ride	몡 타고가기 통 타다
tourist	몡 여행자, 관광객
site	몡 장소
fill	통 가득 차다, 채우다
advise	통 조언[충고]하다
take a deep breath	심호흡하다
air	몡 공기; 공중, 허공
visit	통 방문하다
amazing	혱 놀라운
landscape	몡 풍경
be full of	~로 가득 차다

valley	몡 계곡
cave	몡 동굴
hidden	휑 숨겨진
no wonder	당연히 ~하다
thousands of	수천의 ~
weather	몡 날씨
space	몡 공간
explore	동 탐험하다
wildlife	몡 야생동물
excellent	휑 훌륭한, 탁월한
calm	휑 침착한, 차분한; 잔잔한

UNIT 16 *The Environment*

go out	(불 등이) 꺼지다
accident	몡 사고; 우연
by accident	우연히
event	몡 행사
earth	몡 지구
plan	동 계획하다
fund	몡 기금
protect	동 보호하다
turn off	(불 등을) 끄다

pollution	똉 오염
success	똉 성공
silly	쪵 어리석은
make a difference	변화를 가져오다, 차이가 있다
save	똫 절약하다
choice	똉 선택
have an effect	영향을 미치다
throughout	쩐 ~의 도처에
wild	똉 야생
promise	똉 약속
symbol	똉 상징
uncomfortable	쪵 불편한
drop	똉 물방울
ocean	똉 바다
Switzerland	똉 스위스
goal	똉 목표
damage	똉 손상
natural	쪵 자연의
continue	똫 계속하다
encourage	똫 장려하다
government	똉 정부
hunter	똉 사냥꾼
guard	똫 지키다, 보호하다

smoke	몡 연기
detector	몡 탐지기
detect	동 탐지하다
invention	몡 발명품
have in common	공통점이 있다
common	혱 보통의, 평범한
space	몡 우주
research	몡 연구, 조사
product	몡 제품
space station	우주 정거장
warn	동 경고하다
signal	몡 신호
spacecraft	몡 우주선 (= spaceship)
material	몡 재료, 물질
astronaut	몡 우주 비행사
lessen	동 줄이다
shock	몡 충격
cost	동 ~의 비용이 들다
get to-v	~하게 되다
daily	혱 매일의
competition	몡 경쟁
cure	동 치료하다

serious	형 심각한
illness	명 병
opinion	명 의견
make sense	말이 되다, 이치에 맞다
die of	~으로 죽다
hunger	명 기아, 굶주림
resource	명 (~s) 자원
yet	부 아직
solar	형 태양의
crowded	형 붐비는
curiosity	명 호기심
safety	명 안전(성)

UNIT 18 *Technology*

luckily	부 다행스럽게도
sunlight	명 햇빛
be filled with	~로 가득 차다
heat	명 열
heat up	뜨겁게 하다, 데우다
surface	명 표면
escape	동 달아나다, 탈출하다; 새어 나가다[들어가다]
geothermal	형 지열의

(power) plant	몡 발전소
steam	몡 증기
fan	몡 팬, 선풍기
generator	몡 발전기
generate	통 발생시키다
electricity	몡 전기
release	통 방출하다
windmill	몡 풍차
solar panel	태양 전지판
effectively	뿐 효과적으로
require	통 필요로 하다
ideal	혱 이상적인
location	몡 장소, 위치
treasure	몡 보물
beneath	젼 ~ 아래[밑]에
source	몡 원천, 근원
danger	몡 위험
power	몡 동력, 에너지; 전기 통 동력을 공급하다, 작동시키다
take up	차지하다
fog	몡 안개
precious	혱 소중한
civil war	내전
device	몡 장치, 기구
run	통 작동하다
charge	통 청구하다; 충전하다

28

provide	동 제공하다
thanks to	~ 덕분에
contact	동 연락하다
in need	어려움에 처한, 궁핍한
campaign	명 캠페인
donate	동 기부하다

UNIT 19 *The Arts*

artwork	명 예술품
cultural	형 문화의
value	명 가치
valuable	형 가치 있는
move	명 이동 동 이동하다
museum	명 박물관, 미술관
international	형 국제적인
careful	형 조심하는, 주의 깊은
care	명 조심, 주의
leave	동 떠나다; ~한 상태로 놓아두다
pack	동 포장하다
ensure	동 반드시 ~하게 하다
be designed to-v	~하도록 제작되다
shake	동 흔들다, 진동을 가하다

climate	명 기후
controller	명 조절 장치
work	명 (예술 등의) 작품
experience	동 경험하다
lastly	부 마지막으로
security guard	보안 경비원
priceless	형 매우 귀중한
insure	동 보험에 들다
insurance	명 보험(료)
thief	명 도둑 (복수형 thieves)
overseas	부 해외로
least	형 가장 적은 (little의 최상급)
flash	명 번쩍임, (카메라의) 플래시
photography	명 사진 촬영
allow	동 허용하다
take a picture	사진을 찍다
hurt	동 상하게 하다
light	명 빛
canvas	명 캔버스 천
display	동 전시[진열]하다
outdoors	부 실외에서
necessary	형 필수적인

People

slave	몡 노예
state	몡 (미국 등에서) 주(州)
run away	도망치다
beat	통 때리다
whip	통 채찍질하다
master	몡 주인
throw	통 던지다
object	몡 물건, 물체
nearly	뷔 거의
crush	통 으스러[쭈그러]뜨리다
scar	몡 흉터
injury	몡 부상
injure	통 부상을 입히다
offer	통 제공하다
bravely	뷔 용감하게
continue	통 계속하다
soon after	곧
go through	~을 겪다
bill	몡 지폐
front	몡 앞면[앞부분]
replace	통 대신하다, 대체하다
president	몡 대통령

respect	몡 존경 똥 존경하다
vote	똥 투표하다
appear	똥 나타나다; 나오다
admire	똥 존경하다, 칭찬하다
courage	몡 용기
belief	몡 신념, 확신
equality	몡 평등